I0884406

Leading for Tomorrow

Leading for Tomorrow

A Primer for Succeeding in Higher Education Leadership

Pamela L. Eddy and Elizabeth Kirby

Foreword by Adrianna Kezar

Rutgers University Press

New Brunswick, Camden, and Newark, New Jersey, and London

Library of Congress Cataloging-in-Publication Data
Names: Eddy, Pamela Lynne, author. | Kirby, Elizabeth, author.
Title: Leading for tomorrow : a primer for succeeding in higher education leadership / Pamela L. Eddy, Elizabeth Kirby.
Description: New Brunswick, New Jersey : Rutgers University Press, 2020. | Includes bibliographical references and index.
Identifiers: LCCN 2019052742 | ISBN 9780813596792 (hardback) | ISBN 9780813596808 (epub) | ISBN 9780813596815 (mobi) | ISBN 9780813596822 (pdf)
Subjects: LCSH: Universities and colleges—United States—Administration. | College administrators—Professional relationships—United States. | Educational leadership—United States.
Classification: LCC LB2341 .E335 2020 | DDC 371.2—dc23
LC record available at https://lccn.loc.gov/2019052742

A British Cataloging-in-Publication record for this book is available from the British Library.

∞ The paper used in this publication meets the requirements of the American National Standard for Information Sciences—Permanence of Paper for Printed Library Materials, ANSI Z39.48-1992.

www.rutgersuniversitypress.org

Manufactured in the United States of America

In memory of Kelly Ward—consummate leader, mentor, colleague, and friend who served as a shining example of what leadership should be in practice. To Betty, who has long been a trusted friend and coconspirator on the quest of rethinking leadership. It has been a grand journey. Thanks a million.

—Pamela

To my husband, Kris, an exemplary educational leader who sparked my own interest in leadership and who provides ongoing support and encouragement. To Pam, who has had many important roles in my leadership journey—colleague, role model, mentor, and friend. "Go raibh maith agat."

—Betty

Contents

Foreword

Leading for Tomorrow: A Primer for Succeeding in Higher Education Leadership contributes immensely to the field and helps address a needed knowledge gap facing aspiring leaders. At this juncture in time, effective college leadership is critical and could not be more important for stewarding the higher education enterprise forward to meet the many challenges and external demands facing the sector. This is both a historical and current problem of tragic magnitude as we remain underresourced as a sector when it comes to both leadership resources and development. The authors point out the critical need for skilled leaders who have the capacity for leading change and the need to garner support of foundations and government agencies to fund research and resources. The dearth of attention to leadership is reaching a crisis point.

This book becomes a life vest for what seems like a sinking ship! One of the high points of the book is its focus on student success. The question often not asked is, leadership for what? In a recent scan I conducted of leadership programs across the country, very few—only about 8 percent—had any focus on student success. If leaders (and those who are providing leadership development) do not focus on the core mission of the institution, our institutions will be lost. Yet too many leaders are singularly engaged in fund-raising, budgeting, and priority setting and neglect to put student success at the center of these activities. Without a greater focus on student success and leaders appreciating the growing ecology around student success, campus leaders will not serve institutions well. Leaders must have a clear vision for student success and organize all the work of the campus—its units, committees, data systems, professional development, and technology—in service of student success.

This book also argues for an equity-minded approach as an essential feature of higher education leadership. Equity mindedness requires leaders to be attentive to disparate impacts of policies and programs that they create and to ensure that diverse learners are not hindered and in fact are enabled to succeed. In the past few decades, there has been attention to diversifying leadership—a very needed direction—and the book's emphasis on equity is a natural extension of this important work.

The authors address many often-avoided leadership topics that are critical for leaders to create the environments necessary for student success. For example, an entire chapter focuses on conflict management and will help leaders as they navigate change processes and shifting priorities. The book contains very strong reviews and discussions of change theories that will help leaders navigate this challenging arena. For campuses to reorient in ways that are different from the status quo, some campus groups will feel that they may be losing—as the nature of their work changes. Leaders have to be able to lead their institutions through some challenging conversations. Furthermore, the book reviews the importance of leaders being data savvy and gaining familiarity with existing surveys and data sources that can be used to guide evidence-based decision-making to support change. There is much new information here that is not presented in any previous text.

While resources for leaders often talk about the importance of communication, this volume provides a more in-depth and nuanced discussion that explores issues of framing around communication that help to rethink our language and nonverbal communication and what it might convey. The discussion will help leaders to explore and reconsider their communication approach. Another often-discussed set of leadership topics—relationships and networks—are discussed with attention to why and how relationships facilitate leaders' work and goals and help create collective efforts that are central to leaders working on change.

In addition to providing many new angles for exploring leadership in higher education, the book provides a core foundation to guide leadership practices and principles to enhance leader effectiveness, such as a review of Bolman and Deal's leadership frames, a synthesis of leadership theories, and an introduction to organizational culture. The book is brought to life with case studies, reflective questions, resources, quotes, and sections on "making this personal." Each part of the book makes the ideas practical and tangible. It makes a valuable textbook or self-study guide; it can also be a great resource for training sessions. I found myself drawn into the case-study scenarios that reflect so many situations I have experienced. Other scenarios drawn from the media made me rethink these very visible cases and the leadership successes and failures they represent. Those who pick up this book will find it easy to read, engaging, and inspirational. Enjoy this valuable resource.

Adrianna Kezar
Dean's Professor of Leadership and codirector of the Pullias Center for Higher Education University of Southern California

Leading for Tomorrow

Introduction

The higher education sector faces many challenges due to declines in public funding, changing student demographics, demands for increased accountability, and a growing public sentiment questioning the value of a college degree. Occurring concurrently is a changing of the guard in leadership of these institutions as long-serving leaders retire (Gagliardi, Espinosa, Turk, & Taylor, 2017). This book serves as a primer for new and emerging leaders at all types of institutions—community colleges, comprehensive colleges, minority-serving institutions, research universities. True, each of these types of institutions possesses unique features that require leaders to have a contextual understanding about to lead most effectively. However, many of the issues leaders face are not unique to them or their institutions—they only feel that way when the pressure is on.

The purpose of this book is to illuminate the challenges that new leaders in higher education may experience. Using case-study vignettes, we outline the type of situations new leaders may encounter in higher education. In particular, we focus on individuals moving up from the faculty ranks to their first administrative position, but the information presented is equally valuable for leaders who are new to positions throughout the institution. Research tells us that most new leaders emerge from faculty ranks with little, if any, administrative experience or leadership training. Thus, novice leaders are frequently blindsided by unexpected situations and the unintended consequences of their actions. It is our hope that this book provides practical advice and strategies for success.

Moving up the academic leadership ranks often occurs when faculty members enter the administrative ranks by becoming department chair or the director of a unit. The traditional hierarchy in higher education shows leadership moves from department chair, dean, vice president, and then president. Even though this route is changing with more hires from outside of higher education (e.g., business, politics), the traditional route of advancement still represents the majority. Emerging leaders in student affairs follow similar steps to advancement, typically moving from coordinator positions to director to associate dean or dean to vice president. Some vice presidents in student affairs transition to presidencies too, but the VP role is often viewed as the pinnacle of leadership in this area.

Other books address some of the specific skills required in new leadership positions, such as dealing with budgets (Barr & McClellan, 2011), understanding legal implications (Kaplin & Lee, 2007), or planning for meetings (Harvard Business Review, 2014). Our book takes a unique approach by compiling and building an overarching set of skills and strategies for new leaders that apply to a wide range of topics that are explored in a series of case-study vignettes. The use of these example scenarios allows for consideration of various approaches to leadership, helps identify areas requiring more leadership development, and provides evidence-based research to strengthen skill sets. Ultimately, it is important for new leaders to develop an authentic, ethical approach to leadership.

The book begins with an overview of some basic leadership and management concepts—in essence, parts to help in building a skill set and playbook for aspiring and new leaders. Additional references and websites are provided throughout to provide resources for in-depth background or to dig into some particularly nettlesome issues. Each chapter includes case examples for the chapter topic area. Each vignette is followed by a list of questions to prompt critical reflection. The sections conclude with a range of illustrations of possible ways to resolve the case problem. Care is taken to provide burgeoning leaders with a range of responses or suggestions that underscore the multiple solutions available and to highlight how each person needs to develop her or his own authentic approach to leadership.

Historically, colleges and universities have relied on leadership hierarchies (Northouse, 2015), but we argue that the challenges facing today's institutions require a different approach to leadership. Namely, we posit that networked leadership is needed. Networked leadership builds on connections, both inside the institution and with external partners. Moving forward, leadership throughout the institution marks the wave of the future. Because midlevel leaders tend to be longer serving than top-level leaders (Eddy, Garza Mitchell, & Amey, 2016; Gagliardi et al., 2017) and faculty leaders understand most clearly what works in the classroom, tapping into the expertise of a range of leaders helps the institution on the whole.

In addition to the reliance on single leaders at the helm, a divide between academic affairs and student affairs is long standing. Yet increasingly it is important to develop partnerships between the two areas to best support student success. Whitt and colleagues (2008) identify a set of principles of good practice that best support academic and student-affairs partnerships. Many of the high-impact practices that influence student engagement and academic success require academics working in tandem with their student-affairs colleagues (Kuh, 2008). For example, first-year experience programs, learning communities, student life, and service learning all contribute to academic success (Frost, Strom, Downey, Schultz, & Holland, 2010). A study of academic and student-affairs partnerships at eighteen institutions found specific outcomes included acclimation to the institution, engagement, student learning, and academic and career decisions (Nesheim et al., 2007). Courageous leadership helps foster these types of connections within colleges (Tardanico, 2013).

The following section provides a review of the changing landscape of higher education, in particular focusing on major policy issues with which institutional leaders are grappling. Finally, we summarize the need for building innovative cultures on campus based on an equity mind-set as this environment best supports student success.

Transformative leaders focus on disrupting current practices by questioning who is left out by the way policies are employed or the structures in place (Shields, 2010). Leaders must focus on what best supports *all* students.

Changing Higher Education Landscape

For the past dozen years or so, the American Association of State Colleges and Universities (AASCU) has assembled a list of the top-ten policy issues for a given year. In 2018, for the first time, the list contained changes in federal policy as the top issue. The political landscape, after the 2016 election, resulted in changes to the tax codes, which when coupled with state revenue stagnation, resulted in fiscal pressures on states. The uncertainty of state funding for higher education continues to be an issue for college and university leaders. Also, at the federal level, there is continued uncertainty regarding immigration policies that may make it more difficult for international students to attend U.S. colleges. Finally, at the federal level, the Higher Education Act (HEA) is up for reauthorization, which could also result in changes affecting higher education operations (AASCU, 2018).

Next on the AASCU 2018 top-ten list were concerns regarding the sluggish state revenue growth. Due to competing demands for state revenue, higher education leaders need to make the case for funding of higher education and link state funding support of higher education to the outcome of education as a springboard for economic growth. College affordability (number 3 on the list) has been a perennial concern since the inception of the AASCU top-ten list (showing up as tuition pricing or tuition policy in previous renditions of the report). Economic and workforce development (number 4 on the list) emerged as a policy issue over the past several years, in particular targeting mid-skill-level employee preparation. The tug-of-war occurring at the federal level over undocumented and DACA students (number 5 on the list) impacts campuses differently depending on the size of this population of students and state legislation.

On the AASCU top-ten list at number 6 is the issue of guns on campus. This concern first surfaced on the list in 2013 as gun violence at schools around the country resulted in the loss of life. Institutions with campus-based restrictions on guns and concealed weapons are challenged by some state legislation extending gun policies that force campuses to allow guns.

Changes in state populations require institutions of higher education to react and adjust (number 7 on the list). As outlined in chapter 7, several states have restructured their higher education systems as a result of population swings and changes in high school graduation rates. Connected to the changes in enrollment prompted by population changes is a focus on performance-based funding (PBF) and college completion (number 8 on the list). Despite the desire to use policy levers such as PBF to increase completion rates, research highlights that PBF does not result in intended outcomes (Hillman, Tandberg, & Fryar, 2015; Umbricht, Fernandez, & Ortagus, 2017).

The political context that resulted in federal policy making the top-ten list as a prominent state higher education policy issue also contributed to item number 9 on the list—campus free speech. Campus reactions to controversial speakers on campus and the associated student activism resulted in many colleges creating free-speech zones. The white nationalist march at the University of Virginia, "Unite the Right," resulted in the death of one person and the declaration of a state of emergency by the governor (ABC Action News, 2018).

The final item on the top-ten list in 2018 was combating campus sexual assault. At the time of this writing in early 2019, proposed changes to Title IX were in the comment phase (see United States Department of Education, 2016). The #MeToo movement spread rapidly after the public allegations against, and subsequent firing of, Harvey Weinstein (Kantor & Twohey, 2017). College campuses were not immune to these issues, with several campuses noting an increase in sexual-assault complaints and individuals publicly reporting claims of sexual harassment or assault (Felton, 2018; White, 2018). The high-profile cases at Michigan State University and Ohio State University

(Crowe, 2018; Hansen, 2018) serve as a warning for other college leaders of the need for vigilance regarding student and staff safety from sexual harassment and assault.

Accessing AASCU's top-ten list in January of each year should become a common practice for all college leaders. This outline provides a snapshot of key issues facing colleges across the nation. Leaders need to understand the type of leadership skills required in the changing higher education landscape. Moving forward, leaders must work to build a culture of innovation on campus that allows for flexibility, nimbleness, and the ability to adapt to address these changes.

Innovation for Student Success

Leadership in higher education differs from that found in business and industry, as the focus on student-centered practices diverges from a focus on customers and profits. True, institutions of higher education need to focus on a range of accountability measures, including student retention, graduation rates, a balanced budget, and access and support for underrepresented students. But the metrics and means differ. The preparation of students for the world of work and democratic citizenship requires particular approaches depending on institutional academic cultures and processes. This book makes the argument for the need of transformative leaders in higher education—individuals who disrupt what is taken for granted with regard to power and privilege that perpetuate inequities (Shields, 2010). In this day and age, the headlines are full of college leaders running afoul of the law and public morals and using their privilege for personal gain. Now more than ever, ethical leadership is required. Aspiring and new leaders must always have in the forefront the four ethical paradigms—the ethics of justice, care, critique, and profession (Shapiro & Stefkovich, 2016). These leaders must be courageous and must tap into a network of leaders both within and outside the institution for real change to occur.

Building an equity mind-set provides a means to assure that all students are considered in decision-making regarding admissions, academic programming, and student supports (Bensimon, 2006).

Student-centered practices that take into consideration the experiences of *all* students, not just those who are traditionally successful in college, must undergird programming to obtain the end goal of student success. Policy makers, parents, and students often question the need for a college education, in particular with the rising costs for tuition. When campuses build a culture for student success for all, outcomes improve (Wyner, 2014). It is the commitment to equity that helps achieve these end goals. Part of this process is a focus on innovation.

With innovation comes risk—hence the need for courageous leaders! Focusing on innovation requires knowing current processes and structures, building a commitment to change, and relying on a team to accomplish identified goals (Kotter, 2014; Tierney, 2014). Being ready to tackle the complex issues facing higher education today requires developing a broad cadre of leaders.

CHAPTER 1

Leadership and Learning on the Fly

Historically, leadership positions in higher education academic departments are filled by individuals who emerge from faculty ranks and have little, if any, administrative experience. The lack of training and preparation in critical areas such as personnel and human resources, strategic planning, and organizational management provide newly minted educational leaders with little experience on which to draw. In many cases, the lack of positional authority to supervise for these new front-line administrators has created a loosely coupled system in which a myriad of problems arise and, more frequently than not, are brushed aside. With multiple balls in the air, new higher education leaders must decide which problems to address first.

At a time when leadership in higher education has become increasingly more complex, administrators are less prepared to take over the helm. Traditional faculty and administrator roles are changing, the scope of demands on colleges and universities is increasing, time spent on development of faculty and leaders is scant, and there is a significant void in the literature regarding academic department governance and leadership effectiveness (Bess & Dee, 2014; Bryman, 2007; Hearn & McLendon, 2012). In 2004, Gmelch noted that the development of academic leaders is of critical importance and that "the academic leader is among the least studied and most misunderstood management position in America" (p. 69). More than a decade later, little has changed, and this book helps to fill the void.

What has changed is the environmental context in higher education. Academic leadership in higher education has become increasingly more complicated due, in part, to a convergence of an unprecedented number of environmental factors. In the past two decades, diminishing support through state appropriations and increased competition and growth from the for-profit higher education sector have strained public institutions. Declining revenue and resources, coupled with increased accountability and compliance expectations, has meant doing more with less. Additionally, other factors related to student debt, time to degree completion, and likelihood of employment after graduation have resulted in greater public scrutiny of the cost and value of four-year degrees (Archibald & Feldman, 2010; Lambert, 2014). The national recession from 2008 to 2011 exacerbated this climate of uncertainty and called greater attention to the return on investment of a college degree. Add unstable enrollments and changing student demographics to this context, and the result is an increasing level of stress on institutions and challenges to the status quo (Hoover & Supiano, 2016).

Technology is another major factor that has disrupted the higher education environment (Christensen, Horn, Caldera, & Soares, 2011). Traditional ways of teaching and learning have been challenged (Barr & Tagg, 1995; Weimer, 2013). Student demand for online and hybrid programs has increased (Major, 2015), resulting in increased administrative pressure on faculty to create more online offerings and to expand revenue streams for the institution (Lambert, 2014). In addition, traditional bricks-and-mortar buildings and offices are underutilized (Carlson, 2009), which has altered work dynamics. Faculty can access resources online, conduct online office hours, and teach in the comfort of their own home. Likewise, administrators and staff can accomplish many work-related tasks from the home office. The prevalence of anywhere and anytime access to technology and social media, has significantly changed socialization patterns, communication methods, and human interactions throughout the campus community (Moran, Seaman, & Tinti-Kane, 2011).

Given the changing higher education environment, leaders face new challenges in managing the campus workforce and in achieving organizational goals. However, leadership development has been lacking for a long time, and because of these changes facing colleges, attention to leadership preparation, recruitment, and mentoring is in critical need across higher education institutions today. Colleges and universities need highly skilled and knowledgeable academic leaders to effectively manage the challenges and opportunities that arise when organizations are in transition or experiencing periods of significant change (Eddy, Sydow, Alfred, & Garza Mitchell, 2015). The student-centered focus of higher education leadership presents a unique aspect for college leaders that is not covered in business books on leadership (Buller, 2014).

Exacerbating the need for leadership development is the unprecedented number of faculty retirements within the baby-boomer generation and the resulting increase in the hiring of contingent, non-tenure-track faculty replacements (DeZure, Shaw, & Rojewski, 2014; Kezar & Gehrke, 2014). A comparison of the percentage of the number of tenure-track and non-tenure-track faculty over four decades illustrates the gradual shift away from tenure-track faculty positions in higher education, which has traditionally been the breeding ground for future academic leaders. In 1969, the faculty ratio was 78.3 percent tenure-track to 21.7 percent non-tenure-track, and this comparative reversed by 2009, when the ratio upended to 33.5 percent tenure-track and 66.5 percent full- and part-time non-tenure-track (Kezar & Maxey, 2012). The pool of tenure-track faculty is steadily shrinking, and subsequently so is the pool of future academic leaders. This reality has serious implications for the profession. Cultivating leadership within a shrinking pool of faculty candidates will require shedding the decades-long practice of placing inexperienced individuals in leadership positions without adequate training or skills for success and having them learn on the job. The fast pace of change removes the luxury of the historical learn-as-you-go strategies. Institutions need to tap on leaders throughout the college to enact the types of strategic initiatives and innovation demanded today. As well, new leaders will also come from outside of higher education (Richmond, 2015) as hiring boards seek leaders with business acumen and a fresh approach to solving academic problems.

The purpose of this book is to illuminate the challenges that new higher education leaders may experience and to provide practical advice and strategies for success. The changing environmental context of the higher education landscape clearly helps to establish why a focus on the preparation of academic leaders is an important consideration. A cornerstone in preparing for a leadership position is to acquire a good understanding of leadership theory and to develop strategies for success.

Learning Objectives

- Leadership theory/constructs
- Organizational culture
- Leadership succession
- Leadership development

Overview of Leadership Theory

Leaders in higher education, as well as in any other sector, must know how to lead effectively in a wide range of contexts. There is a vast amount of research and literature devoted to the study of leadership (Amey, 2013). Yet novice leaders may feel overwhelmed navigating through the plethora of books and articles without clear direction as to how to situate their own needs or context within the options available. This short overview helps to synthesize and condense the larger literature base.

Learning how to lead is a dynamic and fluid process, ever changing, and negotiated depending on the organizational context and constituents. As leaders work with others within the organization, they must learn to recognize the cues and signals of power dynamics and relationships (Bolman & Deal, 2013). Leaders must also know how to facilitate role shifts (Leisyte & Dee, 2012), which include the art of stepping up and stepping back in empowering others to do the work. Over time, and through practice, leadership steps become more intuitive and authentic (Bornstein, 2014).

Understanding the evolution of organizational and leadership theories and concepts is a helpful way for today's leaders to recognize some of the prevailing and influential thoughts and practices. Theories provide a conceptual framework to support various assumptions and generalizations related to a particular phenomenon, which, in this case, is leadership and organizational management. They can provide explanatory frameworks that serve to guide thinking about the topic of effective ways to lead. Theories contribute to the advancement of knowledge and often change over time through ongoing research and testing of the basic constructs inherent in a given theory.

Kezar and Carducci (2009) have described the revolutionary progression of academic leadership as one in which conceptions have fundamentally shifted from a primarily leader-centric view to a "vision in which leadership is process centered, collective, context bound, nonhierarchical, and focused on mutual power and influence processes" (p. 2). Command-and-control styles of leadership have evolved over time to collaborative forms of leadership that empower others throughout the organizational system. Servant leadership, which operates from leaders working to serve others as opposed to operating from a position of leader first, provides one basis for working in this type of collaborative way (Wheeler, 2012)

Mapping the volume of research and literature related to organizational and leadership theory is beyond the scope of this book; however, an overview of seminal theories and perspectives from the mid-nineteenth century through contemporary times highlights the theoretical landscape. Table 1.1 presents a historical timeline of the evolution of leadership theories and depicts predominant principles and concepts that contributed to the various organizational and leadership perspectives of the time.

Table 1.1. Evolution of Leadership Theory

Leadership theory	Tenets of theory	Additional references
Great man theory, 1850–1900	In the mid-nineteenth century, the prevalent leadership theory held that great leaders are born and not made. The theory grew out of a male-centric era in which the view of great men was as heroes, destined for leadership.	Brown (2013) Heifetz (1994) Kezar & Carducci (2009) Twombly (1995)
Trait theories, 1900–1950	Similar to the great man theory, trait theories built on the idea that identification of a specific set of leadership traits provided individuals with the capacity to lead.	Dinh et al. (2014) Kezar & Carducci (2009) Northouse (2015) Zaccaro (2007)
Behavioral theories, 1950–1970	Behavioral theories focused on the correlation between behavior and effective leadership. This focus represented a shift away from leadership based on characteristics to leadership based on actions.	Bass & Stogdill (1990) Conger & Kanungo (1987) Cyert & March (1963) Northouse (2015) Wheeler (2012)
Contingency theories, 1960–1980	Contingency theories of leadership emerged in the 1960s and broadened the notion of leadership beyond the individual leader to include context. Effective leadership styles and behaviors were contingent on the situation.	Fiedler (1967) Peters, Hartke, & Pohlmann (1985) Yukl (2002)
Transactional theories, 1970–1990	Managerial models of leadership that involve a transaction between leaders and subordinates form the basis of transactional theories of leadership. This perspective emerged in the late 1970s. The level of employee motivation is contingent on the nature of the transaction or reward.	Avolio, Bass, & Jung (1999) Eagly, Johannesen-Schmidt, & Van Engen (2003) Kuhnert & Lewis (1987)

(*continued*)

Table 1.1 *(continued)*

Leadership theory	Tenets of theory	Additional references
Transformational theories, 1980–2000	These theories emerged at the same time as transactional theories and apply to a form of charismatic leadership that builds motivation and moral purpose among followers to transcend personal interests for the collective good.	Bass (1985, 1991, 1997) Bass & Avolio (1993) Bass & Riggio (2006) Burns (1978) Yammarino, Spangler, & Bass (1993)
Networked leadership, 2000–present	Leadership built on collective input of many emerged at the turn of the twenty-first century. Increasingly complex organizational contexts require leadership throughout the organization.	Amey (2013) Eddy, Sydow, Alfred, & Garza Mitchell (2015) Gronn (2002) Hickman (2010) Lipman-Blumen (2000)

Great Man and Trait Theories

"Captains of the industry are born and not made" (F. Taylor, 1911, p. 8). The notion that leaders are bigger than life held sway in the early days of the industrial revolution. One of the earliest command-and-control leadership theories, the "great man theory," emerged in the mid-nineteenth century. This theory ushered in a trait-based perspective, arguing that leaders, typified as "great men" or heroes, possessed various attributes that distinguished them from nonleaders. The premise behind this theory was that leadership was a set of innate qualities generally ascribed to men in such terms as boldness, strength, vigor, and power (Amey & Twombly, 1992). Identifiable traits included a variety of physical, emotional, and social characteristics deemed necessary for effective leadership. The thinking was that superior individuals, born with a discrete set of traits, were destined for leadership roles in society. Leadership research remained focused on the identification of individual traits until the 1930s, when researchers began turning their attention to specific behavioral styles of leaders and, in turn, how leaders treated their followers (Day & Antonakis, 2012).

There has been a resurgence of interest in the correlation between traits and leadership effectiveness in recent years. Zaccaro, Kemp, and Bader (2004) proposed a model based on an integrative set of traits demonstrating cognitive ability, social capability, and dispositional tendencies. In addition, executive search firms for academic leaders also look for specific traits in individuals that correlate to potential success. For example, the Aspen Institute (2014) created a "toolkit" of qualities that effective leaders should possess. This return to trait theory runs the risk of excluding leaders who do not quite fit the mold of commonly accepted leadership traits. Focusing instead on the way leaders continue to learn as the context changes may result in better alignment of skill sets for today's complex environment (Amey, 2013).

Behavioral Theories

Behavioral leadership theories emerged in the late 1930s and spanned into the 1990s, with a focus on examining the behavior of leaders. Early research (Lewin, Lippitt, & White, 1939) focused on the link between leadership style and employee motivation, specifically understanding how authoritarian, democratic, and laissez-faire leadership styles influenced the performance of subordinates in the workplace. Further, seminal leadership studies in the 1950s (Halpin &Winer, 1957; Katz & Kahn, 1952) influenced contemporary perspectives that focus on the identification of specific behaviors to include in leadership development trainings (Blake & Mouton, 1994). Blake and Mouton (1994) developed a leadership grid based on two areas of concern, one for production and the other for people. Five key leadership styles emerged in this grid. Team management was one of the leadership styles identified as the optimal way to lead (Lunenburg & Ornstein, 2012). In this case, leaders have a high concern for people and a high concern for production; on one end of the continuum, with a focus on concern for people, is servant leadership, in which the leader acts as servant to others (Wheeler, 2012). However, behavioral theories, like trait theories, are limited in scope and fail to take into account the complex array of variables at play and the influence such variables have on academic leadership today.

Contingency Theories

Contingency theories offer more complex understandings of leadership and are based on the notion that leadership behavior is contingent on the situation. Leaders may apply different styles depending on the context and circumstances in a given situation. Bensimon, Neumann, and Birnbaum (1989) noted the overlap between behavioral and contingency theories and concluded that there is a consensus that no single approach or style of leadership is best because of the wide range of internal and external variables involved. Two decades of extensive research on the topic of contingency theories produced and refined Fieldler's Contingency Model (1967). This model considers how multiple factors influence leaders and the way they lead, including task structure, positional power, leadership motivation, group performance, and effectiveness (Fieldler, 1967; Fielder & Chemers, 1974, 1984). Various combinations of these factors may apply to a particular situation. For example, in an immediate crisis, a leader would be more likely to adopt a command-and-control, or authoritarian, style, particularly in light of any threats to the safety and security of the workplace. Eddy (2010) has noted, however, that one of the difficulties with contingency theories is that an individual's preferred leadership style is firmly entrenched. Leaders may be unable to modify their preferred style as situations change, a consideration that is inconsistent with the core element of contingency theories: the leader's ability to adapt to ever-changing circumstances.

Transactional Theories

Transactional leadership theory centers on transactions made between leaders and subordinates, with the intention of benefiting both

(McCleskey, 2014). Transactions based on the mutual agreement of "give and take" can be both constructive and corrective in nature. Leaders assume positional power and focus on effective management of the organization as they make transactions with employees, whereas the motivations of employees depends on the value and perception of the reward in the transaction. Kellerman (1984) noted that transactional leadership is only as effective as leaders' ability to meet the changing expectations and needs of their followers. When the reward no longer is present, employees often stop holding up their end of the work.

Transformational Theories

Transformational leadership research has dominated the field since the 1980s (Diaz-Saenz, 2011; Northouse, 2015) and was first popularized by Burns (1978). Transformational theories suggest that instead of using transactions to appeal and motivate followers to action, leaders make a connection with followers that aligns with followers' values and builds on a sense of shared morality of what is the right action to take. Bass (1985) refined thinking about transformational leadership and incorporated concepts of charisma (House, 1977) into this extended understanding of the theory. Three key methods are used by transformational leaders to motivate followers:

1. Raising followers' levels of consciousness about the importance and value of specified and idealized goals
2. Getting followers to transcend their own self-interest for the sake of the team or organization
3. Moving followers to address higher-level needs (Bass, as cited in Northouse, 2015)

The core of transformational leadership is to move followers past a focus on their own self-interest to band together to accomplish outcomes for the greater collective. The reason followers are willing to focus on the larger good is that transformational leaders inspire commitment to a shared vision, by exemplifying high standards of moral and ethical conduct focused on doing the right thing, and provide followers with space for innovation through listening to their individual needs. Transformational leaders are perceived by followers as more effective (Lowe, Kroeck, & Sivasubramaniam, 1996). Transformative leaders differ from the reform-minded transformational leaders, because the focus of the latter is on changing systems that "create or perpetuate inequity and injustice" (Shields, 2010, p. 564).

Networked Leadership Theories

Moving beyond thinking of single, positional leaders who inspire others to action are concepts of team leadership or networked leadership. The idea of collaborative leadership (Astin & Astin, 2000) or distributed leadership (Bolden, Petrov, & Gosling, 2009) breaks from traditional, hierarchical forms of leading. Bensimon and Neumann (1993) outlined the possibilities inherent in using team leadership and the various roles that team members hold, as well as the complexity of this work and the institutional culture required to support teams. The construct of connective leadership (Lipman-Blumen, 1996) builds on three sets of skills that include mastering and understanding individual abilities (direct), supporting and contributing to others' tasks (relational), and maximizing interactions (instrumental). Undergirding effective ways of building collaborative leadership is a culture of trust, transparency, and focus on team outcomes.

More recently, the idea of networked leadership (Eddy et al., 2015) builds on Helgesen's (2005) web of inclusion that moves the focus from hierarchical leadership to connective leadership. Social network theory (Scott & Carrington, 2011) shows how connecting critical nodes or hubs of expertise can help achieve greater outcomes. Where networked leadership differs from collaborative leadership is the way in which hubs and connections occur both within and outside the institution. The flexibility of today's higher education environment, the expansion of technology, and the interconnectedness of the global economy require an expanded way to think about leadership and demand recognition of connections external to the institution.

This overview of leadership theories provides brief background information. Entire books are devoted to each of the topics listed. Even though the theories outlined appear in the order of their development and prominence in the field, it is important to note that many theories are in operation and practice concurrently. Despite the conclusion that trait theory does little to predict effective leadership (Lord, De Vader, & Alliger, 1986), in practice, many people in the field still believe that a certain array of traits or skills predict ultimate leader success. The resurgence of lists of traits in leadership development programs highlights how many leadership models are in operation at the same time.

Newer conceptions of leadership that acknowledge and build on the contributions of many people in the organization, with a focus on student-centered leading and social justice, require a shift in historical thinking about leading and an examination into historical organizational structures. Changing the architecture of organizational hierarchies begins to move thinking about leadership past top-down models. Networked leadership moves toward intentionality in setting up connections rather than happenstance organizational relationships. "It is not merely *who* is in the network but *how* and *why* the connection is made that is important. And leaders must select *what* information is used to chart and navigate plans" (Eddy et al., 2015, p. 117). The bigger test in thinking about leadership theory is what really works in practice.

Theory into Practice: A Leadership Framework

When individuals are oriented to foundational and contemporary leadership constructs, more effective leadership emerges. Black (2015) has noted that testing existing leadership frameworks to determine their relevance in particular higher education settings and circumstances can improve how individuals learn to lead. Theoretical and conceptual frameworks can help leaders move from a basic understanding of theory to application in practice, encouraging room for reflections and increased learning. Bolman and Deal's (2013) organizational frames provide a useful example for a leadership framework.

According to Bolman and Deal (2013), "A frame is a mental model—a set of ideas and assumptions that you carry in your head to help you understand and negotiate a particular territory" (p. 10). Individual mental maps develop based on prior experience, knowledge, and one's worldview. These maps are powerful and influence the approach that one may take both in responding to a situation and in problem-solving. Learning how to utilize multiple theoretical organizational frames and to view circumstances through different lenses helps leaders develop a broader understanding of the issues at hand and navigate more effectively throughout the organization.

A key leadership tool is being able to move and change perspectives on the basis of emerging needs. Research shows that multiframe perspectives are most evident in seasoned leaders and in community college leaders (Bensimon, 1990b). The more time leaders have had on the job, the more situations they have encountered and the broader range of outcomes they have considered. For example, community colleges receive less funding than other types of institutions do, and because of their community-oriented missions, community college leaders frequently wear multiple hats. An individual may simultaneously be the director of continuing education and the director of teaching and learning.

Bolman and Deal (2013) describe four distinct organizational frames, summarized briefly in table 1.2. Even though these frames are presented as distinct, multiple frames of orientation, in reality, several are often in play at once. Understanding one's predominant leadership frame and another individual's favored frame of reference can provide insight into the best way to build a relationship with that person. Thus, if the dean is someone who relies heavily on rules and

Table 1.2. Bolman and Deal Frames

Structural frame (Architecture metaphor)	The focus of the structural frame is on the architecture of the organization. Leaders using a structural frame tend to rely on rules, regulations, contracts, policies, strategic plans, goals, and other documents. Organizational design tends to be more formal as evinced by units, subunits, and systems (Bolman & Deal, 2013, p. 21).
Human resources frame (Family metaphor)	The focus of the human resources frame is people. Leaders using this frame strive to understand their employees by examining such aspects as one's strengths, weaknesses, motives, emotions, desires, and fears. Organizational desgn tends to be more informal and family-like (Bolman & Deal, 2013, p. 21).
Political frame (Jungle metaphor)	The focus of the political frame is the organization as a competitive arena. Issues of power and control of resources, competing interests, strong versus weak, and inequity all contribute to a jungle-like organization that at times can feel ruthless and threatening. Leaders within this frame rely heavily on conflict resolution, problem solving, and negotiation skills (Bolman & Deal, 2013, p. 22).
Symbolic frame (Theater metaphor)	The focus of the symbolic frame is on meaning and faith in a spiritual sense. Leaders operating within this frame focus on rituals, ceremony, storytelling, symbols, and culturally embedded practices (Bolman & Deal, 2013, p. 22).

past precedent, a department chair requesting a change in practice could provide a rationale based on current policy and established procedures for modifying policies. Due to the dean's preference for operating within a structural frame, this approach would probably be more favorable than requesting from a human resources or symbolic approach would be.

A link in the web resources at the end of the chapter provides a self-test for you to identify your individual leadership orientation in each of the four frames (See Frames Quick Self-Rating Scale). In addition, the case study in this chapter provides an opportunity for you to analyze the scenario utilizing the four frames.

Case #1: Out with the Old; In with the New (Part 1)

To begin to apply the ideas presented in this book, case studies help to provide a context for application. Each case presents a realistic context that new leaders may encounter. A set of prompts points out particular areas of the case in which you can contemplate your own work context and how to apply the information in the chapter. It is important in this review to consider what elements of the case relate to real situations you might encounter and how the discussion points can apply to your personal situation and context. The case study in this chapter provides an opportunity for you to analyze the scenario presented by utilizing Bolman and Deal's (2013) four frames. Think about different approaches from the structural, human resources, political, and symbolic perspectives.

Letting go can be difficult for some leaders, especially regarding relinquishing power and control. This case explores the behaviors of a department chairperson, Sally Moore (all names and scenarios are fictitious). This leader ruled with an iron fist, drove out new faculty members, and cultivated a culture of fear and mystique throughout her two terms in the office. Moore thrived on power and control, and during her tenure, department faculty were kept very isolated from one another. Moore regularly rebuked attempts made by other programs and departments within the college to collaborate, as she was of the opinion that people in other areas were incompetent and that their programs lacked quality and rigor. Not only was Moore arrogant as the leader of her department, but over time she became hypercritical of any policies, procedures, or personnel that were not under her direct supervision. Communication channels were frequently blocked, and critical information received by Moore through weekly meetings with the dean and other department chairpersons never reached department members. The negative skewing of the select information shared with the department resulted in the department faculty developing a very myopic and distorted view of the college and university at large. Moore overplayed the perception that her role was one of a warrior needing to protect departmental resources and keep administrative action at bay.

Coupled with Moore's authoritarian leadership was a changing university landscape. Unique external and internal conditions within the university, college, and department created the environmental context for decision-making. In this instance, the department was experiencing a transition from a predominantly veteran faculty to predominantly new and untenured faculty. New and untenured faculty are vulnerable and more likely to be complacent when trying to navigate through an unknown culture. Initially they may be more amenable to a bureaucratic leadership style, as highly directive behaviors complement their need to know and understand organizational norms and practices. However, over time, when novice faculty members mature in their roles and when there becomes a strength in numbers, faculty who once embraced directive behaviors will often find such leadership stifling and intolerable.

Sally Moore's tenure as department chairperson ultimately ended, and she returned to her faculty role, despite her willingness to continue to serve as chairperson. Even though there were several senior faculty who, at one time, may have aspired to the role, no one was now willing to serve as department chair because of the shared assumptions and negative perspectives about administration that had been cultivated throughout the former chairperson's tenure. The department opted to post the position for a new department chairperson and ultimately selected a leader who was the direct opposite of Moore. The new chairperson was male, midcareer, and collaborative in nature. Tom Smith had an upbeat personality and was student focused. He was aware of previous challenges within the department and began his tenure with optimism and high hopes for faculty empowerment and program improvement. Even though Smith had not served in a formal leadership role prior to taking over as department chair, he was experienced in developing new programs and had expertise in online teaching and learning. The department majority was hopeful that an external candidate would bring a fresh perspective and provide direction and momentum for innovation and change. In particular, the department wanted to expand its online offerings and felt Smith's expertise in online teaching and learning provided a needed resource.

The next academic year started out on a high note; however, no one had anticipated the level of anger and resentment that the former chairperson had for the department and, in particular, for the new leader. Smith's first year as a new leader was a baptism by fire. Moore, using the very few alliances she had with faculty and staff, focused her energy and power in subtle ways to create roadblocks for Smith's proposed initiatives and to submarine these change efforts. Using the rigid policies and procedures she had implemented and relying on the default adage of "this is the way things are done around here," progress was stalled. Moore devoted hours studying and citing the department bylaws and the university's faculty agreement in attempts to thwart change. Department meetings became a public forum for long-winded diatribes and ridicule as Moore and her small group of supporters used past precedence and contractual arguments to block progress. "You can't do that" became the department mantra, and while in most instances the arguments proved to be unfounded or based on historical fiction, it was only after many wasted hours of investigation and fact checking that any minimal forward movement occurred.

Department faculty became increasingly frustrated and began to view Smith as weak. The initial high hopes for departmental change were quickly dashed as Smith's time became consumed by mediating fights and putting out fires. The new chairperson was soon under attack by two camps: the minority who had allegiance to Moore and the majority who were dismayed by the rocky leadership transition and constant in-fighting. By the end of the academic year, two faculty members resigned and went to other institutions, and one retired, which further crippled departmental programs and diminished the leadership effectiveness of the new chairperson.

Guiding Questions

The following questions help to point out how new leaders might begin to understand new scenarios using the various leadership frameworks available. Take a few minutes to contemplate your response to each of the following questions.

1 How do departments give rise to leaders like Moore, and why do you think her behavior was tolerated for such a long time?
2 Issues related to power and control are inherent throughout the case. What would you do to address the behavior of Sally Moore, the former chairperson? How would you advise Tom Smith, the new chairperson, to move forward?
3 A strong academic leader does not always transition seamlessly into a strong managerial leader. How do we develop strong academic leaders in higher education? In addition to role-specific training, what would you add to a professional development plan?
4 Consider how you analyzed the case using each of Bolman and Deal's four frames. Was there one frame in particular that you thought would be the best approach to understand the underlying dynamics of the case? Did you consider a multiframe plan of action? As a leader, how would reframing a problem help you determine solutions?

Case Discussion

In this case, the selection process for the new chairperson is in direct contrast to one in which a department openly discusses, plans, and prioritizes leadership succession. Ideally, the incoming chairperson would have already served as an assistant chair, cochair, or in another leadership capacity before transitioning into the role. As evinced in this case, negative perceptions of administrative roles kept faculty from aspiring to leadership opportunities and forced an external selection of candidates. Who would want to enter into a situation filled with such negativity? Given the administrative naiveté of the department faculty, they selected a colleague with promising qualifications but with no experience in an actual leadership role.

Another important consideration for new leaders is the existing culture of the institution. Understanding how to read and navigate the culture of an organization or unit is another critical skill for academic leaders. Leaders who understand and apply multiple lenses to situations are able to generate a broad view of the potential stakeholder and organizational perspectives, responses, and tensions in a given situation. The ability to reframe situations for others is further enhanced when the leader also understands the contextual layers unique to each organizational culture. In institutions of higher education, the organizational culture can vary widely from college to college and within the vast array of departments and units on campus, as subcultures develop their own assumptions and shared meanings. A leader's failure to read the culture accurately can lead to unintentional missteps when behaviors are misconstrued as insensitive within the surrounding culture (Bryman, 2007).

Organizational Culture

Deeply rooted in anthropology and the history of the institution, organizational culture is a complex set of cultural dynamics based on such things as shared values, underlying assumptions and beliefs, norms, and observable practices and behaviors. Organizational culture has been the focus of research for decades (Hofstede, 1998; Tierney 1988). Schein (1992) defines organizational culture as "a pattern of shared basic assumptions that the group learned as it solved its problems of external adaption and internal integration, which has worked well enough to be considered valid and, therefore, to be taught to new members as the correct way to perceive, think, and feel in relation to those problems" (p. 12). Cultures are deeply entrenched systems of group behavior that help to explain why things are done the way they are in a particular environment. In this sense, culture is viewed as a dynamic process, and how the group behaves constructs reality. Thus, the maintenance of culture is reinforced or changes depending on group actions.

So how does a prospective leader interviewing at a higher education institution get an idea of what kind of culture prevails there? When you know what to look for, scanning the environment is a helpful technique. Schein (1992) discusses uncovering the culture by examining three different levels: artifacts, espoused values, and basic underlying assumptions.

- Artifacts are visible structures or processes that one can see, but they can be difficult to understand without knowing the context. Artifacts come in all shapes and sizes and include such things as symbols, logos, architecture, myths, stories, rituals, and ceremonies (Schein, 1992). Walking around the campus, observing the artifacts and customs you witness, studying the history of the institution, and asking questions to discern the meaning of what you see may help you to get an initial sense of the culture at a new place.
- Espoused values refer to the articulated philosophies, beliefs, or norms of an organization (Schein, 1992). These values may be spoken or written and can be found in publications, websites, and documents, as well as graduation speeches, presentations to the Board of Trustees, or conversations with stakeholders. However, it is important to know that espoused values are meaningless unless they become embedded into the fabric of the institution. Here, the question to ask yourself is, "Are the campus members actually 'walking the talk' of what they espouse?"
- Even though artifacts and espoused values offer visible cues regarding the culture, Schein (1992) believes that to fully understand and predict behavior, one must learn the basic underlying assumptions of the organization, as these constitute the essence of the culture. These assumptions generally consist of taken-for-granted and unconscious behaviors adopted by the group. They are relatively invisible unless challenged, which then provokes a defensive response (Schein, 1994).

Leaders who want to change the culture must first recognize the basic assumptions and understand how they came to be and then utilize this knowledge to mitigate the frustration felt by the group when challenging those assumptions. Kezar (2009) notes, "Leaders will be more successful if they play the role of organizational anthropologist, getting to know the underlying values, history, and traditions of their campus as well as the key individuals they work with" (p. 17).

An image often used to illustrate the levels of culture is an iceberg. The portion of the iceberg that is visible above water represents artifacts, the visible clues about an institution's culture. Yet lurking below the surface are espoused values and beliefs of individuals within the organization. With some attention and focused observation, these values might surface. It is the hidden, deep assumptions that people hold that are more vexing. Without targeted attention, reflection, and questioning, these values remain hidden and can prevent change. Think of how the *Titanic* crashed into the unseen portion of the iceberg.

Being able to navigate organizational cultures is difficult. Berquist and Pawlak (2008) offer a conceptual framework composed of six cultures that they identify as prevalent in higher education institutions today. A brief description of the cultures and related leadership styles can be found in table 1.3.

Understanding the dynamics inherent in each of the cultures proposed by Berquist and Pawlak (2008) contributes to an increased understanding of how internal and external factors shape cultures over time. Although the six cultures are described as distinct, it is likely that each culture will include dimensions that are also predominantly found in other culture types. Exploring cultures is intriguing because so much of the culture hides under layers of socially constructed behaviors that accumulate over time and exist long after the original creators of the culture have left. Leaders benefit when they possess an understanding of the operating culture(s) within the organization. Individuals seeking leadership roles should be thinking about their fit within the prevailing culture and how they might develop leadership expertise that is transferable across different cultures.

Table 1.3. Culture and Leadership

Type of culture	Description
Collegial culture	This culture is disciplinary focused, with a strong emphasis on faculty research and scholarship. Faculty value autonomy, academic freedom, and faculty governance. A weakness of this culture is "a lack of organization and coherence" (Berquist & Pawlak, 2008, p. 73). Leadership is informal and mindful of a strong faculty governance structure.
Managerial culture	This culture is highly structured and goal oriented and values student achievement. There is an emphasis on efficiency and managerial competency of both leaders and faculty and less focus on the personal and financial needs of employees. Leadership styles are formal and directive.
Developmental culture	This culture is mission focused and emphasizes professional learning and development for all members. Leaders in this culture model servant leadership and are generally indirect and collaborative.
Advocacy culture	This culture values confrontation, fair bargaining, and equitable policies and procedures. Leaders in this culture focus on accountability and performance assessment.
Virtual culture	This culture uses an open system, which is flexible and shifting due to technological advances and rapid changes in the global network economy. Leadership styles are entrepreneurial and adaptive to changing conditions.
Tangible culture	This culture reflects the institution's historical roots and traditions. Symbolism, spirituality, and a strong sense of community characterize this culture. Faculty are standards driven and focused on traditional teaching and learning. Leadership styles are formal and steeped in carrying out long-standing traditions.

Schein (1985) described leadership and culture as "two sides of the same coin" and contended that "the only thing of real importance leaders do is to create and manage culture" (p. 2). The adage "culture eats strategy for lunch" is one take on Schein's work and underscores the importance of leaders understanding culture. Unlocking the keys to the culture, and deciphering the cultural codes of conduct within, is a prerequisite for future learning and change within the organization. In an effort to help leaders learn more about the elusive aspects of a culture, there are a number of informal and formal ways to conduct a culture analysis of an organization. Examples include culture audits, observations, structured interviews, and a variety of survey instruments.

Case #1: Out with the Old; In with the New (Part 2)

The department was in trouble despite Tom Smith starting as the new chairperson. Programs were adrift, enrollment was sinking, and the constant turnover of faculty destabilized the unit. Smith blamed himself for the problems and met with the dean to offer his resignation. The dean was equally frustrated and weighed his options. He could bring in an interim chair from another department, repost the position and start over, or take a more active role in both mentoring and building the leadership capacity of the current chair. The dean committed to at least one more year with Smith as chairperson and required Smith to meet individually with other college leaders and to examine the structure, practices, and policies utilized in those departments where productivity was high. In addition to Smith's weekly meetings with the dean, webinars, and targeted leadership trainings, a peer mentor in another college agreed to work closely with him in the coming year.

Smith was also able to secure a new faculty position to fill a vacancy in the department. He worked closely with the dean throughout the search process and hoped to attract a strong candidate to begin shifting the culture. Careful consideration went into the makeup of the selection committee, the site visit for the interview, and final negotiations with the candidate, as the new faculty member could be instrumental in stimulating change.

Simultaneously, Smith needed to revitalize the department and create conditions for renewal. He met with faculty members individually to talk about their experience in the department and to solicit ideas for how to advance various initiatives. Through one-on-one conversations, Smith was able to find common goals and identified individuals who were willing either to facilitate small-group work or to participate in one or more of the department's change initiatives. Using a strategy of divide, empower, and conquer, he implemented short-term ad hoc working groups to tackle programmatic and department issues. The faculty divided into small learning communities that were assigned different issues to examine, research, and generate recommendations that would be reviewed by the whole group. As chair, Smith was also an active participant in each of the groups. Collectively, faculty members felt empowered and discovered that they had a voice in decision-making.

Faculty meetings slowly shifted away from groupthink and complaining sessions. At each meeting, the leader of every small group provided a progress update, action items, and next steps, which in turn instilled a sense of ownership and accountability for all members. Over time, the power base of the previous chair dissipated as leadership was cultivated throughout the department. The new chair gained trust by building relationships and working closely with each group. The problem-solving structure that Smith implemented gave credibility to his leadership as department members saw steady progress. Three years later, the department began thriving.

Guiding Questions

Contemplate the role of culture in the changes that occurred in the department. In particular, consider what type of culture was in place.

1 What are some of the different ways that academic professionals, like Smith, can find their leadership voice? How do positional leaders effectively build leadership within the ranks?

2 Leadership and followership are two sides of the same coin. What role and responsibilities do followers have to their leaders?

3 In this case, the dean chose to support the new chair. Considering the case, design two alterative directions the dean could have taken to resolve this dilemma. Discuss the potential pros and cons of each.

4 As a newcomer to an organization in a leadership role, craft five questions that you would ask to begin to understand the unit culture beyond what can be detected on a superficial level.

Leadership is an action, not a title, and the ability to lead can be found in every person.
—Shapiro, 2005, p. 1

Case Discussion

The case study in this chapter illustrates the importance of planning for leadership succession and leadership development. Faculty leadership succession in departments is rarely a seamless process, and at times it can be downright contentious. Motivation to serve in academic leadership positions is divided, with some faculty members not having the desire or the interest in taking on the duties and responsibilities of the chairperson and other faculty members viewing the position as an opportunity to serve and advance department initiatives and programs. In some instances, department members engage in a selection process that requires a lot of cajoling and convincing before a reluctant individual agrees to step up to the task and take a turn at leading. In other scenarios, individuals may openly campaign for the vote, for reasons that range anywhere from total self-interest to purely altruistic motivations. Department bylaws are generally very clear on procedures to elect a new chair, but rarely is there a well-defined plan and process for leadership succession. The existing culture of the department and the university also influence how leaders are selected and how leaders succeed.

Previous research (Carroll & Wolverton, 2004; Gmelch, 1994) showed that while only 3 percent of department chairs receive leadership training, approximately 80 percent of the decisions in higher education are made at the departmental level. Learning to lead on the fly quickly leads to potential frustration and wreaks havoc on organizational productivity and innovation. The case study in this chapter is an example of leadership problems at the department level gone awry. An inexperienced department chair without the knowledge and skill set necessary to manage conflict and change was set up for failure when transitioning into a troubled department with a disgruntled former leader as a departmental member. Not understanding the existing departmental culture or history at the beginning of a new leader's tenure creates additional stumbling blocks.

Preparing leaders at all levels is important if we are to ensure that there will be a sufficient number of people to lead in institutions of higher education in the future. Research conducted by the American Council on Education (2012) found that 58 percent of college presidents are over the age of sixty-one. We have already seen the beginning of a wave of retirements, with more to follow. The attention on succession planning for presidents is generally considered a must, but careful selection of leadership positions at all levels would enhance the overall quality of the institution. Formal training and internship programs offer one avenue for leadership development. Leadership development can also occur on campus through institutionalized trainings, mentoring, and fellowship opportunities. Long, Johnson, Faught, and Street (2013) state, "The future success of quality leadership at institutions of higher education largely depends on the implementation of a succession management plan" (p. 77). Focusing on how best to prepare leadership talent is critical for the future of higher education.

Making This Personal

In this chapter, a range of leadership theories and organizational frames have been introduced. Reflect on how you can apply the information in this chapter in your own leadership preparation.

- As you think about your own work environment, how would you define your role and the role of others around you?
- How do the leaders in your organization model leadership behavior? Are they effective?

Leadership is not a solo act. It involves others and is played out through interpersonal relationships with followers in a unique cultural context. Knowing this, it is important to consider how you can develop working relationships with others and strengthen your own networks and ties.

Higher education has done very little to train and prepare leaders within the ranks. At your institution, what kind of leadership training is available for faculty and staff? Have you been a participant in training designed specifically to cultivate leaders? If not, are you prepared to engage in self-study, seek out targeted professional development, and engage in ongoing reflection regarding your capacity to lead? The lack of formal succession plans in higher education needs to change. First, senior leaders must assess anticipated turnover in positions and identify a list of positions that are likely to need new leaders in the next five years. Second, intentional leadership development of a broad array of faculty and staff should occur. Many institutions build Grow Your Own leadership programs to help develop a large group of individuals for future leadership roles. Finally, individuals can jump-start their own development by taking part in campus-based or other professional development workshops. As new structures are created in higher education, all campus members need to help in moving the campus forward. Midlevel administrative leaders and faculty leaders will take on particularly critical roles in higher education, and providing them with the best tools possible provides a winning scenario for the institution. Leadership is a dynamic process marked by continual growth and change. The leader in you today is only the foundation for the leader you can become in the future.

Key Chapter Points

- Leadership is multidimensional and enhanced by the ability to reframe situations for others using multiple perspectives.
- Leadership relies on followers and networks to be most effective.
- Organizational culture is complex and socially constructed over time. Leaders need to understand the culture of their workplace in order to change it.
- Effective organizations commit resources to build leadership from within and to plan for succession.

Web Resources

- American Council on Education resources:
  https://www.acenet.edu/Research-Insights/Pages/Senior-Leaders/Toolkit-Resources-for-Administrators.aspx
- Aspen Institute's Global Leadership Network:
  https://www.aspeninstitute.org/programs/aspen-global-leadership-network/
- Frames Quick Self-Rating Scale:
  http://www.bolman.com/frames_selfrating_scale.htm
- Timeline of leadership theories:
  http://www.leadership-central.com/leadership-theories.html#axzz4VNDmkHWL

Leadership Training

There are a number of training programs for leaders at all levels in higher education. In addition to those found below, you will also find leadership programs within specific discipline or subject areas. In addition to face-to-face trainings, there are a great number of online courses and webinars focused on leadership development for targeted skill areas.

- Academy for Innovative Higher Education Leadership: https://georgetown.asu.edu/
- American Council on Education leadership programs: http://www.acenet.edu/leadership/Pages/default.aspx
- Berkeley's Executive Leadership Academy: https://cshe.berkeley.edu/events/executive-leadership-academy
- Center for Creative Leadership: http://www.ccl.org/Leadership/index.aspx
- Harvard Management Development Program: https://www.gse.harvard.edu/ppe/program/management-development-program-mdp
- HERS Leadership Training for Women in Higher Education: http://hersnet.org

CHAPTER 2

Courageous Leadership during Times of Change

Leadership—it's all about the people. Much has been written about leadership, strategies for leading, and tactics for success, but at the center of all this writing is how leaders relate to others and how leaders help change campuses. How leaders set the stage for interacting with faculty, students, community stakeholders, and boards of trustees influences the potential for change and success on campus.

Take a minute to think about the leader in the case example in chapter 1. Clearly, the actions by Sally Moore, the first department chairperson highlighted in the case, damaged some relationships. She was combative and operated using punitive responses in her effort to maintain control. Undoubtedly, authoritarian approaches to leadership often damage relationships and make others reluctant to contribute to change efforts in what is perceived as a no-win situation. The new department chair, Tom Smith, had a rocky start during the leadership transition but was eventually able to build relationships and initiate a change in culture. This chapter focuses on the role of courageous leadership in achieving positive change and picks up on the discussion of networked leadership outlined in chapter 1. Particular attention is paid to leveraging the various leadership frames and the role of building trust during the change process.

Learning Objectives

- Courageous/collaborative leadership
- Relationships within leadership frames
- Building trust
- Strategies for change

Just like the case in chapter 1, today's headlines are replete with votes of no confidence of college leaders, the toppling of chancellors due to their inattention to matters of race, and the difficulty of filling what some people see as untenable top-level leader positions. This chapter focuses on ways leaders can build credibility, how they can value and empower others through collaborative and meaningful leadership practices, and how leaders can harness the power of social and emotional intelligence within social systems to push the needle on campus change efforts.

Kouzes and Posner (2011) emphasize that "leadership is a relationship" and highlight the critical importance of making meaningful connections among people to build positive and engaging work environments (p. 2). Using strategic networking and authentic leadership practices to develop others can help leaders build effective teams and allies, both within the institution and inside other partnering organizations (Eddy & Amey, 2014). Through collegial and supportive relationships, individuals can be motivated to change, grow, and advance common goals in an organization (Black & Gregersen, 2013). How leaders harness this potential makes the difference between success and failure.

Taking as a given that leaders need to build good relationships, it is important to understand how relationships and roles in the college may look different depending on the leadership orientation of each individual. To discuss this further, in this chapter we turn again to the four frames that Bolman and Deal (2013) identify for leaders to use in their approaches to their work. At the core of each of the frames is how mental models (Senge, 1990) influence an individual's worldview. Mental models serve as shortcuts for people that build on unconscious thought processes (Dane & Pratt, 2007; Gladwell, 2007), and understanding more about the default mode of thinking for each of the frames aids in using the best-aligned strategies for building relationships. Relationships are at the core of collaborative leadership.

Power differentials exist in higher education, as witnessed in the case in chapter 1. The hierarchy of colleges and universities includes different levels of power that emerge due to positional authority. Power differentials between people can breed distrust and lack of commitment and can leave the leader truly "alone at the top." In this era of social media, power has become available to the masses. Consider the increased use by student protesters of various social media platforms, such as Facebook, Twitter, and online forums, to build support for their cause. Numerous hashtags also exist that rally supporters around particular issues (e.g., #BlackLivesMatter, #MeToo). Administrators quickly realize the ways in which campus issues can go viral.

Heimans and Timms (2014) argue that there is a difference between old power based on hierarchy and authority and new power that is more fluid and available regardless of position. Indeed, new power "is open, participatory, and peer driven" (Heimans & Timms, 2014, p. 50). Leaders must be prepared to operate in an environment in which power is not vested in authoritative roles. Instead leaders must use this new power that recognizes leadership throughout the institution and that builds on relationships. This leveling of the playing field with respect to power contributes to networked leadership that relies on multiple leaders at various locations within the organizational hierarchy. Tapping into this larger network provides ways to leverage change and foster innovation (Kotter, 2014). The key to managing power is practicing courageous leadership.

Courageous Leadership

Campus stakeholders, external policy makers, and the public are looking for courageous leaders to make the kind of frame-breaking change that many people think is required in higher education (Kezar, 2014). Courageous leaders can lead institutional transformation. Inherent in this type of leadership is risk taking, but with risk comes the potential of failure—loss of revenue for the institution, firing of presidents, and loss of confidence in leadership by parents and students. Despite the risk, transformational leadership creates opportunities for courageous leaders and followers to work together to effect change, inspiring people and tapping into higher ideals to move as a team to reach goals (Burns, 1978). The ability to work collaboratively provides leverage for courageous leadership to emerge, and these courageous leaders can become transformational leaders. The foundation for courageous leadership requires ethical leadership in decision-making (Shapiro & Stefkovich, 2016). Operating from a paradigm in which justice and care drive decisions that support students, the institution, and campus members is critical.

What makes an individual a courageous leader? Tardanico (2013) identifies ten traits that leaders can embody to model behavior for others. Even though we caution about thinking of leadership as a mere listing of attributes given how complex it is to lead, a list can serve as a handy reminder of ways others may view leaders. Tardanico's list includes the following:

1 *Confront reality head-on:* Take the institution at face value, rather than hiding reality and putting on a good face for others.
2 *Seek feedback and listen:* Creating communication loops helps leaders get true information on the state of affairs, and this feedback includes hearing about things that are not going well.
3 *Say what needs to be said:* Crucial conversations mean confronting tough issues and dealing with them in a straightforward manner rather than tiptoeing around real problems.
4 *Encourage push-back:* Building a culture that allows for dissent and debate provides an environment for all ideas to be heard and discussed. This approach ultimately results in better decisions.
5 *Take action on performance issues:* Just as in saying what needs to be said, leaders need to take action to prevent the emergence of a drag on the entire organization.

6 *Communicate openly and frequently:* At the heart of all change efforts is transparent sharing of information. When a leader does not know an answer, the leader must say so—and be clear about what needs to change.

7 *Lead change:* Instead of accepting the status quo, look for ways to improve and change the organization, the people, and the processes. More on the change process follows in this chapter.

8 *Make decisions and move forward:* Collaboration in higher education provides an opportunity for incorporating multiple perspectives. Courageous leaders work with others to reach a decision and then act on the decision.

9 *Give credit to others:* The basis of collaborative and transformational leadership is a focus on the team and others. Sharing credit is a low-cost way to establish motivation.

10 *Hold people (and yourself) accountable:* High expectations set a bar for everyone to meet, and making it a stretch provides a way to achieve momentum for change.

At the core of courageous leadership is the ability to assess the environment, set goals, get buy-in, and bring everyone along. What makes it tough is that individuals must be held accountable, poor performance must be called out, and action and decisions need to occur. It is easy to see why change is hard to achieve!

Networked leadership focuses on building connections both on campus and off campus with stakeholders. This form of leading creates opportunities to move units, schools, and universities forward in reacting to the type of change buffeting today's institutions of higher education (Hickman, 2010). Building on the social networks created from relationships both within and outside the institution leverages relational networks, and shared leadership can leverage change initiatives on campus (Eddy et al., 2015).

Simply, relationships are critical to the change process. Today, colleges and universities are complex organizations that are under a constant siege of change (Kotter, 2014). Trying to juggle multiple initiatives, stakeholder demands, and public cries for accountability requires leaders to be nimble and to move innovation forward quickly. But single, directed leadership approaches are no longer enough. There is no longer a hero(ine) that will come in to save the day. Instead, institutions need to rely on the talents of *everyone* in the organization to move forward and to make lasting change. An exploration of ways to build the networks required for change follows.

Building Networks: Relationships in Organizational Frames

According to Bolman and Deal (2013), "framing involves matching mental maps to circumstances" (p. 12). Leaders must build relationships with individuals in the organization to obtain buy-in for change efforts. A starting point for leaders is first understanding their own perspectives; research highlights that seeing multiple perspectives occurs more often when leaders are more seasoned or when they lead community colleges (Bensimon, 1990a). Longevity on the job provides more experience with a range of situations requiring problem-solving skills that connect with individuals from different perspectives. Community college leaders are likewise situated in a position that requires agility with dealing with a range of backgrounds, given the needs to work with PK–12 institutions, four-year colleges, and local businesses and industry. This type of leadership flexibility requires working with ease with individuals from all four frames. Experience on the job provides exposure to a wide range of situations, solutions, and missteps. Encountering a range of circumstances and interacting with individuals with different points of view provides a chance for leaders to think about the various outcomes of their actions.

Understanding the favored frame of reference for an individual can provide insight into how a leader can best build a relationship with that person. Thus, if someone likes to rely on rules (structural frame), dealing with that individual requires that you understand the policies in place and the process for changing the policies. Valuing individuals and making the organization's core beliefs apparent relies on empowering employees (human resources frame). Building coalitions to achieve a set agenda involves bargaining and negotiating with others to meet their interests (political frame). How leaders frame situations can appeal to others and get them to contribute (symbolic frame). A link in the web resources listed at the end of this chapter provides a self-test for readers to understand their own favored frame, beyond any initial ideas gleaned from the information just outlined.

Increasingly, the turmoil of change on campus calls for leaders with negotiating skills and comfort in dealing with conflict. Indeed, a political frame views organizations "as alive and screaming political arenas that host a complex web of individual and group interests" (Bolman & Deal, 2013, p. 163). The decline in resources for higher education results in a need to do more with less, requiring leaders with agility to build alliances and coalitions via their networks to address complex challenges.

Building relationships with others requires having a better understanding of what motivates them and guides their behavior. Argyris and Schön (1996) point out that people *think* they are acting in one way but that their actions highlight a disconnection between what they espouse and what happens in reality. In part, a model of self-protection prevents individuals from introspection and testing their assumptions. This type of behavior lays blame on others and results in defensive behavior that ultimately prevents change. Argyris and Schön propose an alternative model that aligns with the tenets of courageous leadership, namely, that common goals exist, that communication is open and tests assumptions, and that questions are asked to understand what others really think.

Developing courageous leadership requires looking past personal gain and having a focus on the power of the collective. A central component of this approach is understanding the value of relationships. Here, it is important to recognize what motivates others to action and how to harness the power of this action to achieve institutional goals. First, leaders must recognize their own assumptions and reflect on resulting blind spots. Second, it is important to understand that what motivates the leader, as an individual, is not necessarily the same for others. Individuals bring different mental models to their work and operate on different sets of assumptions about how things work. When a leader knows her or his own individual values, such knowledge provides a means for the leader to meet the needs of individuals and build relationships. Understanding the political arena inherent in higher education, and the importance of framing change for others through stories, contributes to relationship building. Finally, building networks and relationships requires frequent and open communication and a continued questioning of underlying assumptions. Recall how critical underlying assumptions are in the part of the iceberg not seen and how it is this unseen and unquestioned aspect of operations that can scuttle the best-laid plans.

Change Theory

Change, at its basic core, requires doing something differently. Lewin's (1947) initial theory of change provided a simplistic process of change, namely, unfreeze, change, refreeze. Unfreezing requires advocating that old ways of doing things are no longer valid and working to motivate individuals to change. The change portion of the model includes the implementation of new ways of doing things, and the refreeze portion involves reinforcing the new ways and institutionalizing the new practices as the norm. This three-stage model proves useful in advocating for change on campus.

Given individuals' reliance on mental maps and comfort with being able to do things right (Black & Gregersen, 2013), the natural inclination of people is to resist change. Resistance occurs because people are afraid of the unknown and of not knowing how to do their work well. People fear becoming obsolete. Thus, they remain attached to the status quo. A plethora of books and articles exist that address how to change organizations. Kotter (2014) has created a popular change model that builds on eight steps. These steps include a set of accelerators for change that all coalesce around a big opportunity: (1) create a sense of urgency; (2) build a guiding coalition; (3) form strategic vision and initiatives; (4) enlist a volunteer army; (5) enable action by removing barriers; (6) generate short-term wins; (7) sustain acceleration; (8) institute change. Kotter (2014) argues that these steps are needed given the poor track record of institutional change—a surprising 70 percent of change initiatives fail. Individuals say they want to change their organizations, but few do so. How can leaders develop the skills required to be successful change leaders?

The vantage point of individuals contributes to their view of the institution; thus, top-level leaders often see more urgency to change compared to those who are working in the trenches (Kotter, 2008). Creating a sense of institution-wide urgency takes work. A false sense of complacency, however, is a hidden risk that can thwart the sense of true urgency. On the one hand, a contingent within the institution can have a sense of complacency that all is well. On the other hand, a second contingent of individuals can have a sense of urgency that change is needed. False urgency emerges in this latter group when change is espoused, but efforts are slow moving. True urgency instead is built when there is a constant state of environmental scanning that presents a true vision of the state of operations and when plans are followed by actions (Kotter, 2008). Kotter (2014) refers to creating urgency as the "secret sauce" (p. 28) that triggers people to change behaviors. Central to creating urgency is how relationships are built and leveraged and the extent to which everyone in the institution shares this sense of needed change.

The guiding coalition involves people from various departments, ranks, and experience levels who all believe in change that supports the big opportunity (Kotter, 2014). Central to guiding coalition membership is the participation of individuals outside the "same old group," which tends to think similarly about how to solve problems and has a narrower view of the processes, procedures, and issues. The first charge of the guiding coalition is to create and clarify a strategic vision for others. In devising a strategic vision, it is important to help frame next steps for others (Fairhurst, 2011). Only when other individuals adopt the strategic vision will the vision become operationalized in such a way that true change can occur. Thus, leaders must get larger numbers of individuals to buy into the strategic vision.

Once the strategic vision is operationalized, it is important for leaders to remove barriers in the way of change (Black & Gregersen, 2002). When early wins in the change process occur, it is critical to identify and widely broadcast such wins to lend credibility to the change that is occurring (Kotter, 2014). How change is framed influences how others begin to understand and make meaning of their role in the process (Eddy, 2003; Neumann, 1995). The ability to sustain the acceleration for change requires the constant reiteration of the sense of urgency for change. The final step in Kotter's (2014) change model is to get the change to stick, which occurs when new processes, procedures, and most importantly behaviors are adopted. Table 2.1 outlines the steps of this change model and shows how relationships connect to each step. Finally, the table contains a column of questions to ask at each stage and tactics to employ to support the outlined change.

Dual System

Networks help increase efficiencies and contribute to innovation, overcoming some of the limitations of hierarchies (Eddy et al., 2015). Recognizing the importance of networks, Kotter (2014) adds to his eight-step model a new aspect that he calls a "dual system" (p. 19). The dual system operates in concert with current institutional hierarchies. The dual system inserts and connects a network in which innovation can occur within the confines of the hierarchy. Kotter argues, "Innovation requires risks, people who are willing to think outside their boxes, perspectives from multiple silos, and more" (p. 15). This networked system is dynamic and flexible, forming groups to address problems, to create innovations, and to take more risks. In business circles, these innovation hubs are often termed "tiger teams." Another way to conceptualize this dual operating system is to envision it as a space that is loosely coupled with day-to-day operations (Weick, 1976). Given the collaborative leadership models advocated earlier, the existence of this dual system within hierarchies highlights how all talent within the institution can be tapped and leveraged for change.

Table 2.1. Courageous Leadership in Kotter's (2014) Change Model

Change model step	Courageous leadership	Questions	Tactics
Create urgency	Confront reality head-on	Is there true urgency surrounding the change?	Identify the *real* problems Present central problem to others
Guiding coalition	Seek feedback and listen	Who should be at the table?	Use feedback loops to determine who should be on the team Be inclusive
Strategic vision	Say what needs to be said	Is there a clear vision around a big opportunity?	Establish a clear game plan Communicate broadly
Volunteer army	Encourage push-back and give credit to others	How do individuals find out about the change? Have we invited people to participate?	Ask people to join Build an environment of trust
Removing barriers	Take action on performance issues	How can barriers be identified?	Show by action that the change is real Conduct a process review to identify bottlenecks
Short-term wins	Communicate openly and frequently	Is there enough of a real win to celebrate?	Publicly celebrate gains Broadly share credit
Sustain acceleration	Make decisions and move forward	What will keep people excited about change?	Make tough decisions immediately Continually assess process and progress
Institute change	Lead change and hold everyone accountable	Is there real, deep change occurring?	Ask questions about assumptions Deal with underlying issues

The change model outlined by Kotter (2014) is but one way to contemplate change. Kezar (2014) outlines different frameworks for change that align with structural, step-by-step changes, with a learning orientation that relies on feedback loops (which bring evidence from current actions back into consideration for future decision-making), with context-based changes, with negotiated change, and with changes to institutional culture. Each of these approaches to change involves certain assumptions about why change occurs, the change process, types of change, tactics for change, and outcomes of change (Kezar, 2014). These various approaches to change are all embedded in the four organizational frames presented in chapter 1 (Bolman & Deal, 2013). Critical to thinking about change is how context influences the change needed and the levers for change that will be most successful. It is important to remember that change first begins on an individual level before reaching the larger institutional change level (Kezar, 2014).

What is often missing in conversations about change on campus is the type of change desired. Incremental, or first-order change, involves tweaks to the systems in place and the ways processes are currently done, whereas second-order change is deep change that requires the questioning of underlying assumptions (Bartunek & Moch, 1987). When leaders talk about change, there is often an inherent assumption that they mean some form of deep or transformational change. Think of the rhetoric of many campus change initiatives and how the language to promote these changes often includes phrases like "new," "innovative," or "transformational." Yet this type of fundamental change requires a change in culture and a change in processes. Indeed, this is why so many change efforts fail—attention to the underlying assumptions driving practices remains unquestioned. Leaders and stakeholders fail to recognize that part of the iceberg lurking below the surface.

Consider how often institutions look for quick fixes to problems, such as seeing technology as a means to address vexing problems on campus, such as advising. For example, colleges spend money on online systems to address common advising issues, thinking that these systems will "fix" how students determine needed classes, class order, and course requirements for their major. Even though this type of change may address issues for some students and improve the advising function, this type of change alone is often insufficient. Missing in this type of change is a deeper investigation of the underlying problems that students face in advising. This type of introspection would ask about what is assumed about the advising function and the way advising is currently handled. Faculty may think they should be in charge of advising because they know their program's curriculum best, advising centers may think their unit is best positioned to advise as they see the larger picture of student movement within programs, and students may think that they are only seen as a number on campus and not know whom to ask about what they should do. All of these perspectives may be simultaneously true, resulting in the quick-fix system of online advising failing to result in any increased student retention or graduation. What is missing is a deeper analysis into why advising may not be working on campus. Understanding how campus culture influences the process and what campus members assume is critical to deeper change.

By now, it should be apparent to you that in order to effect real change, people need to interrogate what they assume about how things work and what they *think* they want to occur and to consider how to get buy-in to the change vision. In order to accomplish any change, leaders must pay careful attention to people and relationships. It is evident in the overview of the change models in this chapter that the only way for change to occur is for people to change behaviors and for all individuals to be involved. Yet we know that people resist change and moving out of their status quo comfort zone.

Resistance to Change

Resistance to change can slow down the change process; thus, it is important to remove the barriers to change. Black and Gregersen (2002) argue that there are three key barriers to change: (1) failure to see, (2) failure to move, and (3) failure to finish. The first barrier, failure to see, is reminiscent of the iconic scene from *Field of Dreams* in which not everyone saw the teams playing on the ball field in the middle of the cornfield. Individuals are driven by the mental maps they hold of the world, and when something new doesn't fit in, they do not see it. The optical pictures that show a vase or two silhouettes illustrates this point as well: what you "see" depends on how you view the picture. In this case, leaders need to help create a new mental map for others to help them understand the urgency for change. Depending on individuals' frames of reference, how a leader helps others see the need for change differs.

Even when people can see the need for change, a challenge remains in actually getting them to move to action—thus the second barrier, failure to move. When facilitating change, the key to moving is getting others to believe in the change. A clear vision and rationale for change are needed, coupled with resources and rewards to allow individuals to actually do what is needed to change. The last form of resistance or barrier is the failure to finish. "People get tired because organizational transformation is fundamentally not about transforming the organization; it is about transforming the people who work in it" (Black & Gregersen, 2002, p. 91). Here, early adopters and change champions help motivate others. Constantly framing the need for change, why change is needed, and what is possible all help during the tough last phases of change. Part of the framing process is providing information to campus members that charts progress and tells the story of the successes in the change process.

Supporting others through the change process requires knowing what matters to them, speaking in terms that align with how they see the world, and institutionalizing the change into the organization's culture. Leaders should take the time to celebrate the wins along the way. In many ways, helping others see the glass as half full is what is needed in the early stages of change efforts. Yet leaders often make the mistake of resting on the laurels of these early wins. Instead, change efforts must be sustained when a new way of doing things is facing resistance or not achieving high levels of success. Critical to the process is to institutionalize the changes so they become part of the fabric of the institution. Changing culture is hard, but this type of deeper change is possible when assumptions are questioned, tested, and changed.

Seeing Change through the Frames

Chapter 1 outlined the basic underlying assumptions of each of Bolman and Deal's (2013) four frames. Unfortunately, each of these underlying assumptions can create barriers to change. A review of each of the frames from a barrier perspective follows. Strategies for overcoming these barriers are presented and provide courageous leaders with points of leverage (see table 2.2).

Table 2.2. Change in Organizational Frames

Frame	Barriers to change	Strategies to motivate	Steps in change process	Learning to change
Structural	Loss of clarity Confusion over rules/processes Lack of direction	Communicate new plans Renegotiate policies and processes	Instill a sense of urgency Form vision and initiatives	Engage in new thinking Unlock barriers in process
Human resources	Anxiety Feelings of incompetence Need for assurances	Train Involve in change process Support psychologically	Enlist volunteers Enable action by removing barriers	Tap into feelings Determine what motivates
Political	Threat to power Heightened conflict Zero-sum views	Create opportunities for negotiating Build hubs to build new coalitions	Build coalition Sustain acceleration	Build alliances Determine common ground
Symbolic	Nostalgia about the past Loss of meaning Need for purpose	Create new rituals Allow space to mourn the past Celebrate wins	Generate short-term wins Instill sense of urgency	Engage in the emotional life of the organization Employ the language of framing

Structural Frame

Because the structural frame builds on ideals of bureaucracy, which include fixed divisions of labor, organizational hierarchies, rules for performance, and technical qualifications to distinguish jobs, the structural frame includes an assumption that operations assure efficiency and predicted outcomes (Weber, 2009). During times of change, barriers that emerge in a structural frame include confusion over goals and disruption to processes as new policies and procedures emerge. In the structural frame, it is important for leaders to point out the need for change and to begin telling stakeholders how the new processes will be an improvement. Leaders need to be clear on what they want employees to do and to give them a sense of direction. Individuals do not like to feel they are doing their jobs poorly; thus, a change in policies or job requirements requires time to adjust and support during the adjustment time, especially when performance is reviewed (Black & Gregersen, 2013).

Human Resources Frame

The human resources frame builds on the assumption that people matter and that organizations and people need each other. During times of change, leaders need to involve stakeholders in the process and to consider multiple points of view. Individuals need reassurance that the institution will still need them after the change has been implemented. Leaders need to build in training programs during the time of transition and to engage emissaries to help support others when the leader is not present (Eddy, 2010). Once the change is outlined, leaders need to determine what motivates various individuals in the college, as people differ on what will get them excited about change.

Political Frame

An assumption of the political frame is that conflict can be negotiated. Multiple interests are at work in organizations, and when interests diverge, conflict emerges. Associated with varying interests are the different levels of power that individuals have at their disposal, including leaders (Morgan, 2006). An area of conflict that may emerge is the presence of workplace bullying, when individuals with more power leverage their power in unethical ways (Lester, 2009). Bullying may emerge too when change occurs and people are uncertain about the future. When individuals see change as a zero-sum game, conflict heightens, as there is a sense that winners and losers will emerge. During times of change, it is important for leaders to provide neutral spaces in which discussion can occur and interests can be voiced so that diverse perspectives can be heard. The emergence of new forms of power, not based on position or hierarchy, allows more types of participatory power and more access to power through new channels (Fortunato, Gigliotti, & Ruben, 2017). Leaders need to be conscious of the range of power used within the institution and consider how best to leverage their own power during times of change.

Symbolic Frame

An assumption of the symbolic frame is that cultural artifacts, including the saga of the college, represent the vision of the college. During periods of change, the nostalgia for the "old days" and retaining the status quo is strong. As with the structural frame, individuals are seeking meaning and trying to make sense of why things are changing and what will happen to them and their colleagues. Leaders shepherding change in this situation must create a new campus story for people to embrace (B. Clark, 1972). It is important to celebrate wins in the change process so individuals can see that the change process is working.

Organizational change can occur in units on campus in reaction to changes in the field that require rethinking how campus processes work. Policy mandates, accreditation requirements, and employer demands may all be an impetus for change on campus. Institutions of higher education have had to grapple with incorporating new technologies, responding to new approaches to teaching that incorporate active learning and inclusive teaching practices, and focusing on changes in practice to improve equity. Departments and academic units are often on the downstream of institutional change efforts but increasingly are also being charged to come up with innovative changes to make their units more relevant and competitive. In particular, an increased reliance on interdisciplinary collaboration requires change to historical patterns of siloed academic departments. Organizational change is ubiquitous on college campuses. Relationships are at the core of the day-in-day-out work of colleges and play a key role in leveraging organizational change. Successful change hinges on getting everyone on board with new initiatives and building trust throughout the organization. The following cases provide an opportunity for you to test out newfound knowledge on some vexing problems. Envision how you would react, what actions you would take, and what advice you would give the leaders in the cases.

Case #2: Father Knows Best: Leading without Input

Historically, men have led colleges, businesses, and political offices. The vestiges of male approaches to leading remain. Part of this remnant is a paternalistic approach to leadership in which the leader makes decisions under the cloak of knowing what is best for the organization. Because of the pressure to create more shared governance, participation is often sought from campus members. But often participation feels more like an illusion than real collaborative leadership (Bensimon & Neumann, 1993). Consider the case of Bob Wright, the president of a small, rural community college in the Northeast: Mountain Town Community College (MTCC).

President Wright started in office at the beginning of what is now referred to as the Great Recession of 2007–2009. The state was cutting funding to public colleges, local businesses were laying off employees, and enrollments were surging. Laid-off employees and others sought to go back to school in search of new credentials to make them more competitive in the job market. This pattern mirrored the typical inverse relationship between a downturn in the economy and an uptick in enrollment at community colleges, as individuals wait out the poor job market by going back to school to brush up on skills or change careers.

President Wright came from an engineering background and was in business for several years prior to making a shift to administration in the community college sector. He started as a dean of occupational programs and quickly moved up to chief academic officer at a suburban community college in the South before starting the search for his first presidency and landing at MTCC. Having done his engineering degree in the North, Wright targeted community colleges in the Northeast when he started his leadership search. What attracted the search committee to Dr. Wright was his experience in the business sector and his comfort level with technology programs. Prior to the recession, the college experienced several lean years as the population dwindled in the region and the regional four-year university started attracting students that formerly would have chosen MTCC.

One of the first actions President Wright took on campus was to engage the college staff in a strategic planning process to determine a focus for institutional change. The president was used to leading projects in his former life as an engineer and applied many of the same principles to the current change process. This case highlights one meeting in particular, when the department chairs, directors, and leadership cabinet gathered to brainstorm about ideas and plans to address the problems associated with the surge in enrollment concurrent with budget cuts. The additional tuition dollars due to higher enrollments did not cover the extra staffing expenses, nor did the additional tuition dollars begin to address the maintenance issues on the campus that had been deferred during the lean years.

The meeting was facilitated by the chief academic officer and the vice president for administration. After two hours, the meeting ended. The director of continuing education and the dean of admissions walked back to their offices debriefing on the session. "It was nice to see how many people spoke up at the meeting about some issues that have been festering for a while," stated the director of continuing education.

Her colleague added, "Yes, it was surprising to see how many good ideas were mentioned. I'm actually looking forward to the next meeting! This just might be a change initiative I can buy into."

The next morning, staff arrived to their offices to find on their desks a planning packet. The document included a 108-point plan to address campus budget issues; next to each item was the name of a department chair or director who was responsible for oversight of execution of the item. The first call that the director of continuing education received that morning was from the dean of admissions. He was fuming. "Did you see the planning packet for change?! I can't believe Wright did this. We were just talking at that meeting. If I knew my name was going to be assigned to the ideas we were brainstorming, I would have kept my mouth shut." The director of continuing education responded, "I really thought the president wanted our input on how to make changes. I guess it was too much to hope for that a new administrator would come in and shake things up for the better."

Guiding Questions

Consider the following questions regarding the case. How might you advise President Wright moving forward?

1 What parts of change theory are evident in this case? Why was there resistance to the plan proposed by President Wright?
2 Given President Wright's background and experiences, what organizational frame do you think he is using?
3 How do expectations impact the interpretation of the events in this case?
4 What is needed to build trust at MTCC?

Case Discussion

Consider how leaders can employ a number of different perspectives. Look at each of the case questions to see how theory translates to practice. This chapter includes a review of change theory and shows how individuals from different frames will understand the change process. Consider each of the frames individually. Individuals using a structural frame will be concerned with the rapid pace of change and what this means for their roles in the process. Resistance will emerge from individuals in the structural frame as they may fear how their performance will be measured and they may fear how new polices will change their roles. Individuals in the human resources frame will feel devalued and think the change process has broken a pact between themselves and the institution because their views were not incorporated in the manner they expected. Individuals in the human resources frame will have high anxiety regarding their roles and relationship with others, potentially leading to high conflict. Individuals in the political frame will begin jockeying for power, leading to new negotiations. Finally, individuals operating from a symbolic frame will wonder how the new story of the college will emerge. The culture in this case appeared ripe for change to occur, but the new planning document has cast the campus story as a leader dictating change rather than looking for broad participation. The president's background in engineering makes it likely that he is operating from a structural frame and that he may feel that the planning document is just what campus members need to understand how the college will change for the better. He underestimated, however, the role of individual feelings and how this top-down mandate would be perceived by campus stakeholders. Initially, campus members felt like they were part of the process of change, but the unilateral move by the president has made them feel disenfranchised.

President Wright can still salvage the change effort by attending to the change process and understanding better the motivations of those who are coming from a variety of perspectives and working within different frames. First, it would be worthwhile to establish an urgency for change. The president may have assumed that it was obvious that there was an urgency to change given the recession and the campus financial status. But it is critical to make sure that everyone has an understanding of what is happening and that the situation is really dire. Long-serving campus employees may think this current downturn is similar to others in the past and think that, as in the case of other recessions, the college will rebound. The president needs to create a compelling story for change. Second, once input has been secured, President Wright still needs to include a range of individuals in the process. Those who favor a structural frame need to become involved in changes in processes and policies; those who come from a human resources frame need to be motivated to participate and feel that their viewpoints and perspectives are valued; those who are in a political frame require a place to negotiate the multiple interests at play and a process that guides the negotiation; and finally, those who are in the symbolic frame need the creation of a new campus saga, one based on the anticipated positive outcomes of the change. It is important that President Wright rebuild trust on campus and attend to the underlying cultural assumptions on campus. Like many campuses, long-serving employees have seen several presidents leading the college during their tenure and may take the path of resistance, thinking that they can "outlast" the current president who is advocating for change.

Trust

As noted in the preceding case, trust is central to the change process. Trust building occurs on an individual level and also emerges on an organizational level as part of the institutional culture. Tschannen-Moran and Hoy (2000) reviewed four decades of research on trust, with a focus on trust and schools, and concluded that trust supports reform efforts and collaboration but that obstacles exist in building trust. These obstacles include different interpretations and routes of communication in diverse settings, the existence of distrust, and rotating staff and leaders. In times of change, trust can be broken or questioned as old alliances and relationships undergo negotiations into new roles. Knowing your leadership frame of preference, how would you build relationships? What might be a blind spot for you?

In situations in which networked leadership is in operation, there are several moving parts. Individuals draw on their own social capital with others during these shifting times (Coleman, 1988). Because social capital differs by person, however, a change process can mean a loss of capital by some as they renegotiate new roles and processes. Campus leaders, in particular, expend their own social capital in advocating for change, all with the assumption that the change is for the better. Depending on what change means for individuals, trust may be built or broken. Thus, it is important for leaders not to assume that because their last change initiative was successful and reinforced campus trust, all change initiatives will have the same effect. For example, a change on campus that results in the elimination of jobs impacts trust negatively compared to a change initiative that results in expansion of programs and an influx of resources, which positively impacts trust.

Ratnasingam (2005) reviewed literature on trust and presented a typology that distinguishes four types of trust, namely, technological perspectives of trust (emerges based on the belief that the infrastructure of the organization supports the goals and values of campus members), economic perspectives of trust (builds from cost-benefit analysis among stakeholders that determines that the interdependencies of collaborating are beneficial), behavioral perspectives of trust (relies on relationship trust that transfers to believing organizations will fulfill obligations), and organizational perspectives of trust (relies on best business practices to create interorganizational trust in which partners are satisfied with outcomes). Ratnasingam's research found that the types of trust can change over time. For example, when goodwill is built due to competence and predicable roles and outcomes, relationship trust builds. Thus, during times of change, it is critical to keep lines of communication open so that everyone understands what is going on and their role in the process—even when they are not necessarily good at their new roles. Support during this time of change builds goodwill that can support trust in the leader and in the change process.

Key building blocks exist for leaders to build collaborations on campus. According to Kouzes and Posner (2010), four key behaviors help build and strengthen trusting relationships:

- *Honesty and candor:* Leaders say what they mean. You will never wonder what they are "really" thinking.
- *Accessibility and openness:* Leaders tell you what works for them. They keep their agendas open, and you know who they are. They share information and resources.
- *Approval and acceptance:* Leaders value people and diverse perspectives. You can count on being heard without judgment or criticism, making the leaders easy to talk to. They facilitate relationships with others.
- *Dependability and trustworthiness:* Leaders do what they say they will do. They keep their promises and you know that you can count on them. (p. 312)

Closely linked to notions of honesty and trust is ethical leadership, which is reviewed in chapter 1.

Case #3: The Sky Is Falling!

The Midwest was hit hard when manufacturing jobs left the region and went to offshore companies. The lucrative jobs working in the local plant were no longer available. As a result of the loss of business, the city of Urban Hub looked deserted, with shuttered buildings and for-sale signs peppering the city and anemic sales at department stores and local shops. The president of Urban Hub University, Brenda Foster, was worried. She had been the president of the institution for fifteen years and during that time frame had overseen an expansion of programs and increased enrollment. But the past five years had been rough. She felt like all the gains she had made were being chipped away. Enrollment was down, donations to the endowment had flatlined, and the unionized faculty had gone without a pay increase in the last contract. The state just instituted performance-based funding that linked key performance indicators (KPIs) such as the enrollment of underrepresented students, students' persistence of enrollment until graduation, and graduation rates to institutional budgets.

President Foster knew that she had to jump-start the college and contemplated some potential change initiatives that would help meet the KPIs. She called a meeting of her leadership cabinet; cabinet members included the provost (Anne), the vice president of administration (Kyle), the vice president of student affairs (Sally), the executive director of advancement (Ben), and the director of institutional research (Felix). Foster opened the meeting stating, "We're under the gun to figure out how to meet our KPIs for this fiscal year and get the university squarely in the black. Where should we start?" Kyle was the first to jump in: "Brenda, we've got to take a detailed look at the budget and figure out the processes each unit is using to come up with their budgets. The devil is in the details. I think we'll save a bundle if we stick close to our knitting." Meanwhile, Sally was shaking her head: "Kyle, you're aiming at the wrong place. We've got to figure out what will keep our students happy and staying at the college. I hear that our competition just put in a new rock wall—we've got to invest in student amenities to draw kids to campus." Anne couldn't believe what she was hearing. She offered, "Folks, you are both wrong. We have to pay attention to what is going in our classrooms. If we don't pay attention to what students are learning, how faculty are being supported in their teaching, and how students are making it to program completion, we may as well hang it up now!"

Meanwhile, Ben and Felix were engaged in a sidebar conversation. Ben said, "Felix, were you able to compile that list of STEM alumni for me? We've got an initiative under way to help expand the Innovation Corridor to help with career shifters, and I really need to get my hands on some of our wealthy alum and shake some money loose from them." Felix quickly retorted, "Ben, you can't be serious about that initiative!

We all know that business is leaving the area, and this shouldn't be our focus. Anyway, I've not had time to run that report because I'm busy with the latest accreditation demands for data. Really, how much longer can we keep being asked to do more with less?!"

President Foster leaned back in her chair as the meeting spun out of control. Just how was she going to get a handle on identifying potential programs that would be innovative, meeting KPIs, and addressing all the needs of the campus?

Guiding Questions

Consider what President Foster might do to enhance courageous and collaborative leadership. What issues emerge with collaboration in practice?

1 How can a clear action plan be created for Urban Hub? What are the campus priorities?
2 What type of leadership frame did each member of the cabinet favor?
3 Has urgency for change occurred that will allow the campus to engage in successful change?
4 What advice would you give President Foster to support and develop her leadership team?

Case Discussion

You should consider your own orientations to leadership. Are the suggested alternatives tied to preference, or might other leadership approaches also make use of these solutions? Consider the culture of the institution. If campus members always feel like the "sky is falling," what type of options might be evident to the leadership team? Suggestions for addressing the problems in the case should recognize that individuals cannot drastically change their own orientations or initial approaches to how they see problems. Knowing this, it is important to consider what type of questions might be posed to the team to get them to question the assumptions they brought to the meeting.

Individuals coming from each of the organizational frames would have different approaches to building trust to address the issues facing Urban Hub. Those using a structural frame would look to technological perspectives of trust, focusing on refining institutional structures and policies to assure reliable results from change initiatives. Leaders using a human resources frame would rely on behavioral perspectives of trust, as relationships are central to them. Those using a political frame would look to economic perspectives and determine the best ways to negotiate among varying parties to achieve benefits for all. Individuals relying on a symbolic frame would use organizational perspectives of trust that emphasize the institution's culture (Ratnasingam, 2005). Knowing your preferred frame, consider in advance how you would approach change. Considering the different frame approaches builds ready options to use when faced with situations requiring trust building, with all leaders building on a foundation of honesty and ethical leadership.

Making This Personal

You have had a chance to practice your own leadership approach as you analyzed and thought about the case studies in this chapter. As we have argued, it is important to understand the various ways individuals approach new situations, both for yourself and for understanding the perspectives of other points of view. The adage of oil and water not mixing remains true, but in today's world, it is important to understand and deal with individuals who differ from yourself.

As you have reflected throughout this chapter, begin thinking about your own assumptions. How do you typically approach issues at work? Is the glass half empty or half full? Do you think everything will work better if people just follow the policies in place and work within the system? Consider a problem or issue that came up for you in the past six months. Using the frameworks and theories outlined in this chapter, how might you take a bird's-eye view to see the issue differently? What would you have done differently? What *can you still* do differently to change the interaction?

Your challenge now is to reflect on your own frame and leadership approach and contemplate what you'd like to try that is different and how you might expand your use of multiple perspectives. Change is hard, both on an individual and an organizational level. You have read in this chapter about a range of theories and approaches that may help you in better understanding some options.

Key Chapter Points

- Change starts at the individual level and builds on the power of relationships through use of courageous leadership.
- Building urgency and plotting a direction is central to creating effective plans.
- Risk-taking in change requires a safety net for the inevitable failures that will occur.
- Trust in relationships creates a particular context for change.
- Knowing your own preferences for leadership helps identify how best to relate change to those who are operating with different frames.

Web Resources

- "Barriers to Innovation and Change in Higher Education": https://pdfs.semanticscholar.org/d513/141cb6af397d22a68d99fa9264875f888312.pdf
- Bolman and Deal's Leadership Orientation Inventory: http://fs25.formsite.com/josseybass/form29/index.html
- Communication Styles Inventory: http://www.leadershipframing.com/test.php
- "Effective Organizational Change in Higher Education": https://evolllution.com/opinions/effective-organizational-change-higher-education/

- Kotter's 8-Step Process for Leading Change: http://www.kotterinternational.com/the-8-step-process-for-leading-change/?gclid=CPD91rLZncoCFQdafgodIv8JSw
- "The Role of Networks in Organizational Change": http://www.mckinsey.com/insights/organization/the_role_of_networks_in_organizational_change
- "Ten Reasons People Resist Change": https://hbr.org/2012/09/ten-reasons-people-resist-chang

CHAPTER 3

Communication

Talking about the Walk

A range of communication networks exist in institutions of higher education (Monge & Contractor, 2001). Among the networks in use, new leaders most often have immediate access to connecting with others through a history built on shared meaning, proximity, and mutual interest. Leveraging access to the existing communication network can allow new leaders a voice in setting the course of change. The role of framing—how leaders tell the story—is especially important, as this form of communication influences how stakeholders and employees understand what is going on. Yet embedded in framing are power differentials based on position, gender, race, and ethnicity (Morgan, 2006).

This chapter explores communication theory, communication networks, and the role of framing. The unique challenges of developing and utilizing communication networks and framing in the context of today's social media environment are addressed. Increasingly, social media is proving the undoing of sitting leaders. With social media, the power differential is critical. Social media power is diversified and held by many as opposed to a few, which can level the playing field

(Heimans & Timms, 2014). The chapter includes tips for you to learn more about harnessing the power of social media to help in change initiatives. A section of this chapter includes a primer on how to build a personal communication network. Here, we review the role of nonverbal communication. Individuals often have tells or shifts in body language that signal discomfort, anger, distress, and a range of other emotions. The ability to pick up on nonverbal communication aligns with emotional intelligence in leadership (Goleman, 2005). As well, social media increasingly serves as a means to connect with others, both on and off campus. Thus, this chapter concludes with a discussion of how to maintain a social presence, how to curate one's online profile, and how to react to campus issues that go viral. Building a social media presence is important, but so too is the leader's reaction to the way the campus is cast, online and in print, and the way such communication influences the reputation of the institution and reinforces how others come to understand what is going on around campus.

Learning Objectives

- Communication theory
- Framing as a leadership tool
- Building a communication network
- Hearing what is not said

Communication Theory

Organizational communication is an entire field unto itself. Higher education communication theory is a unique subset of the broader field that applies principles of organizational communication in the context of the college setting and sheds light on skills that are useful for leaders within this setting. Higher education organizational structures often contain inherent barriers because disciplines are often siloed. As a result, higher education leaders often fail to share information across knowledge domains, leading to missed opportunities for learning among all campus members. So what can aspiring leaders learn from the broader study of organizational communication patterns? A central lesson centers on learning *how* information is communicated within organizations. *How* information is gathered from the surrounding environment, processed, and shared is critical to institutional success (Sutcliffe, 2001). In an environment of uncertainty and ambiguity, *how* leaders are able to help campus members make sense of what is going on can make a difference in outcomes.

Types of Networks

There are five basic types of information-sharing networks within colleges: chains, Y-networks, circles, wheels, and stars (Lunenburg & Ornstein, 2012). A link in a chain helps illustrate the ways in which information is shared back and forth between individuals. The chain is the building block of a communication network and is the simplest form of information sharing—between two individuals. Thus, in a chain, the chances are higher that both individuals understand what is being communicated.

Building on the chain information-sharing pattern is the Y-network. The natural hierarchy of organizations makes the sharing of news via a Y-network quite common—the president tells the cabinet, who tells the deans, who tell the faculty. Here, information flows from the top down and sometimes back up the reporting chain. In the Y-network, it is easy to identify barriers that result from differing interpretations and miscommunication.

Tying together the ends of the Y-network forms a circle network. Yet, like the Y-network, it is still the leader who controls the information that is passed around the circle. Moreover, like the chain network, individuals are communicating and receiving information from only a few people. It is easy to envision how the deans may be on one part of the circle, faculty leaders on another, and the leadership cabinet located on still another part of the circle.

The wheel network, instead, is a variation on the circle network that seeks to remove barriers to information sharing by placing the leader in the center and in contact with more individuals within the college.

This type of network begins to open up lines of information sharing, and this can begin to move beyond the hierarchy and rank-based information sharing.

The final pattern of communication network is represented by a star or an open network. In this case, individuals have open access to others in the organization and are not limited in communication access by their position. Think of leaders who state that they have an open-door policy and how this allows access to communication. The use of social media follows an open-network framework, as anyone can share or follow to gain access to communication. The star network provides leaders with input from a wide variety of stakeholders and, as a result, removes the barrier created when information is filtered through various sources. Aspiring leaders need to contemplate how to keep their networks as open as possible not only to establish this practice early in their career but also to obtain feedback on their own development. It is important to hear the good, the bad, and the ugly to be best informed on how to lead and move forward.

Language Interaction

Not only are the routes of communication important in organizations, but so too is the language involved in interactions among individuals. The communication field is replete with a number of communication theories and approaches to understanding language (Jablin & Putnam, 2001). Hymes (1974), a sociolinguist, argued for the multidisciplinary study of language and connected organizational communication with linguistics. In fact, Hymes developed a handy mnemonic for outlining how individuals engage and communicate with one another. He offered the mnemonic of "SPEAKING" as a means to understand language in schools (W. Baker, 2012; Charity Hudley & Mallison, 2010) and social settings. Table 3.1 provides a summary.

The mnemonic applies naturally to college leadership and helps in understanding why some gaffs occur for individuals. Misreading the room or not understanding the seriousness of an interaction can result in miscommunication and even unintended offense.

Table 3.1. Interacting as a Leader

	Definition	Leader role
S	***Setting and Scene*** define the backdrop of the physical place that communication is occurring and situate the formality of the exchange.	The setting dictates for the leader the implicit rules of interactive exchanges. Consider how a board meeting or convocation set the stage for particular speech that is acceptable versus an exchange that occurs during a walk across campus. What is acceptable speech differs based on the setting. For example, a leader speaks differently in a closed meeting with subordinates (more informally) versus when giving the state of the college address (more formally).
P	***Participants*** include the person speaking and those who are listening. Here, those listening may be the intended audience and others who happen to overhear the conversation.	When leaders give speeches, it is not only the intended audience who is listening but also those in the vicinity. Critically, staff are often present when the leader is speaking but often are invisible as part of the audience. Think about the custodial staff hearing a speech to incoming parents or wait staff hearing discussions over meals during Board of Trustee meetings.
E	The intended outcomes, or ***Ends***, of verbal interactions represent the goals or purpose of the exchange. Disconnections may occur for the speaker and the participant.	Even when leaders think they are clear on the desired end goals of an initiative or project, they must contemplate how the listener/participant is hearing the intended message. Here, framing of the message is especially important. For example, "The college is in a budget crisis that is unmatched in our history" versus "We are in for a rough patch, but together we will get through it" provides different ways to understand the belt tightening that is being advocated.
A	The ***Act*** sequence ties together the form of the message and the content.	The leader sets the tone in the way language is linked together, and this orients the listeners' expectations. For example, "Greetings and welcome to this celebration!" versus "Today we are recognizing several campus members" conveys different understandings of the act. Institutional context sets the stage for acceptable act sequences.

	Definition	Leader role
K	The ***Key*** in a speech act sets the tone or spirit of the message and, in doing so, provides clues regarding how to situate the message.	Leaders can set the tone of a speech exchange with their word choice and by setting the scene of the exchange. This helps key others into the message. Think about how a leader may address a group of parents by using stories and humor to set them at ease, whereas a leader's tone shifts when addressing the campus after a campus tragedy.
I	***Instrumentalities*** refer to the modes of communicating the speech act. These modes might include written communication, verbal communication (speaking), signage/logos, or signaling symbolically the intended message.	Leaders typically want to engage in multiple modes of communicating, as campus members may have their own preferences. The forms and styles of engagement will differ depending on the speech event. Consider how formal proclamations are made to honor individuals or occasions relative to more local vernacular when speaking to someone at a sporting event.
N	***Norms*** of the group and societal expectations guide the language and tone used in speech acts.	The campus culture and norms dictate what is considered typical for exchanges. Consider how regional stereotypes of speech convey the norms of the fast New York City talker versus that of a slower southern drawl. Norms also set the stage for taking turns in conversations—including how loud conversations get and when it is time to listen versus jump into conversations. Certain norms also apply with respect to the type of language used by the leader, and word choice is often based on gender. Missteps can occur when leaders enter a new context using norms from their last institution rather than acknowledging and understanding their new institutional norms.
G	***Genres*** of speech acts align with different type of events.	Leaders should be mindful of the genre of speech act involved for their various speaking obligations. Talk at the water cooler is a particular genre compared to a meeting of the faculty assembly. As well, the opening of football season and a speech to alumni at a tailgate are one genre, whereas a presentation to prospective students or parents presents a different genre. Genres range from the informal to formal, and each has a different purpose.

Consider the example of the president and chancellor at the University of Missouri in November 2015. The president, Tim Wolfe, resigned after a series of racial incidents on campus resulted in protests, including a student hunger strike and the university football team's threat of a game boycott. Similarly, Chancellor R. Bowen Loftin, who oversaw the Columbia campus, was also forced out of office after misreading communications (Svrluga, 2015).

Using the SPEAKING framework provides a way to understand the breakdown in communication at the University of Missouri. The *setting* in Missouri involved recent racial unrest and rioting in Ferguson, Missouri, after "Michael Brown, an unarmed black teenager, was shot and killed on Aug. 9, 2014, by Darren Wilson, a White police officer, in Ferguson, MO, a suburb of St. Louis" ("What Happened in Ferguson?," 2015). Students from the University of Missouri participated in subsequent protests in Ferguson, and racial tensions on campus grew. The university witnessed student protests in 2015, when a group, Concerned Student 1950, called attention to a series of racial incidents on campus. *Participants* included Concerned Student 1950 members, campus leaders, and eventually the larger higher education physical and online communities. Jonathan Butler, a graduate at the university, staged a hunger strike that drew widespread attention to the issues on campus.

The *end goals* of leadership were no doubt to ally student concerns, yet when students blocked President Wolfe's car during homecoming, he refused to speak to them. Shortly thereafter, the student group posted a list of demands, one of which was that Wolfe apologize for the homecoming encounter and resign from his post. From the students' perspective, the *act sequence* of the president was dismissive of their concerns, as they felt the ongoing racial tensions were not receiving the type of attention needed. Likewise, the *key* involved in framing the message on campus indicated that the president was not meeting the needs of his audience—here the Concerned Student 1950 group. Pointedly, it was reported after a meeting the group had with the president that "Wolfe verbally acknowledged that he cared for Black students at the University of Missouri, however he also reported he was 'not completely' aware of systemic racism, sexism, and patriarchy on campus" (Izadi, 2015). The *instrumentalities* (modes of communicating) by campus leaders were in more formal settings and meetings with students. The students, on the other hand, made use of various forms of social media to share their list of concerns.

The *norms* of exchanges with leaders and students in Missouri are steeped in a long history of racial inequities. Likewise, historical relations with campus leaders and students typically are more formal, especially in the South. *Genres* of speaking based on context would support more informal opportunities to engage. The fact that the president did not engage with the student group when his motorcade was stopped during the homecoming parade was complicated by the need to maintain order and a perception of capitulating to protester demands. This positioning resulted in the president seeming inaccessible, which was reinforced in the formal meeting with students when Wolfe disagreed that systemic racism occurred on campus.

Using the SPEAKING framework to review this example, it is apparent how important it is for leaders to understand the context in which they are communicating with stakeholders. Student unrest on campus and vocal advocacy is increasing. Leaders need to think how they will deal with new norms evolving as a result of social media broadening attention to campus issues.

Individual and System Influences

As evident in the example from the University of Missouri, outside societal issues influence campus life. Not only must leaders be concerned with the culture of communication on campus, but they must also be attuned to the way larger events influence how messages are received on campus. Deetz and Simpson (2003) discuss how dialogue is a process through which individuals try to express meaning to others. Yet, within dialogue, there is a context of self and other. An individual's understanding of situations is based on one's own experiences and one's reactions to these experiences, whereas others may have different background experiences and therefore different reactions to situations. Thus, interactions can reproduce the dominant social norms, and it is important to recognize that within these exchanges individuals are presumptive about the perspectives of others. President Wolfe, a white man, did not recognize or understand how others, particularly black students, experience the world, and conflict ensued. It is important for leaders to understand that there is no singular truth of experience; understanding the perspectives of others helps dialogue and avoids conflict.

Just as others are influenced by norms and changes in society, so too are individual leaders. How individual leaders make sense of situations influences how they frame the situation to others (Weick, 1995). Certainly, understanding self and other perspectives is an important first step. However, an equally important second step is for leaders to be aware of their influence in communicating and framing scenarios for others on campus. How a leader frames the situation for others can influence how others understand and interpret what is going on. Knowing and identifying the type of communication networks in place at the institution proves helpful as the way information is shared can influence who is privy to key issues on campus. As well, knowing the elements and influence of the SPEAKING process can help in communicating messages on campus.

Nonverbal Communication

Consider how much is conveyed in a glance or by striking a certain posture. Anyone who has spent time around teenagers understands the message expressed with the rolling of the eyes or the shrug of a shoulder. Leaders need to understand how much is communicated by their nonverbal interactions with others. As the term implies, nonverbal messages are those conveyed without using words or speaking out loud. Instead, nonverbal communication is sent by visual cues, such as the body language noted in the example just given, by distance between self and others, by appearance, by tone of voice, and by touch (Giri, 2009). Indeed, words make up only part of the impact of communication, with nonverbal communication making up the bulk.

"Mehrabian noted the impact of communication across the three forms as verbal, 7% (words); vocal, 38% (tone of voice, inflection); and visual, 55% (nonverbal physical behaviors)" (Giri, 2009, p. 691). Notable here is how gender, race, and culture influence how others understand and interpret nonverbal communication.

Women leaders are judged differently from men, even when offering the same initiatives (Butler & Geis, 1990). In part, the judgment is based on how the pitch of a leader's voice influences how others react. Over time, for example, the pitch of women's voices has lowered because of the preference for lower-pitched voices in leaders, given the links with lower pitch and strength (Klofstad, Anderson, & Nowicki, 2015; Tigue, Borak, O'Connor, Schandl, & Feinberg, 2012). How individuals speak in tone, volume, and pitch influences how others react to what is said. Think of the scenario of union negotiations. Here, a man might assume the posture of striking the table, using a loud voice, and deepening the pitch of his voice. A woman using these same strategies would be judged differently and thus would instead use different strategies.

Likewise, other nonverbal clues like body language and distance between speakers make a difference when engaging with others. Here, culture influences the norms of comfort with how close individuals stand to one another when interacting (Watson, 1970). Americans typically like more space when engaging with others—consider the quip "You're in my space!" that connotes a dislike for getting too close. How often a speaker touches another person when speaking is also dictated by culture and gender. Direct eye contact may be seen as aggressive in some cultures but seen as neutral in others (Akechi et al., 2013). Understanding differences in cultural norms is therefore important, especially as U.S. colleges are becoming increasingly diverse and campuses more internationalized.

Framing

Framing in communication complements the construct of organizational framing (Bolman & Deal, 2013) presented in chapter 1. Just as in organizational framing, communication framing involves individual foci and views. Pointedly, Fairhurst and Sarr (1996) argue, "Leadership is a language game, one that many do not know they are playing" (p. xi). How leaders opt to frame situations builds a view that others see. Thus, in contemplating how you frame situations for others, a helpful way to think about it is how you are helping others to make sense of what is going on. Sensemaking (Weick, 1995) is built on several steps, the first of which is making sense of how you understand the situation yourself. In studying transformational change, the American Council on Education investigated successful change processes and uncovered the critical role leaders played in the sensemaking process on their campuses (Eckel & Kezar, 2003). What is said by a leader matters to how everyone understands what is going on and how they interpret it. Importantly, this framing guides actions on campus.

Central components of framing are language, thought, and forethought (Fairhurst & Sarr, 1996). Language and word choice draw attention to the central issues at hand and help others figure out how to understand the gist of what is communicated. The use of metaphors is a popular mechanism and shortcut for connecting new ideas to familiar ideas. For example, in times of crisis, metaphors about putting out fires, building a plan of attack, and heading for the lifeboats all conjure up the immediacy of action.

Forethought provides a chance to think in advance of responses, and it is important for leaders to first make sense of what is going on before framing for others. According to Fairhurst and Sarr (1996), leaders "must know how to handle a wide range of people and situations in split-second moments of opportunity, when there is not time for carefully scripted speeches—only time to break into the conversation and frame" (p. 10). In this way, the clarity of the message comes through. Once leaders know what they want to say, it is easy to react when they are called on to provide quick responses to the media, campus members, and other stakeholders. Think back to the lack of response from President Wolfe when confronted by the student protesters. Being equipped with some advanced preparation of a response could help in similar situations.

The ways leaders communicate build on their networks, the influence they hold with others, and their leadership approach. Depending on the leaders' network, *whom* they deal with dictates *how* they approach the situation. Fairhurst (2001) outlines how leaders might use coercive pressure when interacting with constituents rather than using coalition-building tactics with peers. Coercive pressure and coalition-building tactics are two sides of the same coin, with differences emerging relative the power differentials among the actors (Morgan, 2006). Also playing a part is the leader's approach, as "coercive pressure" may look different for an authoritative leader versus a servant leader. Finally, influence matters. A midlevel leader holds different types of networks and influence relative to an entry-level leader or top-positioned leader. Influence is tied to how clearly a leader articulates a vision to others and how much buy-in occurs as a result.

When leaders help craft a vision, they underscore how the current status quo falls short, and they paint a picture of a better future. This involves frame breaking. According to Fairhurst (2001), frame breaking can help move change forward to achieve the vision. Here, creating a new understanding for others relies on leveraging the values of the culture and the collective identity of the group. History can play an important role in this process. How framing connects to individuals' institutional memory may trigger either support or rejection of new ideas. Consider when longtime leaders retire and someone new is hired. Often, a first step by new leaders is to create a strategic plan to lay out a vision and the steps to get there. Yet, if this plan sits on a shelf, campus members will be reluctant to believe any future leader who espouses the value of a collective plan because of their history of experience with a leader who constructed an ineffective plan.

Framing tactics that show promise for change include "experienced predicaments" and "possible futures" (Fairhurst, 2001). Experienced predicaments consist of the quandaries and dilemmas that leaders and organizations face, which might occur due to budget shortfalls, administration scandals, or changes in the economy. The predicament of communicating an urgent need to change based on differences between the current state and possible future outcomes creates an important wake-up call. Consider how leaders use data to point out the need for change and the story created as a result. Imagine the quintessential graph with a red line pointing downward, and fill in the blank for the scenario of declining finances, dropping enrollment, or loss of faculty to retirements. The counterpart to these predicaments is highlighting possible futures to solve these problems. Depending on how leaders communicate the vision, the possible future dictates how others react. Others will buy in when they believe the picture painted by a leader (Black & Gregersen, 2002).

Power and Framing

What is also important to recognize in framing change is that individuals hold different types of power, and these differences result in different types of framing for change. First, gender and race contribute to how others are perceived, given the ways in which both are socially constructed. It is easy to call up situations that negatively typecast women if they are "too" forceful and act "unladylike." Similarly, for leaders of color, mental maps of expectations run rampant with stereotypes (C. Steele, 2011). Gender and race represent one form of power (Morgan, 2006); however, these roles can also provide leverage. Consider that research highlights that women's collaborative style typically results in better organizational outcomes (Bass & Avolio, 1994) and that when equity is embraced, better teamwork and results follow (Bragg et al., 2014). But it is also important to recognize that there is power outside of top-level positions. Thinking about power only in the hands of the people in charge represents "old power" based on inflexible organizational structures, whereas Heimans and Timms (2014) highlight that "new power" is open, participatory, and distributed throughout the organization.

Access to social media proves a significant means to communicate and frame change and can serve as a source of distributed power. As was illustrated in the example at the University of Missouri, the use of social media by students and the public generated a context in which attempts to address change by the chancellor occurred. Leaders need skill in navigating in an environment in which power is diffuse and in managing their message (and those of others) on social media.

Yet another source of power is being able to "read" a room using the four frames of Bolman and Deal (2013). Leaders possessing this skill can intentionally address the needs of others who might be operating from a different frame and might need to hear about change in a particular way. Recall the information presented in table 2.2 that highlighted how to address resistance in each of the frames. Thinking about these levers for movement builds a particular type of power for those who are able to see through a lens that is not their own preferred approach. Following are some pressing predicaments facing leaders and some alternative framing options.

Framing a Crisis

All leaders will face a crisis of some type. Some problems are more localized (e.g., a hurricane hits campus, damaging buildings and displacing students), while others are larger, more sector-wide concerns (e.g., meeting completion targets or addressing issues emerging from the #MeToo movement). Regardless of the source of the crisis, leaders must be prepared to handle any of the fallout from the crisis. A misstep in not understanding the scope of the issue or misidentifying the main concerns of stakeholders may damage the reputation of an institution and its leaders.

In light of recent public scandals in higher education, Perlmutter (2018) offers commentary for a crash course in crisis communication. At the heart of Perlmutter's commentary is differentiating a crisis from crucial yet ultimately routine matters and awareness of how fast events can spiral out of leaders' control. Early warnings of a spiral may emerge on social media, necessitating some form of social media monitoring.

Framing a crisis requires proactive preparation and honesty when communicating to others about the issue.

"Crisis communication demands that you get ahead of the story" (Perlmutter, 2018), and the way to do this is by thoughtful advance preparation and knowing how and when to communicate with internal and external audiences. Unfortunately, the typical bureaucracy and hierarchy of colleges create barriers to quick reaction. Campus members must feel empowered to speak up and to jump up the reporting chain when they witness internal problems or hear of issues from external stakeholders. Consider that campus members do not want to learn about a crisis by hearing about it on the evening news.

Preparing to communicate about a crisis needs to occur proactively, before leaders need to use these skills. It is important for leaders to be visible during a crisis and to be open and honest in their communications and their reactions to the crisis (Ulmer, Sellnow, & Seeger, 2017). Attending in advance to building a positive reputation and willingness to listen and react to issues provides goodwill during times of conflict. At no point should leaders attempt to cover up or deny problems. Indeed, "a virtuous response to a crisis by the organization's leaders may be the most effective in generating support and renewal" (Ulmer et al., 2017, p. 148). How leaders handle crises sets the stage for their personal career trajectory but most importantly for the way the institution fares postcrisis.

Framing Accountability

With over thirty states having some form of performance-based funding (PBF; Friedel, Thornton, D'Amico, & Katsinas, 2013), how leaders talk about institutional outcomes and ways in which the college will meet accountability metrics matter for the way others approach their work. Take for example a step-by-step approach to framing (Eddy, 2010), in which leaders can have a master plan that contains a series of steps but may only discuss one at a time with campus members until they are ready for the next step. The focus is on incremental steps and a linear approach to meeting goals. In the case of PBF, once metrics are established, for example, increasing the percentage of students retained or the number of students that graduate, a plan or road map can be presented to the campus regarding how to achieve the desired outcomes. A leader in this case would discuss how institutional data are going to be reviewed to determine the areas in persistence to degree completion that show places for improvement. This might be retaining students between freshman and sophomore year or, for community colleges, getting students to enroll full-time. Leaders can frame the urgency of attention around the reward of additional institutional funding. This type of framing is very transactional and relies on a reward (in this case, more institutional funding) to motivate campus members to change.

These types of small changes rather than wholesale changes can help alleviate fear among campus members who are nervous about change (Black & Gregersen, 2013). Focusing on public accountability for how the college or university is doing also involves managing the meaning of the message (Fairhurst, 2011). Here, campus leaders must realize the continuous need to remind faculty, staff, and community stakeholders of how they are changing to improve outcomes and the steps in place to achieve improvement in campus metrics.

Framing for accountability may focus on the specific incremental steps required to achieve a change in outcomes.

Consider how leaders can frame these achievements: posting on Twitter changes in graduation rates or running a website story on the achievements of students. Celebrating these short-term successes will highlight for others the attention of the leader (and the campus) to accountability improvements (Kotter, 2014). Leaders may employ different approaches to this framing depending on how the message aligns with their own beliefs. New leaders may need time to understand better how their messages are received, and seasoned leaders may find a need to update their message to maintain relevancy. Recognizing that sensemaking is ongoing in the steps to accountability (Weick, 1995) positions leaders to be attentive to how they frame their messages.

Framing Student Success

Inherent in the institutional focus on accountability are achievements in student success. Wyner (2014) identifies leader commitment to student success as a cornerstone for campus improvements. Transformational change efforts hinge on the ways in which leaders frame new initiatives to stakeholders (Eckel & Kezar, 2003). In part, this type of visionary framing (Eddy, 2010) relies on leaders focusing campus attention on what is possible. Often, this means creating a picture of what attainable futures might look like rather than what the current reality presents. When leaders focus their framing on student success, they direct campus attention and decision-making to the question, How does this support student success? This type of framing acknowledges that success may require different types of supports for different students. In the community college sector, for example, some students require the challenge offered by an honor's college curriculum, whereas others require differentiated teaching pedagogies that meet their preferred approaches to learning in developmental course work. Building an urgency for change begins to provide leverage in how stakeholders understand new mental maps for supporting students and supports the argument for resources to bolster what works (Fairhurst, 2011; Wyner, 2014). Central to the framing here is a commitment to success for *all* students.

Framing student success requires a visionary focus on policies, procedures, and approaches to teaching and learning that accommodate a range of learners—not just those who have been historically successful.

Framing student success contains at its core an inherent social justice and equity message (Bragg & Durham, 2012; Wyner, 2014). When colleges shifted away from elite education to mass education, access to higher education was a societal priority (Thelin, 2011). Over time, the accountability movement shifted attention to outcomes—in particular, graduation and completion rates. The balancing act of access and accountability, however, sets up challenges for community colleges in particular, given how "success" is measured (Bragg & Durham, 2012). The wide-ranging and conflicting missions of community colleges (Dougherty & Townsend, 2006) result in different measures of success for students (Mullin, 2012).

Mullin (2012) investigated how student success was measured in community colleges and noted distinctions dependent on either the individual student or the institution as the unit of measure. This differentiation highlights the importance of how leaders frame student success and the ways in which leaders focus attention on what they mean by "success." On an individual level, success might mean that students take enough classes to acquire skills that allow them advancement at their current job. By comparison, at the institutional level, success may be measured by increased pass rates of a gatekeeper course, which translates to more degree or certificate completion.

The fluidity of circumstances around success requires leaders to feel comfortable with a level of ambiguity, to possess the framing skills to help campus members make sense of uncertainty, and to focus on success for all students. Transformational leaders look to disrupt what is taken for granted to improve organizational effectiveness. "Transformative educational leadership begins by challenging inappropriate uses of power and privilege that create or perpetuate inequity and injustice" (Shields, 2010, p. 564). How leaders communicate a social justice agenda on campus matters.

More frequent communication between leaders and others on campus creates more opportunities for framing. Even though the overarching message is the same—how can the institution help students succeed?—the ways in which leaders deliver this message may differ depending on the audience. A leader will speak to the faculty differently than to financial-aid personnel or advisors, as the language of the groups is different due to their roles in supporting student success.

Framing Organizational Learning and an Inquiry Mind-Set

At the heart of a college education is a focus on learning. Just as critical to leadership success and fulfilling the institutional mission is a focus on organizational learning. Organizational learning requires some change in process or institutional approach based on feedback loops that use evidence to make changes in the system and operations of the college. Huber (1991) argued for a behavioral rather than a narrow concept of organizational learning when positing, "*An entity learns if, through its processing of information, the range of its potential behaviors is changed*" (p. 89, italics in original). An inquiry mind-set is required to build in the type of feedback loops and learning required to continuously improve the institution and thereby the processes necessary to meet its strategic goals and objectives. Here, continuous dialogue among stakeholders and leaders helps in shaping the revised story for the campus. How and where leaders create the space for this dialogue to occur is important, and how inquiry, and inevitably failure, is structured matters to outcomes and campus buy-in (Wyner, 2014). Connective framing brings together the campus to jointly build the campus story (Eddy, 2010), in this case around inquiry.

Framing for inquiry requires providing the adaptive space necessary for organizational learning to occur.

Depth of organizational learning differs, as Argyris and Schön (1974) highlighted when they differentiated between single-loop learning and double-loop learning. Single-loop learning focuses on fixing problems, whereas double-loop learning concentrates on changing structures and systems through questioning underlying assumptions that contribute to how things are done. Improvements in efficiency are possible with single-loop learning; however, when assumptions are questioned about *how* things are done or what is *assumed* about operations, deeper change occurs with double-loop learning. This type of critical questioning of underlying systems provides feedback to leaders to help support organizational learning. Here, building an inquiry mind-set and culture can aid in helping others collectively improve.

Linked to building an inquiry mind-set is adaptive leadership. "Adaptive work consists of the learning required to address conflicts in the values people hold, or to diminish the gap between the faculties people stand for and the reality they face. Adaptive work requires a change in values, beliefs or behaviors" (Heifetz, 1994, p. 22). Leaders in positions of authority may use framing to help others identify what should be changed, whereas leaders without authority can help highlight blind spots that others might miss. Adaptive leadership (Heifetz, 1994) also allows for reactions to unexpected scenarios and situations and may require different leadership approaches from those that are used when things are running smoothly.

Often "the task of leadership consists of choreographing and directing learning processes for an organization or community" (Heifetz, 1994, p. 187). In getting others to adapt to new beliefs, it is important for leaders to connect with others by listening and finding shared values. Those who operate from a connective frame use dialogue to bring together campus members to investigate assumptions and to discuss what is helping or hindering change in the organization (Eddy, 2010). Connective framers work collaboratively with constituents across campus and frame issues from multiple perspectives so that campus members can see not only the next steps but also the future direction of the college. At the heart of this work is building an inquiry mind-set and choreographing ongoing sensemaking to help support organizational learning. According to Duffy (2008), thinking strategically about how to communicate for change connects elements of the institution's vision, mission, and strategic goals to the larger community needs and gives campus members purpose to the work they are involved in doing. Here, ongoing and continuous questioning creates new understandings of what is possible.

How leaders frame issues on campus matters to how other campus members and stakeholders understand their roles and how they make meaning of what is happening. First, leaders must recognize their own preferences in communicating and determine how they are making sense of the scenario. For example, a leader who was a first-generation student who received financial aid but also had to work to support herself may make sense of student success differently than a leader who came from a family of college graduates and did not require financial aid. Yet, for all of the framing needs just outlined, individuals must help their campus members understand the path forward. It is important to use a range of framing approaches to help get everyone on the same page. Consider how the frame in use needs to shift based on *what* is being framed. Continue to reflect on how to leverage information on communication theory on campus to support change.

Framing Change

How leaders frame change often dictates how others understand the next steps and changes required. As argued in chapter 2, creating urgency is an important part of the change process. A central component of change is creating new mental models for individuals. The mental maps that individuals hold help them quickly take thinking shortcuts. For example, think how young children learn that stoves might be hot or to wait at a crosswalk when the light is red. The maps we hold create our worldview. Individuals coming from other cultures may not hold these maps in their minds and face challenges as a result. As well, hanging onto outdated mental maps may prevent change from occurring. Recall how the famous scene in *Field of Dreams* showcased how people slowly see the ball field when they believe it is there aligns with the notion of "I'll see it when I believe it" (Weick, 1976, p. 2). Thus, framing change requires shifting mental maps and communicating a new future to stakeholders.

According to Black and Gregersen (2002), there are three brain barriers created by the mental maps that individuals hold: the failure to see, the failure to move, and the failure to finish. For change to occur, leaders need to help others move past outdated mental models. To aid in framing change, leaders must show campus members contrast between current ways of doing things and new ways of doing things. This type of attention is what Kotter (2014) labels "increasing urgency." Yet contrast isn't always enough. Black and Gregersen (2002) argue that leaders must also confront others with the contrasts to avoid slippage into "old" mental maps. Here, confrontation can take the form of repeated discussion about the contrast between old thinking and new thinking, with a focus on the core essence of the change. People can get lost in the details without this type of focused reminder. Also, individuals are often afraid to try new things because they are initially bad at new tasks. This type of implementation dip, in which a new practice initially results in worse outcomes, has long been documented (Herold & Fedor, 2008), but it is tough to get people to stick with something new if they fail. Thus, leaders must frame the end goal well and support campus members with resources and rewards along the way (Black & Gregersen, 2002). Here, think of Kotter's (2014) setting of a strategic vision and short-term wins. Small steps help move people. Finally, leaders can address the failure to finish by enlisting early champions in initiatives and charting progress. Enlisting an inquiry mind-set aids in setting the stage for the ability to document improvements. When individuals believe in the change, more jump on the bandwagon, and in the process, new mental maps are formed. How leaders frame this change for others matters in how much others support and work toward improvements and change.

Case #4: It's All about How You Ask

This case looks at a lesson learned by a department chair who was trying to cajole her faculty into changing curriculum for a doctoral program at the university. Think about the type of communication network in place, the form of framing used, and how change occurred.

Lorraine Stark was the department chair of educational leadership at a large regional university that was recently reclassified by the Carnegie Foundation as a research university. The small doctoral program in education was one of the first advanced graduate degrees at the college and emerged from a need to train area superintendents. Now the program offered a distance-delivered program and included programs for higher education leaders as well. The original architects of the curriculum design of the program were two men who were retired school superintendents. This program required seventy-three credits to complete, including ten required core classes that made up almost half of the program. One of these required classes was taught by one of the two original faculty members. The course work that had once served the program well was now outdated and not aligned with competitor programs.

Stark, a recent hire, examined the curriculum and was particularly struck by how many of the core classes would have been designated as electives in other programs. The class taught by one of the retired superintendents was somewhat ironically on the topic of communication. Having researched the institution's policies to change curriculum, Stark brought a proposal to the department that would streamline the program and eliminate the former superintendent's pet course. Her male colleague who taught the class was indignant—and loudly voiced his disagreement with the proposal. Stark was surprised during the meeting when those who had been complaining to her about this course sided with the male faculty member teaching the course. The proposed curriculum did not pass.

Regrouping, Stark tried a different tactic. She took a page from Kotter (2014), who advocates for increasing urgency by showing people what is needed. Stark canvassed the top education programs in the country and the competitors in the state to determine how they organized their doctoral program with core classes, research, and electives. With these data in hand, she had the print shop create a banner that fit an entire side of the conference room and on it created a table that showed the curriculum of all the comparison programs and that of the department. The core classes were color coded to show alignment—for example, all leadership courses were blue, all policy courses yellow. Stark stood at the front of the conference room to review the chart on the wall and to argue again for the needed curricular change. This visual highlighted apparent patterns, and importantly the faculty member's pet course was clearly an outlier. Once the department saw how out of line the curriculum was compared to others, and when the dialogue focused on how to improve the curriculum to best support students, the tone of the meeting changed. Now it was harder for the lone faculty member to argue the merit of his course as a core course. In the end, the course was kept as an elective option, but the curriculum now contained a new core set of courses that aligned more with other programs.

Guiding Questions

As you consider this case, ponder for a minute what lessons Lorraine Stark learned about communication. In particular, think about how the initial failure of her proposal occurred and how this misstep could be avoided.

1. What type of communication network is in place?
2. How did the framing of the curriculum change between the two meetings?
3. What type of nonverbal communication was evident in this case?
4. What type of mental map did the department chair create that helped in the change process?

In considering this case, it is important to address how new leaders can best read the room to know how to communicate with others about issues. Thinking ahead about a communication strategy can avoid missteps.

Case Discussion

Contemplate the material presented in this chapter on framing and consider how Stark followed the steps of language, thought, and forethought (Fairhurst & Sarr, 1996). Think of the use of language in saying that the "required" course was not core to the curriculum. How did this use of language set up a confrontational situation among the faculty? If Stark was thinking of the larger scenario of alignment with other programs, how might she have taken a better pathway on forethought when first proposing the change?

Critical in communicating a change is the need to consider why something must change and what would motivate others to see the same perspective of the need for change. Here is where use of the Bolman and Deal's (2013) organizational frames comes in handy. Think how Stark might present the need for curricular change within each of the four frames. What would appeal to someone in a structural frame compared to a human resources frame? How could she have symbolized the change as a refreshing of the curriculum and a means to contribute to increased enrollment? What was missed in the political frame that would have helped in the first round of the proposal? Seeing what others are seeing makes it easier to frame situations for self and others. As you consider your own leadership, how can you remind yourself to think of the perspective of others when communicating? Where can you create space in your day to allow for reflection on what went well in your recent conversation rather than what didn't go well?

Building a Communication Network

Key to leadership development is contemplating how to build a communication network. As evident in the earlier section about communicating in times of crisis, it is important for leaders to have plans at the ready to communicate their message. These messages might intend to get campus members excited about a new change initiative or to launch a partnership with community agencies and industry. How the message is communicated is almost as important as the message itself. Given the leadership frames reviewed in chapter 1 (Bolman & Deal, 2013), it is important to understand how leaders in the different frames might leverage their messaging to others. Equally important is understanding that the audience for the message will "hear" what is said filtered through their own frame. It is, therefore, important to communicate in ways that listeners from a range of frames will hear the same core message.

Building a communication network entails using a variety of communication tools. Eddy (2010) outlined how leaders need to talk the frame, walk the frame, write the frame, and symbolize the frame. How leaders send their messages through the communication venues on campus requires thinking about widespread disbursement and staying on message. Thus, when leaders talk about items on their agenda, they must convey the same message when involved in informal conversations walking around campus and in formal and informal writing about the issue. As well, the words chosen for communicating to others will hold particular symbolic value. Consider how long-established colleges have leaders who reference their historical roots and how community college leaders focus on ways in which the college is supporting the community and its citizens. Understanding the culture of the campus matters in how leaders communicate in their network.

Leveraging Your Leadership Frame

Being true to your own leadership frame provides a means to communicate authentically. Consider how those who lead from a structural frame may opt to communicate via more formal means and how using standard operating procedures and policies to convey messages is common. Alternatively, those who communicate from a human resources frame want to make sure that they relate their messages to the people in the college and to external stakeholders. Here, more personalized forms of communication might be more common. Those who operate from a political frame will consider how their message influences coalitions and may want to test out their messaging in advance of a broadcast of the final communication. Finally, those who operate from a symbolic frame will focus on the meaning of the messaging and the format. Thus, attention might be given to the way a logo is created to symbolize a new plan or how a story conveys the intent of a new initiative. Regardless of frame preference, individuals can choose to frame an issue differently depending on the audience and the context.

It is important for leaders to understand that their audience is made up of individuals who come from a variety of frames and that others may like to hear the messages differently. It is important for leaders to remember this range of receivers for their messages and the need to enlist others operating in diverse frames to help spread the word. For example, if a leader finds that it is more difficult to figure out how to symbolize a message, the leader should call on someone else who is adept at this for the task. If it is not the leader's style to buy donuts and hold small meetings with campus members to discuss the latest college plans, the leader should get someone on the leadership team with this orientation to help out. The key here is that leaders need to attend to *all* stakeholders even when this causes the leader to move out of his or her own comfort zone.

Role of Social Media

The leader's online presence is often the first way that others begin to form initial impressions of the leader. The first action that many search committees take in their initial review for open positions is to conduct an online search of each applicant. A leader's personal online presence (POP) builds the leader's personal brand (Labrecque, Markos, & Milne, 2011). The ubiquitous access to social media in its varied forms means that individuals are always in a position to be recorded. These media recordings can then make their way online and can often be taken out of context or presented in a less flattering light.

How can leaders be mindful of their online presence, and what can they do to combat attacks? Leaders can frame their own story, and

Table 3.2. Curating an Image

Google yourself	**The first step in building your online presence is to understand what already exists online about you. A quick online search of your name can show what others will see if they are trying to find out more about you. Consider what shows up at the top of the list and if it is flattering or not.**
Find your voice	**It is important to find your own voice and to communicate in ways that are authentic. Knowing there are certain norms for online forums, make sure you are attentive to what allows for the most positive attention to your points versus merely looking to make a splash. Determine what it is that is important for you to say.**
Self-promotion: build capital, not hubris	**Many individiuals are taught not to brag about their accolades or to draw attention to themselves. The intention of self-promotion in building your online presense is not hubris but rather to share your knowledge with others. This type of leverage builds your social capital on the basis of being an authority and expands your reach.**
Combat online attacks	**It is important to establish online alerts on your name and/or your institution's name so that you are aware if there are attacks on your reputation.**

their reactions can be a step in this direction. Consider the steps in table 3.2 for curating an online image.

From the beginning of any new position, leaders must be planning how to deal with conflicts and to handle attacks, both personal and on the institution. It may seem like this issue is only a problem for the top leadership ranks, but increasingly attacks on faculty members, association leaders, and the institution overall highlight that everyone needs a plan. Be mindful of the leverage of social media. What does your online presence say about you?

A number of facets influence communication on campus. In part, how the communication network is structured dictates how information is shared. Individuals have more or less access to shaping the meaning of messages depending on whether they are in formal positions of leadership or informal positions of leadership. It is important for leaders to understand their own preferences for communicating, as their approach will elicit particular responses in those who operate from other frames. Recognizing that the ways in which leaders encode their points when communicating with others is influenced by how they decode the information can help avoid misunderstandings. Of particular importance is the knowledge of how much is communicated beyond the spoken language. Leaders should consider having themselves recorded on video to provide a review of how they come across to others and to note how their tone and nonverbal body language comes across.

Case #5: The President versus the Faculty Blog

This case provides an example of communication gone bad. Think of the role of social media and how much the leader understood the responses that others had to her communication and leadership approaches.

Back in 2006, a presidency was toppled due to unrest initially sowed by a faculty blog. This case provides an understanding of the critical role of communication on campus, in particular because it was one of the earliest instances of the use of social media intersecting with campus decisions. Back in the early 2000s, Jan Dublin began her tenure as president of a regional comprehensive university in the Southwest, Southwest College. The college began as a two-year vocational and liberal arts transfer institution, but in the early 1990s, the college started offering four-year baccalaureate degree programs.

In President Dublin's first year on campus in 2003, she made a series of unpopular decisions. One of the first casualties of administrative firings was Jamison Stanley, then the provost and vice president of academic affairs. Stanley had been in consideration for the presidency, but he was not selected. In an interesting turn of events, Stanley was later selected as the president of Southwest and served in this capacity from 2008 to 2012. In the early days of Dublin's presidency, the local paper reported that "two-dozen other top staff members quit, were fired or were asked to resign." It was against this backdrop of campus unrest that an anonymous faculty blog was started.

The blog first appeared in 2005, and it served as a forum for individuals to express discontent with Dublin's leadership and to air complaints about campus culture. The blog master used the pseudonym "Silence Dogood." Readership of the blog increased as the dissent and distrust on campus grew—ultimately resulting in the president and chair of the faculty senate asking for an intervention by the state's system of governance. The team of mediators arrived on campus in December 2005. Their report was released in February 2006 and cast blame on both sides of the issue. Pointedly, the report noted problems in campus governance that were "characterized by a high incidence of mutual suspicion, lack of civility and frequently hostile discourse, [and] loss of credibility of both the administration and the faculty leadership."

The president was urged to change her leadership approach and counseled to become more collaborative in the hopes of building trust on campus. Communication between the president and the faculty senate remained tense, and individuals were reluctant to speak up for fear of being fired or marginalized. The outside report called for improvements in the governance structure that would include the firming up and following of academic senate rules and policies. Despite these intervention efforts, by mid-June 2006, President Dublin resigned her post.

Guiding Questions

Consider the role of communication in campus leadership as you reflect on the following questions. Given the role of faculty agency, how can faculty leadership instigate change? In particular, contemplate the increase in social media in the first decade of this century, when this case unfolded. How can campus leaders respond to the heightened access to social media?

1. As an advisor to the president, what plan of response would you have suggested? How might this plan be different at the beginning of the president's tenure as opposed to after the call for outside mediation?
2. What type of leadership approach do you think the president used on campus? What type of communication frame was employed?
3. Now that the president has resigned, what should be the first moves of the next campus president?

Case Discussion

This case provides another example of social media contributing to the downfall of a sitting leader. Consider how the faculty blog reinforced the lack of trust among faculty toward the president and how the president did not appear to be listening to the faculty. When a leader comes from a more structural frame, there is a reliance on the hierarchy and rules and procedures. Yet this singular approach chafes faculty members, as they desire collegial interactions and shared governance. The answer here is not to ask the leader to become someone she is not—this strategy rarely works. Instead, a leadership council can help in providing a wider variety of leadership approaches such that messages going out from the central administration address the needs of a range of individuals.

If faculty seek a collaborative environment, one in which all voices are heard, it is important to set up within the structure a mechanism for this to occur. One option might be a biweekly open session for exchanges. Another option could be a president walking through different academic buildings to allow for happenstance conversations. Still another option is the use of emissaries to act as a conduit of the president's message and in turn faculty feedback. At the core of many issues of conflict is merely the desire to be heard. Providing opportunities for these exchanges matters.

The president highlighted in this case example was facing a vote of no confidence and working with campus members in a climate of distrust. Contemplate the options available to the president in this case and consider how the leader might handle being new to a campus. How might a leader learn about campus culture and what type of communication works best? All campuses have long-standing leaders, some of whom will not meet the needs of a new president. How might change in leadership begin to happen without firing everyone with whom a leader disagrees? The ubiquitous nature of social media means that a leader's every move will be tracked. How can leaders begin to control the messaging? Suggestions for addressing the problems in the case should recognize that individuals come to their work from a number of leadership and communication frames. Knowing this, how can leaders assure open communication and in the process recognize their own blind spots? Understanding better the context of a campus can provide a range of options for framing change on campus.

Making This Personal

This chapter has provided background on communication processes within institutions and discussed the implications for leaders. Contemplate the type of communication network that is in place in institutions. How can leaders take advantage of the SPEAKING process to understand better how others understand what the leader is trying to say? Communication involves both sending messages and receiving them. Think about leaders who may have made assumptions (right or wrong) when interacting with others. Knowing that leaders are making an impression by their nonverbal actions can also make them more alert to their behaviors and those of others. Leaders should take a minute at their next meeting to ask themselves a few questions. What is observed about the way people talk with one another? What hidden tensions are present? What type of power plays are present?

The ubiquitous nature of technology has heightened the role of social media in college relations. Nearly every week, a campus news story goes viral. It is critical for leaders to have a plan in place to deal with social media. Leaders must know their online presence and curate their social media accounts. As leaders move up the career ladder, they are more often called on to be the voice of the college. Consider how leaders prepare for video interviews, podcasts, and answering questions on the fly. Creating a campus communication plan is a first step.

Key Chapter Points

- Different communication networks exist in institutions, and understanding what format is in place can inform how leaders receive and send messages.
- Understanding the process of communicating via theories like SPEAKING can aid in intentionality of communication on campus.
- Curating your own social media presence is important, as it reflects on the campus.
- Having a communication plan in place to deploy during times of campus crisis is important for all leaders.
- How leaders opt to frame messages to the campus community and college stakeholders sets the stage for how the message is heard.

Web Resources

- Finding your communication style:
  https://outsmartyourbrain.com/4-dominant-communication-styles/; https://www.leadershipiq.com/blogs/leadershipiq/39841409-quiz-whats-your-communication-style
- Leaders and social media:
  https://thenextweb.com/contributors/2017/05/25/leadership-social-media-7-essential-tips-new-leaders/#.tnw_MeoHqysB
- The Power of Communication:
  http://thepowerofcommunication.net/
- *The Power of Framing*:
  http://www.leadershipframing.com/TPOF.php

CHAPTER 4

Conflict Management

To be ready to lead in higher education, you must understand how to deal with conflict.
—Suárez, 2016

The types of organizational and governance structures commonly found in institutions of higher education are a contributor to work environments that tend to generate and support aggressiveness, which presents a leadership challenge (Twale & De Luca, 2008). Left unchecked, aggressive behavior can lead to incivility and bullying, both issues that have been well documented in higher education (Keashly & Neuman, 2010). New and inexperienced leaders often express the need to know how to manage conflict more effectively in the workplace. As well, understanding how emerging conflict may be linked to other issues and identifying the true source of the conflict are important skills for leaders in higher education, including senior administrators, deans, directors, human resources staff, ombudspersons, diversity officers, legal staff, and others spearheading investigations into workplace conflict.

Conflict is a natural occurrence among social groups, teams, and individuals and can present itself in both positive and negative ways. For example, conflict is positive when it allows surfacing of new ideas or options on a topic or decision, but it is negative when it penalizes subgroups in an organization or creates barriers to accomplishing organizational goals. Buller (2013) offers, "Positive leaders adopt a systems approach, emphasizing the efficient operation of the group as well as the unique contributions of each member" (p. 12). Here, conflict provides an opportunity for the consideration of all voices as opposed to shutting down contrary perspectives. Adopting a solution-oriented approach that listens to the voices of each member and leverages strengths helps move the conflict from being viewed as a "problem" to identification of what is possible through negotiation.

To the contrary, conflict left unchecked leads to job stress, which has been identified as "far and away the major source of stress for American adults" (American Institute of Stress, n.d.). The *2016 Work and Well-Being Survey*, conducted by the American Psychological Association (APA), found that the percentage of people reporting job stress has risen in recent years, with over one-third of employees surveyed indicating they experience stress during the workday. Even though the percentages of working adults reporting positive interpersonal relationships with their coworkers (78 percent) and boss (72 percent) represents the majority of employees, these figures have declined over a six-year period (APA, 2016, p. 25). Health risks associated with stress can take a toll on individuals' physical and psychological well-being, which in turn raises tension in the organization through such issues as work performance, absenteeism, burnout, and high turnover rates (APA, n.d.; Pazzanese, 2016).

Sources of workplace conflict vary widely and include tensions caused by external factors. Concurrent with increases in job stress is the level and frequency of protests on campuses across the nation, with more than fifty schools in 2016 experiencing student protests and demands ranging from calls to right historical wrongs to public apologies and resignations of campus leaders (Dickey, 2016). Environmental conflict emerging from student protests contributes to leaders' stress.

The 2015 findings from UCLA's annual CIRP Freshmen Survey, the largest and longest-running survey of American college students, corroborated this outcome of escalation of protests on campus. The survey findings suggest that participation in demonstrations was likely to increase due to an all-time high in students' commitment to activism and political and civic engagement (Higher Education Research Institute, 2016). Leaders must be prepared to deal with increased, and visible, activism on campus while managing the stress resulting from the conflict.

Those leaders who are most prone to experiencing conflict must anticipate that conflicts will occur and be prepared to respond effectively. The complex governance structures of higher education lend themselves to a wide range of conflicts and disputes among students, faculty, staff, administrators, and stakeholders. Rules, processes, and procedures and complex reporting structures all set the stage for disagreements to occur. Individuals get frustrated when faced with the red tape of bureaucracy, and higher education institution structures reinforce particularly inflexible and often lockstep approaches in procedures and processes. Thus, success in leadership positions in academe requires foundational expertise in conflict management and resolution to address situations that emerge. Even though conflict is unavoidable in the workplace, learning skills to reduce tensions and prevent conflict from escalating to a higher level is possible for leaders.

This chapter introduces the concept of conflict management for the academic leader and focuses on conflict dynamics and understanding types of conflict, management styles, and best practice strategies to resolve conflict and foster positive working environments.

Learning Objectives

- Types of conflict
- Conflict management styles
- Conflict analysis
- Institutional supports for conflict management

Conflict Defined

Conflicts are part of life. Although many people assume conflicts are negative and, therefore, should be avoided, conflict is truly neutral; however, how one engages in the conflict is what can be perceived as constructive or destructive.

—Watson, Watson, & Stanley, 2016, p. xv

Various definitions and descriptions of conflict exist. Conflict is described as an expressed struggle (Donahue & Kolt, 1992) between two or more interdependent people with perceived differences in beliefs, values, and goals or over differences in desires for esteem, control, or connectedness (Wilmot & Hocker, 2011). Yarn and Boyens (2004) state, "conflict is the condition or situation that gives rise to a dispute" (p. 12). The tensions inherent in conflict incentivize individuals to seek resolutions. Pondy (1967) describes minor conflicts as those that create pressure toward resolution and preserve the relationship, while "major conflicts generate pressures to alter the relationship or to dissolve it altogether" (p. 312). There is a push to "play nice" to avoid irreparable damages to relationships, yet unresolved conflicts can escalate in ways that can be destructive to teams.

As each of the definitions or descriptions suggests, social tensions that emerge from issues of identity, resources, power, and ethics are also key factors in conflict and often create the impetus for change (Hickman & Couto, 2006, p. 168). These factors are described in table 4.1 and are exemplified through a faculty lens. Social tensions can be very powerful and have the ability to generate a movement. Think of the 2017 Me Too movement, which was advanced virally through social media to illuminate sexual harassment and sexual assault in the workplace. As a result, individuals felt empowered to report incidents of sexual harassment and assault that in some cases led to firing or

Table 4.1. Factors and Social Tensions through a Faculty Lens

Factors	Social tensions
Identity	Assigning, asserting, and valuing identity Faculty within a department are struggling with their identity given programmatic philosophical differences. Faculty definitions of quality have created an environment of inclusion or exclusion depending on affiliation with one philosophy or another. Elitist behaviors exhibited by one group of faculty has left others feeling devalued.
Resources	Acquisition and distribution of individual or collective resources The college has declining resources and increased resource demands from department and service units. Faculty increasingly scrutinize the distribution of resources as concerns about equity and favoritism abound. Increased social pressure and tensions become focused on subsidized groups unable to contribute to resource generation.
Power	Disenfranchised and authorized power Historically faculty and administration struggle over shared governance issues, academic freedom, and influence and involvement in university affairs. Faculty tensions erupt when the administration replaces a faculty position as a staff position. The faculty then engage in a campaign to discredit the staff member's capacity to perform job duties.
Ethics	Equitable actions and conditions vs. inequitable actions and conditions Faculty make a Freedom of Information Act (FOIA) request for a dean's travel reimbursement. Faculty perception is that the dean is using university resources for self-interest through extensive travel, training, and conferences. Ethics violations frequently align with issues of inequity, inequality, and abuse of power.

Adapted from Hickman & Couto, 2006, p. 169.

criminal charges for those accused. In the higher education workplace, academic leaders must embrace creative tension needed for adaptation and innovation yet recognize when conflicts escalate in ways that can be destructive to their teams.

Destructive Conflict

When conflict is mismanaged and disputes are left unaddressed, a typical outcome can be the loss of talented people in the workplace (Watson et al., 2016). The cost of replacing this loss of talent tallies up with recruitment, training, and a learning curve. Additionally, conflict can quickly escalate and lead to a wide range of destructive behaviors such as the following:

- Negative emotions
- Blocked communication
- Increased negative stereotyping of those with whom we are in conflict
- Reduced coordination between people who have to work and live together
- A shift toward autocratic leadership when discussion-based decision-making breaks down
- Reduced ability to view other perspectives and a breakdown in empathy and vision (Eunson, 2007, p. 2)

Constructive Conflict

Effective management also requires the understanding that conflict is a natural occurrence, and while the word often carries a negative connotation, conflict can also happen in functional, healthy ways that are conducive to positive outcomes (Engleberg & Wynn, 2007). As outlined in chapter 2, resistance to change is normal and often generates a great deal of angst in the workplace. However, some level of conflict is what drives change, which is essential to keeping an organization vibrant and growing (Watson et al., 2016, p. 12). The key here is finding the right balance. When people in the workplace begin experiencing discomfort, it can be a signal to organizational leaders that individuals may be open to trying something new (Holton, 1998). Leaders who encourage people to share their diverse opinions, values, and passions and who channel these perspectives into constructive dialogue lay the foundation for creative thinking and shared meaning (Solomon & Flores, 2001).

Outcomes and benefits from constructive conflict include the following:

- Cohesiveness can increase
- Complacency can be challenged
- Differences can be appreciated
- Intrapersonal conflicts can be resolved
- Better decision-making and problem solving can take place (Eunson, 2007, p. 3).

The question in situations of conflict is what leaders can do to promote constructive conflict rather than destructive conflict. First, clear lines of communication are required. Second, leaders must recognize that individuals have different perspectives on scenarios and that shared meaning does not always exist. Third, the nature of conflict means that disagreements are evident, but the handling of these differences influences the outcomes. Finally, the existing organizational culture sets the stage for the perception of emerging conflicts. A toxic culture is more likely to set the stage for destructive conflict, whereas a collaborative culture can generate constructive conflict. The adage "culture trumps strategy" is recast as "culture feeds conflict."

Case #6: Stealing the Limelight

Contemplate the type of conflict illustrated in this case. Consider as you read how you might advise the dean in this case.

The importance of a diverse teaching staff is well documented, as is the racial and ethnic demographic disparity between our nation's teachers and their students. Mark Williams, dean of the College of Education and Professional Studies, created a faculty team to implement a new diversity initiative in the college that was designed to attract minority teacher-education candidates and males to the teaching profession. The initiative was well designed and included incentives for recruiting and retaining minority and male students in the teacher-education program. After three years, enrollment data in the program demonstrated a significant change in the demographic profiles of students enrolled in teacher education.

Dean Williams applied for a state award for innovative strategies in educational equity and was very pleased when the state superintendent of education announced that he had received the highest award for innovation. As a result, the state selection committee submitted the initiative as a model of best practices for national recognition. The university provost and dean were feted at an awards ceremony sponsored by the state Department of Education, with corresponding accolades in the press for the program. The dean also received acknowledgment from the university president and Board of Trustees at their annual meeting.

A few months later, the dean's office nominated the initiative for a national award by a prestigious organization in teacher education, which was successful. Now, in addition to the state recognition, the program received national recognition. Dean Williams was invited as a keynote speaker at the association's national convention to present on the College of Education's transformative practice. Things were looking good for the dean. Yet trouble was brewing, as none of the faculty who were actually responsible for implementing the program were invited to present at the national convention. Instead, the dean's administrative assistant reached out to faculty for the latest program data and names of students whom Dean Williams could feature in *his* presentation.

By this time, members of the faculty team were infuriated and felt that while they did all the work, they were not being recognized in any formal way as being instrumental to the design and implementation of the initiative. The team's well-deserved desire for recognition and acknowledgment of their role in the success of the program was unmet. These negative emotions led to a strained professional relationship with Dean Williams. An outcome of this conflict was the resignation of the program director and faculty becoming unwilling to work on any new initiatives under the dean's leadership. Dean Williams's reputation also suffered across campus as unhappy colleagues cast him in the light of a selfish person, a show horse, and someone inclined to take all the credit so that he could bask in his own glory.

Guiding Questions

Consider the following questions regarding this case:

1. Describe the various social tensions prevalent in this case.
2. In what ways could Dean Williams have prevented this conflict?
3. What steps would you recommend for reducing the ongoing tensions between Dean Williams and his team given the current situation?

Case Discussion

In chapter 2, the constructs of collaborative and networked leadership were introduced. Consider how different this scenario would have been had Dean Williams embodied a collaborative leadership style. Giving credit where credit is due forms the basis of collaborative leadership and is integral to relationship building. Tapping into a leader's network helps build increased relationships, such as the dean did internally in this case. The dean may have provided the initial idea for the initiative, but it was the faculty team's sustained efforts over time that took an idea and transformed it into a successful program.

While Dean Williams basked in the limelight, faculty trust and willingness to engage with him faded. As a result, the program director who was vital to recruitment and marketing quit, which unfortunately put the future success of the program at risk. The dean's reputation across campus suffered, and faculty gossiped about his showboating behaviors. He did not understand how his actions reverberated within a network and how quickly he lost the respect of his team. Negative stereotyping and reduced support and collaboration between people who work together are characteristic of destructive conflict.

As evident in this case, destructive conflict can have a lasting effect and can derail a leader's career. There is an infinite list of potential causes and triggers for conflict, including, for example, differences in perception, competing goals and priorities, opposing drivers for change, resistance to change, individual personalities, and gender or cultural-based preferences. Understanding the basics of conflict and recognizing the first signs of a problem are valuable both personally and professionally, as one can begin to assess the situation at hand and take proactive steps to address issues before they escalate. Recognizing evidence of conflict is the first step in finding solutions.

Conflict is a normal part of life. Differences in perspectives, goals, and experiences all contribute to diverse understandings of seemingly similar situations. At the heart of Bolman and Deal's (2013) political frame is contested spaces that require negotiation. Savvy leaders build the space in which to voice different opinions and provide the opportunity for stakeholders to uncover the real issues driving the conflict. Finding common ground, negotiating compromise, and surfacing the underlying reasons for differences are key to effectively handling conflict.

Yet too frequently leaders enter situations in which destructive conflict has permeated the culture. Instead of conflict providing creative tensions in the workplace, it breaks down trust and builds barriers. Understanding better the ways in which conflict intensifies, developing strategies for deescalating conflict, and building up trust become essential leadership tools.

Conflict Analysis

Practitioners and academics in the field of conflict management face extraordinary challenges in dealing with the various phases of conflict, whether it is rebuilding in the aftermath, stopping conflict in progress, or preventing conflict before it begins. In these efforts, successful educators and practitioners follow a simple precept: effective action depends upon insightful analysis.

—United States Institute of Peace, n.d.

A common problem in effectively managing a conflict lies in how it is diagnosed (Furlong, 2010). Accurate diagnosis of the situation requires framing the conflict in a logical and coherent way. Cheldelin and Lucas (2004) offer a three-part framework for conflict analysis. Level I conflict analysis examines the conflict more deeply to determine what type of conflict is occurring, the cause or causes, the circumstances, and the duration (Cheldelin & Lucas, 2004). Here, analysis is of the conflict's micro issues. A reflective question to ask in surfacing micro issues is, "Is this a recent conflict or one that has been simmering below the surface for some time?" If this conflict has been brewing for a long time, it is a signal that the parties involved have been avoiding getting to the root of the real issues, and this avoidance behavior has made getting to the heart of the matter more difficult. Individuals have already demonstrated, by past behavior in avoiding the conflict, that they have passive tendencies and may be equally as reluctant to engage in conflict resolution.

Level I conflict analysis begins with questions to elicit understanding of the situation:

- How would you describe this type of conflict?
- What is the source or trigger of the conflict?
- What is the duration of the conflict?

- Has the conflict escalated? If so, why? (Adapted from Cheldelin & Lucas, 2004, p. 15)

Level II conflict analysis considers the contextual issues, including identity and situation (Cheldelin & Lucas, 2004). Situational aspects that may be influencing the conflict involve factors such as time, setting, roles, opportunities for discussion and problem solving, or concerns about repercussions. Identity-based aspects that may be influencing the conflict involve factors such as social identities and belief systems. Identity-based factors may focus on individual or group affiliation by gender, race, religion, class, disability, and ethnicity. Examples of identity-based conflicts include accusations of discrimination or bias based on an individual's social identity or affiliation.

Level II conflict analysis begins with questions to examine contextual issues:

- How would you describe the context of the conflict?
- Have personal values or beliefs been questioned in this conflict?
- What are the power dynamics of this conflict?
- Is there a tension between the social identities of those who are involved in the conflict?
- What are the repercussions of the conflict?
- Are there concerns about retaliation? (Adapted from Cheldelin & Lucas, 2004, p. 17)

Level III conflict analysis examines the macro issues, culture, traditions, and structures within an organization (Cheldelin & Lucas, 2004). In this analysis, the internal and external layers unique to each institution of higher education are explored to better understand the shared values, underlying assumptions and beliefs, norms, and observable practices and behaviors that describe the organization culture. As reviewed in chapter 1, cultures are deeply entrenched systems of group behavior that help to explain why things are done the way they are in a particular environment and why a violation of the norms can result in culture clash.

Level III conflict analysis begins with questions to examine issues that may be emerging from a sociopolitical or structural context:

- How would you describe the espoused values, history, and traditions of the institution? What makes this campus unique?
- What are the underlying assumptions of this culture? Have these assumptions been questioned or challenged?
- Have shared values or behavioral norms been violated in some way?
- Has there been a change in the group dynamic leading to conflict? (Adapted from Cheldelin & Lucas, 2004, p. 19)

As you think about your own institution, explore the ways that cultural or historical characteristics are reflected in policy and practices related to the prevention and mitigation of conflict.

Theory into Practice: Conflict Management Styles

Managing conflict effectively first requires an analysis of the conflict, followed by a determination of actions to resolve it (Furlong, 2010). Understanding the variety of ways individuals are inclined to respond to conflict is invaluable for leaders facilitating and managing difficult issues. The Thomas-Kilmann (1974, 2008) framework identifies five different modes for responding to conflict situations and is based on the behavioral dimensions of assertiveness (degree to which you try to satisfy your needs) and cooperativeness (degree to which you try to satisfy the needs of others) in addition to the surrounding systems of the organization, such as culture, structure, roles, and processes. The mode that an individual uses in response to conflict often depends on personal preference, experience, and the situation (for more information, see KilmannDiagnostics.com).

The five modes are summarized as follows:

1 *Competing* is assertive and uncooperative behavior. Individuals operating in this mode are power oriented and pursue their self-interests

over others' interests. They will pursue their position, ideas, and rights and try to win.

2 *Accommodating* is unassertive and cooperative behavior, the opposite of competing. There is a self-sacrificing element in this mode, and individuals may put their own best interests aside. They seem motivated to keep the peace and yield to the will and preferences of others.

3 *Avoiding* is unassertive and uncooperative behavior. Individuals do not address conflict; they sidestep or postpone issues or withdraw to reduce tensions.

4 *Collaborating* is assertive and cooperative behavior, the opposite of avoiding. Individuals work with others to explore the issue and find creative solutions.

5 *Compromising* is a moderate balance of assertive and cooperative behavior. Individuals seek resolution to issues that are mutually acceptable. A willingness to compromise signals a desire to find the middle ground or to split the difference between two competing positions. (Adapted from Kilmann, n.d.)

Table 4.2 offers an example of some of the pros and cons found in each of the conflict modes. The pro column identifies constructive behaviors that can be used effectively to reach an intended goal with an illustrative example. The con column identifies the downside of each of the modes, which can occur when it is overused or perceived by others in negative ways.

Leaders learning to manage people in a wide range of organizational structures understand and anticipate that conflict will happen, recognize contextual cues, and approach conflict in ways that result in beneficial outcomes for both the individuals involved and the organization. Knowing that individuals react to conflict differently can aid savvy leaders in their interactions with others during times of disagreement and as leaders apply solution-seeking strategies.

Table 4.2. Understanding the Pros and Cons in Thomas-Kilmann Conflict Modes

Conflict style	Pros / constructive behavior	Cons / destructive behavior	Example of effective use of this style to meet intended goals
Accommodating "Peacekeeping"	Builds social capital Is cooperative	Creates power imbalances Reduces creativity	The provost agrees to maintain faculty incentives for online course development.
Avoiding "Let it be"	Deescalates by not fanning the fire Takes time to assess and think it through	Detaches Neglects responsibilities Is uncaring	The new dean wants to eliminate course releases given to faculty to complete program assessment work but gets pushback from department chair. With an upcoming accreditation site visit, the dean agrees to evaluate the workload and wait until after the visit is completed.
Collaborating "Win-win"	Builds relationships Fosters trust Generates ideas and creative solutions	Misrepresents interests Leverages relationships for personal gain	The president agrees to invest in sports programs and an arena after stakeholder survey results, focus group, and student committee recommendations all demonstrate support for the initiative.
Competing "Stand up for your rights"	Establishes positional power	Strains relationships Pursues self-interest over others	A department chair who oversees a new doctoral program asserts the right to equal access to resources provided for doctoral faculty in similar programs in the college.
Compromising "Give a little; get a little"	Finds the middle ground Maintains relationship	Takes the easy way out Sits on the fence	The provost does not support a new tenure-track line but provides base funding for a fixed-term position.

Adapted from Kilmann Diagnostics (n.d.)

Emotional Intelligence

Emotional intelligence (EI) is a key competency for high-performing leaders (Rosete & Ciarrochi, 2005). The emergence of EI as a competency builds on the foundational work of Howard Gardner (1983). In 1983, Gardner first published his seminal book on multiple intelligences, which argued that individuals learn, perform, and understand in different ways. He outlined seven types of intelligences: (1) visual-spatial, (2) bodily-kinesthetic, (3) musical, (4) interpersonal, (5) intrapersonal, (6) linguistic, (7) logical-mathematical. Moving beyond a singular measure of intelligence as marked by an intelligence quotient (IQ), this framework expands and acknowledges a full range of individual capabilities.

Salovey and Mayer (1990) built on the framework of multiple intelligences and advanced the concept of emotional intelligence (EI), a term first coined by Payne (1985). Their work distinguished between the emotion of self and the emotion of others. The emotion of self is the ability to accurately appraise and express feelings. The emotion of others is the ability to emphasize with others and includes the nonverbal perception of emotions. Pointedly, the authors conclude that "when people approach life tasks with emotional intelligence, they should be at an advantage for solving problems adaptively" (Salovey & Mayer, 1990, p. 201). Adaptive leaders are able to assess situations (including times of conflict) and come up with solutions and options (Heifetz, 1994).

Goleman (1995) popularized the concept of emotional intelligence. He categorized EI into five areas: (1) self-awareness, (2) self-regulation, (3) social skill, (4) empathy, (5) motivation. Central to the concept of EI is the ability to know yourself and how your actions are perceived by others. You no doubt can readily remember a situation in which you observed someone not noticing signals when interacting with others or not being able to read the room. Self-awareness regarding EI can identify how leaders can build EI skills. Once individuals have this sense of self, there is a need to continue to self-monitor. For example, a leader may discover that others may perceive the leader's excitement to add to a conversation as a rude interruption. Practicing active listening, self-regulating during interactions, and generally employing good social skills become important. This type of behavior also signals to others less reliance on a singular leader and instead underscores the value of leadership throughout the college (see table 4.3).

Table 4.3. Emotional Intelligence Capabilities and Competencies

Capabilities	Competencies	Examples
Self-awareness	Emotional self-awareness	Ability to read your emotions accurately and understand the impact your emotions have in the workplace
	Accurate self-assessment	Ability to recognize your strengths and weaknesses
	Self-confidence	Ability to feel and project self-confidence
Self-management	Self-control	Ability to keep emotions in check and not act on impulse
	Trustworthiness	Ability to build trust by acting with honesty and integrity
	Conscientiousness	Ability to manage your duties responsibly
	Adaptability	Ability to adapt to changing conditions and overcome challenges
	Achievement orientation	Ability to succeed based on intrinsic standards of excellence
	Initiative	Ability to recognize and act on opportunities
Social awareness	Empathy	Ability to sense and understand the emotions and perspectives of other people and act on behalf of their concerns
	Organizational awareness	Ability to recognize and navigate the culture and dynamics of the organization
	Service orientation	Ability to recognize and serve the needs of constituents

(*continued*)

Table 4.3 *(continued)*

Capabilities	Competencies	Examples
Social skills (relationship management)	Visionary leadership	Ability to create and implement a shared vision
	Influence	Ability to persuade
	Developing others	Ability to mentor and guide others to enhance their skillsets
	Communication	Ability to listen, to accurately receive and send messages
	Change catalyst	Ability to enact change by effectively managing resistance and persisting through to sustained implementation
	Conflict management	Ability to deescalate tensions and resolve conflict
	Building bonds	Ability to successfully build a supportive relationship network
	Teamwork and collaborations	Ability to build effective teamwork through collaborative practices

Adapted from Goleman, 2000, p. 80

The influence of EI on leader effectiveness (Kerr, Garvin, Heaton, & Boyle, 2006; Rosete & Ciarrochi, 2005) results in leaders seeking ways to enhance their own EI to help improve their ability to perform. George (2000) proposed specific links between EI and leadership effectiveness:

1 Development of collective goals and objectives
2 Instilling in others an appreciation of the importance of work activities
3 Generating and maintaining enthusiasm, confidence, optimism, cooperation, and trust
4 Encouraging flexibility in decision-making and change

5 Establishing and maintaining a meaningful identity for an organization (p. 1039)

Building a leader's EI requires attention to reflective practice and commitment to appreciating the value that the contributions of others bring to the organization. Understanding others and their perspectives builds space for empathy. Consider how the focus on understanding the four frames (Bolman & Deal, 2013) provides one way to perceive what drives individuals to act in particular ways. The ability to empathize begins with first understanding the actions of others. The role of motivation in EI concerns what motivates leaders' actions and what motivates the actions of others. Chapter 3 on communication provides greater depth on how to relate to others. Using reflective practice in leadership helps self-monitor EI.

Cultural Intelligence

Cultural intelligence has been recognized as an essential intelligence for creating high-performing organizations. As global markets and partnerships across all sectors expand and as demographic shifts create a more diverse workforce, cultural intelligence has become a key leadership competency (Livermore & Van Dyne, 2015; Thomas et al., 2015). While the emotional intelligence framework is conceptually built around self-awareness and understanding how one is perceived by others, cultural intelligence (CQ) refers to one's adeptness in relating and interacting in environments within cultural contexts (Earley, 2002). Cultural intelligence is described as "a system consisting of cultural knowledge, cross-cultural skills and cultural metacognition that allows people to interact effectively across cultures" (Thomas et al., 2015, p. 1102). As cultural outsiders, individuals who possess high CQ demonstrate a seemingly natural ability to interpret cultural norms and values and to utilize appropriate interpersonal skills that align with cultural patterns of behavior (Earley & Mosakowski, 2004).

Cultural intelligence is multidimensional, and theoretical constructs vary as researchers continue to define and measure the capacity individuals have for effective intercultural interactions within cultural contexts that differ from their own. Livermore (2015) conceptualizes a cultural intelligence framework consisting of four interrelated dimensions or CQ capabilities: motivation (CQ-Drive), cognition (CQ-Knowledge), metacognition (CQ-Strategy), and behavior (CQ-Action). These capabilities are defined as follows:

- *CQ-Drive (motivation):* Having the interest, confidence, and drive to adapt cross-culturally. Intrinsic, extrinsic, and self-efficacy are three subdimensions of this capability and refer to the degree to which one derives enjoyment from culturally diverse experiences (intrinsic), the tangible benefits gained from the experience (extrinsic), and the confidence one has to effectively navigate culturally diverse situations.
- *CQ-Knowledge (cognition):* Understanding intercultural norms and differences. This capability refers to a person's knowledge about the variations of culture systems and associated norms and values.
- *CQ-Strategy (metacognition):* Making sense of culturally diverse experiences and planning accordingly. This capability refers to one's ability to use cultural knowledge to plan an appropriate strategy, to accurately interpret what is going on within the cultural context, and to compare the actual experience with expectations.
- *CQ-Action (behavioral):* Changing verbal and nonverbal actions appropriately when interacting cross-culturally. The subdimensions of this capability involve verbal and nonverbal behaviors and refer to one's ability to adapt these behaviors appropriately to diverse cultures. (Livermore, 2015, pp. 30–34)

The CQ framework provides a coherent model for novice and experienced leaders who recognize the need to further develop their professional and personal capacity to engage in culturally intelligent behavior. Like other forms of intelligence, CQ can be developed and enhanced over time in ways that include elements of self-assessment, targeted professional development, coaching, and mentoring. As discussed in chapter 1, theoretical and conceptual frameworks such as

Bolman and Deal's (2013) organizational frames become powerful tools for learning how to shift and change situational views within various contexts. Imagine how leadership capacity can be enhanced as one layers the CQ framework over Bolman and Deal's (2013) organizational frames. The ability to navigate various organizational and cultural landscapes now becomes multidimensional.

Case #7: The Question of Professional Competency

This case study provides an opportunity for you to conduct a conflict analysis of a scenario in which two professors are locked in a struggle over professional competency. As you read the case, think about the perspectives of each person involved and how you might frame your approach to this conflict.

Two professors employed at a large Mid-Atlantic university known for its online and distance learning programs have a long-standing conflict that has recently escalated to an untenable level for Professor Rodgers. Three years ago, the Family Studies Department hired two tenure-track professors, Julia Rodgers and Samuel Alvarez, to support a robust graduate program in child development. The master's degree in child development is a hybrid program delivered at two satellite locations. Dr. Alvarez works directly out of the Florida center, handles student recruitment and admission, and teaches primarily face-to-face courses in the program, whereas Dr. Rodgers is located on the main campus, directs and assesses the program, creates the schedule and identifies instructors, and teaches the introductory course online. The rest of the faculty teaching in the program is a balanced mix of adjuncts and tenure-track faculty. Several times a year, Dr. Rodgers visits the satellite location, and Dr. Alvarez comes to main campus for departmental retreats dedicated to strategic planning and program reviews. Both professors enjoy a good rapport with their students, who are primarily working professionals seeking advanced credentials to bolster their careers.

Dr. Rodgers carefully planned the first course to include an introduction to the program, expectations for research, and an overview of the capstone thesis requirement. All students and faculty teaching in the program received copies of the program requirements and the expectations of course work to build shared program norms and to establish quality of student outcomes. As the program lead, Dr. Rodgers asked faculty for feedback after each course related to any concerns they may have. Early on in the delivery of the program, it was evident that student writing and research were areas of weakness. On the basis of this feedback, Dr. Rodgers made a request to all faculty in the program to reinforce APA style in their writing assignments and guide students to the online writing center if needed. Dr. Alvarez was teaching both the research and capstone courses in the program, which typically contained the most writing and research skill assessment. His feedback about the students was generally positive, and he noted that he held capstone study and review sessions on a regular basis to reinforce research and writing skills.

Students were also required to work closely with their thesis committee, composed of two faculty members. Without exception, faculty committee members began contacting Dr. Rodgers with concerns that the students seemed ill prepared to conduct a research study. Initial thesis drafts were lacking in substance, and faculty felt they needed to reteach basic research principles and formal writing techniques. Faculty threatened to quit serving on the committees and began questioning the students' limited knowledge of research.

Dr. Rodgers brought the concerns to the department chair, shared some of the thesis papers, and asked him how to approach the situation. The department chair, Andrew Lowell, indicated that he would review and contact Dr. Alvarez to discuss the concerns. Dr. Lowell reviewed Dr. Alvarez's course syllabi on file. The assignments for the research class were primarily group projects and take-home quizzes and tests. He questioned the rigor of the course and found that the thesis papers were weak. The chair scheduled a conference call with Dr. Alvarez and discussed the faculty concerns and suggested ways he could strengthen the course.

The next day, Dr. Rodgers received an email from Dr. Alvarez blasting her for going to the department chair and not discussing the concerns with him first. His email carried an angry tone, and he accused her of blaming him for what was clearly the result of lazy students not applying what they had learned. At the end of the email, in capital letters, he told her, "SHUT YOUR DAMN MOUTH!" Dr. Rodgers forwarded the email to the department chair and demanded that he take action, as she felt she was being harassed.

Dr. Lowell contacted Dr. Alvarez immediately and scheduled a three-way conference call the next day to discuss the situation with him and Dr. Rodgers. The conference call went well, and Dr. Alvarez apologized for the email, explaining that he holds himself to high standards and that he had been totally blindsided by the initial call from the department chair. He and Dr. Rodgers talked about steps they could take in the program to strengthen the student capstone projects. Dr. Alvarez also said that he was willing to have students share their thesis drafts with him first, give them more feedback, and then send them forward for the committee review. Dr. Rodgers agreed that she would meet with faculty committee members and ask them to provide students with more targeted feedback and to encourage them to use university support services to strengthen their research proposals and writing. The department chair reminded both professors that they were hired as a team and that he expected them to work closely together to assist the students to elevate the quality of the capstones.

The faculty members serving on thesis committees, however, were not satisfied. They blamed Dr. Alvarez for poor preparation and pressured Dr. Rodgers to change Dr. Alvarez's course assignments. As the program director, Dr. Rodgers wanted to avoid the ongoing complaints from her peers and acknowledged that the majority of student had a limited grasp of both research and thesis writing. When the time came to schedule courses for the next cohort, Dr. Rodgers informed Dr. Alvarez that she would need him to teach two other courses in the program, as faculty from the main campus wanted to take a turn teaching the research and capstone courses.

Dr. Alvarez was very upset about this change and called the department chair. He told Dr. Lowell that students had been privately raising concerns about Dr. Rodgers to him for several years, and he had not taken them seriously until now. He claimed that the students said Dr. Rodgers was a racist and that they wanted to quit the program at the very start because of her repeated microaggressions. The only reason the students stayed in the program was due to his assurances that Dr. Rodgers was really not that bad and that he would help them through. He told Dr. Lowell that he now knows the students were right and that Dr. Rodgers is making arbitrary course-schedule changes and discriminating against him. He told Dr. Lowell that he was going to contact faculty personnel services to file a complaint against Dr. Rodgers.

In the following week, Dr. Lowell received emails and several letters of support for Dr. Alvarez from students in the program. Each correspondence had a very similar format and included a concern about an interaction or experience when working with Dr. Rodgers. When the chair shared the student letters with Dr. Rodgers, she was stunned. She said none of the concerns cited were true, and she felt certain that Dr. Alvarez was soliciting help from students in an effort to sabotage her career.

Guiding Questions

The following questions help to point out how new leaders might begin to analyze disputes and recognize the potential for conflict escalation. Use the following questions to conduct a deep analysis of the case:

1. Identify the behaviors of Dr. Alvarez and Dr. Rodgers that you find problematic.
2. How did the behaviors of others (students, faculty, department chair) further escalate or deescalate the issue? Identify the trigger points for each professor.
3. Conduct a Level I, II, and III conflict analysis of this case.
4. How does emotional intelligence contribute to problem? To the potential solution?

5 How would you describe the cultural intelligence of the various individuals?

Case Discussion

This case study illustrates how quickly conflict can escalate into a serious dispute. Aggressive communication, accusations of racism and discrimination, and the filing of a formal complaint are indicative of a conflict spiraling out of control. The hiring of Dr. Alvarez to support a robust off-campus program resulted in him having a great deal of autonomy, because of his physical distance from the main campus, his department chair, and other faculty. His position was critically important due to his role with student recruitment and admissions for the program. As the on-site program coordinator, he taught students in face-to-face courses and had many other opportunities to interact with them. Dr. Alvarez represented the face of the program and was one constant for the students as their direct link to the main campus.

Dr. Alvarez was working under the assumption that everything was running well. Program enrollments were strong, and student concerns were minimal. From a distance, it also appeared that the program delivery and management were solid, until the first cohort of students began their research capstone projects and were found to be ill prepared to complete them. After two years of smooth sailing, Dr. Alvarez suddenly found his teaching abilities being scrutinized by the department chair. He felt blindsided and blamed Dr. Rodgers for this abrupt change in perception regarding his job performance. He was very angry and responded to her aggressively through email.

In this case, concerns about professional performance and competency are paramount. As you consider the intensity and scope of Dr. Alvarez's behaviors, as well as the strong influence that department faculty had on Dr. Rodgers, it is important to consider the context. From a pragmatic view, ask yourself about how the tenure-track status of both professors creates a strong undercurrent below the surface of this conflict. Tenure has been identified as "the single common cause of serious disputes in an academic environment" (Coffman, 2005,

p. 50), and it results in escalation of the stakes of a conflict. Twale and De Luca (2008) explore issues of faculty incivility and note that "faculty along an academic career path toward tenure and promotion are likely to feel and react more strongly to uncivil or bullying acts" (p. 50). Faculty may feel victimized when concerns about their performance are coupled with untenured status and worries about future job security (McCarthy & Mayhew, 2004). However, while concerns about tenure offer a plausible explanation for behaviors, they do not excuse those behaviors.

Group dynamics also play a role in this conflict. The department faculty's approach to the students' problems in preparation and capacity to complete the capstone was to place the blame squarely on Dr. Alvarez. They assumed an adversarial approach instead of a collegial one. Clearly, there were legitimate concerns about his performance, but the overall response by the faculty appears uncaring. A reasonable expectation for a relatively new and untenured faculty member would be collegial support from the department that hired him. Ideally, a decision to change Dr. Alvarez's course load would have come after faculty mentorship for his perceived failings in teaching research and a more thorough analysis of the program curriculum and delivery sequence. Dr. Rodgers's decision to make the change could be construed as being insensitive and the result of faculty pressure to conform to the will of the group.

Managing conflict is a delicate balance, much like a tightrope walker who takes each step with the knowledge that too much movement in one direction or another can result in a serious fall (Wilmot & Hocker, 2001). In this case, the conflict was spilling out in multiple directions. There was a breach of trust across interdepartmental levels, external constituents, and the students. Emotions were running hot, with various faculty members not feeling that others understood their plight. Group dynamics, tenure concerns, and unexplored issues related to gender and culture exacerbated the situation. The academic leader was now faced with a critical question: What do I do next?

Institutional Supports to Manage Conflict

As evinced in the preceding case, department chairs should work in collaboration and consultation with their dean. Bright and Richards (2001) note that "as the leader of the college, the dean plays the role of chief mediator" and is expected to resolve personnel concerns at his or her level (p. 218). Leaders in academe have a responsibility to manage conflict and need to consider what options are available on their campuses for consultation and support in moving conflicts to resolution.

Given the complexity of the preceding case and the potential for litigation, it is very likely that the dean would need to utilize institutional support systems and resources to assist in mediating the conflict. Institutional support systems to address conflict vary (Coffman, 2005). Descriptions of some of the more common offices and services follow.

Ombudsman

Campus conflicts in the 1960s were the stimulus for the creation of ombudsman offices across universities and colleges in the nation in an effort to provide a neutral space to air concerns and to assist individuals in problem resolution (Warters, 2001). In higher education and other organizations, ombudsman "serve as a confidential, independent, neutral, and informal dispute resolution resource, . . . are accessible to a defined population, and can advocate for fairness" ("Editorial Note," 2013). The ombudsman office provides informational resources and is available to all members of the organizational community. The International Ombudsman Association (IOA) provides a Code of Ethics to guide the growth and development of the ombudsman profession (n.d.).

Faculty Personnel Services

Campus policies provide a guide for practices to follow in times of conflict. The evolution of faculty roles over time (Bowen & Tobin,

2015) highlights changes in governance, processes for interactions, and the establishment of particular norms regarding faculty responsibilities for tenure and promotion. Campuses with unions have formalized contracts that govern the course of action for grievances, but faculty and professional staff handbooks also provide similar guidance on nonunionized campuses. New leaders should spend time reading and understanding the processes in place that govern the campus before they need to use the policies in a time of conflict. Just as critical is the distinction between *actual* policy and *perceived* policy via norms. One often hears when new to a campus, "This is the policy on . . . ," yet many of these "polices" are in fact norms of behavior and are not written down.

Legal Counsel

The proliferation of external rules and regulations has increased the role of campus legal counsel. Compliance rules and policies are in place to keep colleges and universities clear of any infractions. Recently, Title IX implementation required campuses to update policies for sexual assault, gender language, and student and faculty policies regarding sexual engagement. New leaders should understand when to contact legal counsel regarding an employee or student issue, the channels for reporting, and how to document scenarios of conflict as they unfold.

Mediation

When conflicts cannot be resolved internally, involved parties seek mediation. Meditation typically involves a third party, which may first occur internally (e.g., dean level) and, if not resolved, externally. Mediators often meet with each of the parties separately first to determine each person's "story." Next, background information collection and analysis occur to determine a set of agreed-upon facts. Establishing common goals and outcomes helps to move along the process toward obtaining a mutually agreed-upon resolution. Mediation is an iterative process that involves a sequence of meetings designed to move parties to resolution of the conflict within a context of working with an impartial mediator (Moore, 2014).

The various infrastructures embedded in institutions of higher education to address conflict demonstrate an attempt to build conflict competence among individuals. Leaders who acknowledge and anticipate conflicts and who manage them effectively through training and early intervention and in ways that maintain safety and respect (Runde & Flanagan, 2008) build campus environments and cultures that are conflict competent. In summary, "Perhaps the best conflict management systems in higher education have to offer educators is a model for promoting individuals' capacities and responsibilities for making decisions about their lives; for building a sense of community; for fostering mutual respect and cooperation; and for developing a sense of understanding and fairness rather than power as a basis for resolving conflicts and disputes" (Campus Conflict Management Guidelines Committee, 2003, p. 24). At the heart of managing conflict is attention to a collaborative culture, trust among campus members, building effective structures to negotiate disagreements, and attention to both self-awareness and perspectives of others.

Making This Personal

Think about your own approach to conflict. In what ways have your actions or responses contributed to either destructive or constructive conflict? How would you describe your emotional response to conflict situations? Consider the elements of EI and CQ, in self-assessment and in understanding others. Which area contributed to the conflict or how you understood the conflict?

Self-awareness offers leaders invaluable insight into their own leadership styles and behaviors. Professional development in the area of conflict management and resolution is often an integral component of leadership programs. An example of a useful tool that offers individual, group, and 360-degree feedback is the Conflict Dynamics Profile Assessment. Sample profiles can be retrieved at the following site: https://www.conflictdynamics.org/about-the-cdp/. A tool such as this may help you to understand your own personal bias and conflict triggers and to identify strengths and areas for improvement so that you may further develop your skills and fine-tune your approach to conflict.

This chapter has introduced the topic of conflict and conflict management in higher education. As you think about your professional work environment, what have been your observations of conflict or tensions? How were they addressed? Was it effective? In what ways can leaders develop and foster conflict management skills with faculty and staff before interpersonal disputes erupt into intractable problems?

Conflict is complex and unique depending on the individuals, circumstances, and context. Leaders need to be self-aware and understand their predominant approach to managing conflict as well as alternative approaches and available institutional supports. Understanding your role and responsibilities in the organization is also critical. Watson and colleagues (2016) offer seven key competencies for individuals to sharpen in order to develop personal and professional skills in managing all forms of conflict. They propose focusing on the following:

- Being self-aware of your position, attitudes, and reactions to conflict
- Being an active listener to everyone engaged in the conflict
- Being able to manage multiple perspectives on the conflict
- Being mindful
- Being able to find the best frames for understanding the nature and intensity of the conflict
- Being able to create safe dialogues concerning the conflict
- Being able to decide if your chosen behavioral style and intervention strategies are likely to be effective (Watson et al., 2016, pp. 39–40)

While there are many other conflict-related skills that leaders develop over time, these seven competencies offer a starting point for the novice leader who may be wondering where to begin. Research supports that training in conflict management yields promising results in workplace productivity and employee well-being (Overton & Lowry, 2013).

Key Chapter Points

- Conflict in organizations is common and occurs in both constructive and destructive ways.
- Approaches to conflict management involve a number of different options, which are often dependent on the intended goal or outcome.
- Leaders need to understand the multifaceted aspects of conflict and be able to conduct a thorough analysis of the situation to make an informed approach to resolution.
- Leaders must be aware of the conflict management supports and processes in their organization environment that help mediate intractable problems or mitigate serious conflicts.
- Emotional intelligence provides a potential tool in managing and avoiding the escalation of conflicts.
- Cultural intelligence is increasingly important in a global marketplace and helps build effective leadership in institutions.

Web Resources

- Conflict Dynamics Profile assessment: https://www.conflictdynamics.org/about-the-cdp/.
- Conflict Styles Assessment, United States Institute of Peace: https://www.usip.org/public-education/students/conflict-styles-assessment
- "How Emotionally Intelligent Are You?," Mind Tools: https://www.mindtools.com/pages/article/ei-quiz.htm
- The Intercultural Conflict Style Inventory (ICS): https://icsinventory.com/

CHAPTER 5

Strategic Thinking, Planning, and Decision-Making

Organizations are dynamic and complex systems, constantly moving, adapting, and readjusting. This chapter reviews how to build a strong foundation of understanding among stakeholders for data-informed decision-making and systemic improvement, using principles of transparency, coherence, and engagement. Aspects of both traditional and organic strategic planning methods will be reviewed through case analysis. Traditional strategic planning assumes a relatively stable environment. True, there will always be unknowns, but traditional planning occurs in a context in which most of the data are known and rational decision-making can occur (Chaffee, 1983). Strategic planning based on organic evolution assumes that some information remains unknown and that plans need to include the ability to adjust on the fly. The state of constant change in higher education requires strategic planning that sets a direction but is also flexible and nimble (Bryson, 2018; Dooris, Kelley, & Trainer, 2004). But either traditional or organic strategic planning are appropriate options depending on the circumstances.

At the heart of strategic planning is strategic thinking. Historically, budgeting was challenging for leaders responsible for allocating and managing resources, but it was more predictable (Tierney, 2008). Now, effective leadership relies on strategic thinking and planning that ultimately includes aligning resources with actions to advance the vision, mission, and strategic priorities of the institution. Central in this process is establishing what it is that is important for the institution, making plans to obtain these goals, and perhaps most critically, operationalizing the plans. The best-laid plans and thinking on strategy will be ineffective without paying attention to the existing culture and working on building a change mind-set. This requires courageous leadership.

The headlines are full of stories of bad decision-making by leaders and of plans that have gone awry. Scrutiny from the public and stakeholders requires attention to ethical decision-making (Englehardt, Pritchard, Romesburg, & Schrag, 2014; Wood & Nevarez, 2014). As stewards of the institution, leaders throughout the college must make sound decisions, followed by sound actions to implement the decisions. This chapter reviews some of the basics for strategic thinking and planning and covers the role of strategic leadership in decision-making. Making decisions during times of change sets the stage for future direction and hopefully success.

Learning Objectives

- Strategic thinking and planning
- Environmental scanning and goal setting
- Data-driven decision-making
- Balancing competing objectives

Strategic and Deliberate Action

A well-developed process and strategic plan can offer the benefit of stability in a turbulent environment, while maintaining the university's ability to take advantage of unplanned opportunities.

—Goldman & Salem, 2015, p. 5

The concept and practice of strategic planning in educational organizations emerged in the United States in the late 1970s (Keller, 1983; UNESCO, 2010) and has increased in usage over time. Adopted from both a military and business management perspective, strategic planning in higher education coincided with a time when "enrollments began to fluctuate, student demographics started to change, and funding became inconsistent" (Hinton, 2012, p. 7). Ironically, that statement is as true today as it was decades ago. Recent surveys conducted by *Inside Higher Ed* (Lederman, 2018) and Gallop (Jones, 2018) indicate that declining enrollment, a decrease in international student populations, financial difficulties, fewer high school graduates, lower world rankings, decreased funding, and changing demographics are top challenges for U.S. higher education institutions. These and other challenges require higher education leaders to take strategic and deliberate actions and practice strategic thinking to ensure short-term gain and long-term sustainability.

Strategic planning is defined as "a managerial tool to help an organization to improve its performance by ensuring that its members are working to the same goals and by continuously adjusting the direction of the organization to the changing environment on the basis of results obtained" (International Institute for Educational Planning, 2010, p. 10). Much like a wheel on a ship, those who are steering the organization must shift and adjust continuously to remain steady while moving toward the destination. Like a ship, charting a new course requires forward thinking given how difficult it is to turn a large vessel midcourse. In a survey of more than 150 four-year college and university presidents, strategic planning and fund-raising were identified as the top-two most important presidential responsibilities. Additionally, the top-ranking skill and behavior needed for presidents assuming the office was identified as being a strategist (Selingo, Chheng, & Clark, 2017). Cabinet-level leaders, in particular, must scan the horizon to chart institutional direction, but leaders throughout the institution should also consider their roles as scouts and smaller-scale strategists.

The scale of a strategic planning process can be tailored to size and is helpful for units, departments, divisions, colleges, and centers, as well as the overall university. The university typically develops the overarching strategic plan, followed by each smaller unit designing a unit-based plan that aligns with the institutional objectives. Consider how this process looks like a set of Matryoshka nesting dolls—with each of the smaller units mirroring the overarching design of the institution, like the dolls mirror the largest outside decorative shell. Close alignment throughout the university creates cohesiveness in the strategic aims and anticipated plan outcomes.

Cohesive strategic planning done well can produce valuable outcomes for an organization. However, it is important to recognize and anticipate key strategic planning concerns. The International Institute for Education Planning (2010) noted three of the main criticisms with the strategic planning process:

1 There is too much focus on plan development and not enough on implementation.
2 Plans are prepared in a top-down, technocratic way.
3 Not enough consideration is given to the changing environment. (p. 10)

No doubt it is easy to recall a professional experience with strategic planning in which campus members dedicated time and energy to mapping out a plan only to have the plan sit on a shelf. When campus members experience this process a few times, it is no wonder that they approach a new leader's strategic planning process with skepticism. Indeed, Ginsberg (2011) argues that plans are a waste of time, pointing out that they often reinforce the status quo and existing administrative power structures.

The development of an institutional strategic plan can often take months; however, once the plan is adopted, the time and attention spent on implementation is sometimes minimal. It is for this reason that strategic planning should not be viewed as a blueprint or as a strictly linear and outcome-based process. Strategic planning conducted during times of rapid change and unpredictability must remain fluid and responsive. An implementation plan is needed to frequently monitor and track progress, attain goals, and ensure accountability. Hinton (2012) notes, "The implementation plan is revised, amended, and changed frequently to respond to environmental factors" (p. 12). Strategic planning is a journey, not a destination. The initial path may change based on feedback and adjustments along the way. To be most effective, continuous evaluation and goal reanalysis are required.

Strategic Planning Process

Strategic plans for higher education typically have a framework that includes some or all of the following components:

- Reviewing institutional vision, mission, values
- Engaging key stakeholders
- Scanning the environment
- Formulating goals
- Creating strategic objectives and action plans
- Aligning action steps based on institutional values and mission
- Identifying metrics and intended outcomes
- Monitoring implementation and progress
- Revising the strategic plan as needed (Hanover Research, 2013; Ruben, De Lisi, & Gigliotti, 2017)

The strategic planning process at the institutional level is often guided by an external consultant or senior leader with specific experience in facilitating such large-scale efforts. Strategic planning at the school or college level is typically facilitated by the dean, in order to align department goals to college and institutional strategic priorities—think of the nesting-dolls metaphor and the necessary cohesiveness between the overarching institutional planning and that of the smaller units. The alignment of the strategic plan throughout the institution is what is most important to ensure all constituents are contributing to a shared vision and the attainment of institutional goals.

Here is a brief description of core components of the strategic plan framework from a higher education perspective:

- *Vision statements* describe the aspirational goals and values of the institution. The vision statement is what sets the institution apart from others, defines a strategic position, and creates a shared vision for the future (Hinton, 2012).
- *Mission statements* vary widely and are representative of an institution's purpose, principles, and values. They are unique and derived from institutional history, the constituents they serve, funding sources, and aspirations. Mission statements provide direction for higher education leaders as to how resources are allocated to advance core values. "The mission statement ideally provides a blueprint and a touchstone for organizational decision-making" (Ruben et al., 2017, p. 41).
- *Value statements* include words, phrases, or sentences that identify the core values of the institution. These values should be verifiable with evidence and may include values of inclusion, integrity, social justice, and so on.
- *Goals* derive from institutional research and analysis of gap areas. Goal setting is also generated from meaningful and engaged discourse with stakeholders and embodies shared perspectives (Ruben et al., 2017).
- *Strategic objectives* define the actions that guide goal attainment.

- *Metrics* are established for each of the objectives to measure progress and success in goal attainment.
- *Action/implementation plans* are utilized to advance strategic goals and objectives. Resources, such as people, time, space, funding, and technology, are identified, as well as the action steps and the individuals responsible for carrying out the plan. The implementation plans also include timelines for frequent plan monitoring in order to refine and make necessary adjustments. (Hinton, 2012)

In the initial planning stage, strategic planning teams also conduct institutional research, mine data to identify performance gaps, and conduct environmental scans to better understand the current and future context for institutional needs. The process engages a wide range of internal and external stakeholders, tapping into a range of networks.

Strategic Thinking

Mintzberg (1994) argues that strategic planning found in practice turns out to be more about strategic programming—essentially reifying what exists (Ginsberg, 2011). In this case, planning is more about analysis than about forward thinking. Strategic thinking instead focuses more on synthesis. "Strategy making needs to function beyond the boxes, to encourage the informal learning that produces new perspectives and new combinations" (Mintzberg, 1994). Considering strategic programming more fluidly, Mintzberg identifies three required steps: codification, elaboration, and conversion of strategies into practice.

Codification involves putting the range of thinking into clear, concise language that is operational. Clarity in target goals is required. For example, leadership team strategic thinking may determine a general goal that new forms of program delivery are needed. But having a target goal that 10 percent of all course work be offered online provides more specificity and clarity. Elaboration puts specific plans into place to achieve the target goal—in this example, 10 percent of all course work being offered online. Here, the implementation process might identify a ramping-up plan that starts with two programs building online options and ultimately extends to one online program in each major. Finally, conversion requires the leadership team to take a step backward to determine if changes to structures or process are required. In the example of online programming, stepping back might highlight the need for evening advising options or alternative semester start and end times.

Strategic thinking is all about bringing an inquiry-centered mindset to situations that require guidance and direction. "Strategic thinking requires suspending judgment, rather than engaging in a rigorous and challenging examination of underlying premises relevant to the strategic challenge at hand. Ultimately, the purpose of strategic thinking is to support the process of generating a suitable strategic response to the strategic challenge that evoked its necessity in the first place" (Tovstiga, 2015, p. 32). The first step in strategic thinking involves identifying the strategic challenge. Determining a relevant challenge requires knowing the environmental context. Once the challenge has been identified, the next step is framing the issues on which to focus. Once issues are identified, strategic thinking requires development of relevant inquiry questions. Important in this inquiry process is surfacing what individuals and institutions assume, as unsurfaced assumptions can result in thinking falling into a rut of previously tried responses (Sloan, 2017).

Scenario Building

Scenario building is another practice used in higher education to strategically plan for the unexpected (Bradfield, Wright, Burt, Cairns, & Van Der Heijden, 2005). Scenario building includes studying trends, exploring possibilities, and mapping out both intended and unintended outcomes (Schoemaker, 1995). Understanding how the institution may be impacted by a given scenario helps to identify potential problems and contemplate solutions proactively, rather than reactively. The process employed is participatory and completed by teams that identify plausible cause-and-effect scenarios for a particular set of circumstances. The purpose of scenario building is not to predict the future but to provide a snapshot of how the institution would react when faced by any number of opportunities or challenges. Scenario building explores the "what if" question, and the process can help illuminate institutional strengths and vulnerabilities.

Rasmus (2012) notes that organizations that hope to remain relevant need to engage in strategic thinking as well as scenario building to examine the unknowns that can significantly impact and ultimately alter the established norms and accustomed practices of an institution. Rasmus states, "Uncertainty threatens to incapacitate institutions as they choose for change to be thrust upon them, or attempt to avoid or ignore the strategic importance of the changes taking place around them." The number of scenarios that can be examined is limitless. For optimal effectiveness, leaders and their teams will want to examine the status of the institution within the current environment context and prioritize key issues. Possible scenarios might include the following:

- Change in enrollment (decline or increase)
- Change in student demographics
- Facilities in need of renovation or removal
- New facility needs given institutional expansion
- Increased need for counseling services
- Technology infrastructure
- Campus shooting or safety concerns
- Major lawsuits
- Loss of community businesses
- Reduction in federal or state funding
- Closing satellite programs or shifting to online delivery
- Influx of international students
- Legislative mandates
- Accreditation loss or probation
- Catastrophic damage

To prepare for the future, leaders engaging in scenario building should consider the prompt, What will the university look like in the next ten years? Consider the scenario of declining student enrollment: A steady decline in applications has occurred at the institution, due in part to declining high school graduation rates, which are predicted to remain stagnate. If this trend continues for the next five to ten years, identify potential problems that will need to be managed at the institution. For example, a decline in revenue streams may lead to faculty and staff reductions, low morale, elimination of programs, and lack of resources to run programs. What else is likely to occur? How could scenarios be built around these examples?

Understanding what might occur helps leaders identify potential action steps to take to be ready for a range of scenario outcomes. Planning may involve developing strategic partnerships to provide new programming and a new stream of student enrollments. Programs may become prioritized or eliminated based on scenario building. In the short term, university endowments can offset revenue losses, but this type of planning does not provide for long-term solutions. Scenarios that emerge from leaders' use of this exercise will highlight variable futures and serve to provide leaders and stakeholders a glimpse of what could happen within the institution. Peering into alternative realities and contemplating the "what if" question give teams time to shore up vulnerable areas and explore targeted opportunities for turnaround. As you reflect on the challenges facing your institution, what types of scenarios might you envision?

Case #8: Follow the Money

No doubt you can draw from your own experiences several examples of planning efforts that did not turn out as planned. This case provides a scenario to contemplate and consider as you work to apply the concepts outlined in this chapter. A quick scan of the headlines will provide ample alternative examples.

Roger Holiday, dean of the Arts and Humanities College, prepared for his annual review with the provost. Holiday had been dean for five years, but this review would be different from the past ones, as the provost also invited the vice provost of academic management to the meeting. The vice provost, Darlene Harris, joined the university over a year ago, and her primary responsibilities include oversight for all budgetary matters related to academic programs and the development and advancement of the strategic plan. She was hired to turn around long-standing inefficient budgetary practices and, as rumor had it, to push out individuals who were deficient in maintaining their budgets. Dr. Harris had quickly earned the reputation as a no-nonsense, data-driven leader.

Dean Holiday was concerned going into the meeting, as overall enrollments at the university had been declining in recent years and his college was struggling to meet projections. Increased competition from online programs, the exponential growth of a regional community college, and an increase in early college initiatives throughout the state were some of the factors impacting student credit-hour production in his college. He felt prepared to discuss these concerns and planned to ask for additional funds to increase marketing and recruitment efforts. Holiday was also going to ask for two new faculty lines to bolster two of the college's online programs.

The meeting got off to a positive start with an overview of college activity and faculty successes. Faculty in the college were highly productive in research and scholarly activity and engaged in professional associations and networks. The dean also had a number of special projects for faculty that involved international travel for recruitment, coordination of the annual conference for international comparative education, and the development of international student support materials. Over the years, lucrative hiring packages, generous buyouts, and alternative workload assignments had contributed to faculty success, as well as an increased number of supplemental assignments.

Dr. Harris praised the dean for the accomplishments that his faculty had achieved and then zeroed in on the number of supplemental assignments offered in the college. She asked the dean if he was aware that he had the highest number of supplemental assignments in the university. The combined full-time equivalent (FTE) of these assignments was the equivalent of nearly twelve faculty members. Dean Holiday noted that faculty expectations for compensation had increased, but he was not aware of the combined FTE. Yet, despite this high usage of alternative assignments, the dean noted that he still had a steady stream of faculty coming to his door with all kinds of requests for additional funding for buyout assignments and that financial constraints were making it more and more difficult to satisfy their desires. Holiday knew he had a problem with saying no, and he wondered if other deans had similar issues.

The provost told Dean Holiday that he would not be getting new faculty lines and asked for an analysis of the supplemental assignments. The provost added that any additional faculty for the college would need to be funded by a reduction of supplemental assignments. The conversation next turned to a discussion of other areas for improvement. The provost turned to Dr. Harris and asked her to discuss the fiduciary concerns related to Dean Holiday's budget, which had been running in deficit for the past two years. Dr. Harris asked many questions, including how the annual college budget was constructed, who had input in developing the budget, how resource allocations were made, and how often budget expenditures were reviewed. Throughout the questioning, it was clear that managing the budget was a serious weakness for the dean. Dr. Harris also asked about the dean's progress with the college's strategic plan. She noted that all academic colleges, departments, and units were asked to update their strategic plans over a year ago to align with the new university strategic plan.

Dean Holiday acknowledged that although his college report on the strategic plan was nearly complete, it had not been a priority with his department chairs this year. What could he really say? That personally he thought strategic plans were a huge waste of time? That he struggled to get buy-in and wasn't willing to take a top-down approach? The truth was that he only discussed the strategic plan with his team once and never gave it a second thought. Finally, the provost intervened and told Dean Holiday that he would need to schedule another meeting in two weeks and to bring his financial officer with him. Specifically, he wanted the dean to outline his strategic planning process for the college and demonstrate to what extent the college budget supports departmental goals and initiatives.

Roger left the meeting and broke out in a sweat. Was this the beginning of the end of his role as dean? If he got fired, would anyone ever consider him for a leadership position again? His mind leaped ahead to a reduction in salary and benefits and less money for his retirement plan. On his way back to the office, Dean Holiday called his executive assistant and told her to set up an immediate meeting with his financial officer and assistant deans. They should have been on top of this, and he was going to let them have it.

Guiding Questions

The following questions help to understand the role of strategic thinking and scenario building in planning efforts. Use them to reflect on your advice to Dean Holiday.

1 How could Dean Holiday have aligned his college's strategic plan with the institutional plan?
2 What type of process could be instituted to get all of the college members to employ strategic thinking?
3 How might the use of scenario building help provide some options for Dean Holiday?
4 Describe Dean Holiday's leadership challenges and what steps he needs to take to turn things around.

Case Discussion

Dean Holiday felt he was a champion for his college and his faculty given his work to support the scholarship and reach of the college's faculty. Yet he failed to align his efforts to the institution's broader interests and strategic goals. Much of his approach aligned with historical strategic planning that focused on advancing the status quo. By his own account, he ignored aligning the college's work with the institutional goals. The dean was also unaware of the budget consequences of decisions, which had been allowed to continue for years until resources grew tight. The provost was working to apply strategic thinking across the university and to hold units accountable for identified goals. Mintzberg (1994) would argue that the dean was not synthesizing information—if Holiday was doing this wider level of scanning, he would have been aware of the practices in other units on campus through dean's meetings and looking at the institutional data. There is some level of awareness of the challenges facing the university with respect to enrollment but not a more detailed level of thought regarding the programs in place. Taking an inquiry approach and questioning assumptions would result in posing scenario building questions such as, Are the programs meeting the demands of the field? How might we adjust our programming to complement the work done in the community college or in advanced high school classes? How can we look at existing programs and ensure that students are not taking an excessive amount of credits to complete their degrees?

An issue at the heart of this case is the use of human resources. Yes, the faculty has achieved high levels of productivity, but at what cost? What remains unknown is if the structures in place are equitable and how much work each faculty member contributes to credit generation. The dean may opt to bring a range of stakeholders to the table and use an inquiry approach to think strategically about options. A danger lurks in the current tactics Dean Holiday employs. On one hand, it might be argued that he is using an inclusive leadership style as his decision-making is not top down. On the other hand, his actions might be viewed as avoiding conflict and putting his head in the sand. The dean's thought after the meeting to shift blame to the assistant deans does not bode well for outcomes.

Another level of analysis in this case involves the actions of the provost. It is important in the process to identify in clear language the goals and objectives. What remains unknown in this case is how the original institutional strategic plan was conveyed to the deans and other campus members. If there was a lack of clarity, it is not a surprise that Dean Holiday did not take the plan seriously. It is equally likely that the dean failed to hear the difference in the message sent on this version of the strategic plan and merely thought it was like the ineffective plans of the past. His surprise at this juncture would lead you to believe that there was not a clear identification of goals or clear metrics to know that the goals were achieved. However, a critical point in this case is that the college is bound to broader institutional plans and needs to align itself accordingly.

Environmental Scanning

Environmental scanning is a process used to collect environmental data and to analyze it through an organizational lens (Hambrick, 1982). One of the very first steps in the strategic planning process is to widely scan the internal and external environment of the organization. Bukowski and Michael (2012) note that environmental scanning "should be done by just about everyone who wears a managerial hat" (p. 2). Leaders must also be prepared to take environmental scanning to a higher level and seek to understand how the internal and external change drivers identified through scanning may hold future implications for their institution.

We all must become "horizon thinkers" and look into the future together, with good information, diverse perspectives, shared values, and great hopes.
—Sanaghan, 2009, p. 1

A commitment to environmental scanning is needed to understand the environment, to change stakeholder perceptions, and to determine the future trends in enrollments (Smorynski, 2017). For any organization to prosper, keeping a pulse on an ever-changing environment is essential. Environmental scanning at its best allows institutions to predict challenges and opportunities, design strategies or structures to navigate them, and create a blueprint for the future.

SWOT Analysis

There are many tools and data sources available for environmental scanning that can be utilized by a novice leader or scaled up for an experienced leader. One such tool is called a SWOT (strengths, weaknesses, opportunities, threats) analysis. Table 5.1 shows the typical format used when conducting a SWOT analysis.

There are many applications for a SWOT analysis. The range of uses includes a simple brainstorming session for a potential program to a critical analysis of a unit, department, college, or university. When conducting a SWOT analysis, it is important to identify both the *internal*

Table 5.1. SWOT Analysis

SWOT Analysis For: ______________________

Strengths	**Weaknesses**
Opportunities	**Threats**

and *external* strengths, weaknesses, opportunities, and threats. Once the process has been completed, individuals or planning teams will want to ask the following types of questions:

- How can we utilize our strengths to leverage the opportunities we identified?
- How can our strengths be utilized to overcome weaknesses?
- In what ways can we utilize our strengths to diminish potential threats?
- In what ways are our weaknesses making us vulnerable to threats?
- What action steps can we develop to capitalize on our strengths, reduce weaknesses, and take advantage of opportunities?

This type of inquiry-based activity helps synthesize key elements in the larger environment that may influence campus operations and provides a means to identify possible future activities.

PESTEL Analysis

Another environmental scanning tool is called the PESTEL, which stands for political, economic, social, technological, environmental/ecological, and legal. This tool is used to scan the external environment in each of the named areas, using the context of the institution. Conducting this type of environmental scan along each of the PESTEL domains requires examination of the environment from the local, state, national, and international perspective, as applicable. Using a wide lens provides another means to identify changes on the horizon, which can help leaders plan more effectively.

Following is a description of the PESTEL categories. Each listing includes factors that drive change:

- *Political:* governmental regulations, policy changes, political movements, shifts in the political environment
- *Economic:* unemployment, economic growth or decline, inflation, recession, interest rates

- *Social:* demographics, social norms, population growth and decline, social-cultural changes
- *Technological:* emerging technologies, artificial intelligence, robotics, automation, impact of technology on work
- *Environmental/ecological:* natural disasters, global warming, climate change, environmental regulations, organic and natural food
- *Legal:* legislative changes, sexual harassment laws, health & safety laws, tax laws, employment regulations.

Table 5.2 provides an example of how a PESTEL analysis that uses supporting evidence can help strategic leaders to identify priorities and plans for the future.

Table 5.2. PESTEL Analysis Example

PESTEL factors	Source of evidence	**Impact** L (low), M (medium), H (high), U (unknown)	Implications
Political	Institutional policy change—sexual misconduct / reporting requirements	M	Campus training for all stakeholders annually
	Elected administration in White House / state governor	H	State and/or federal legislation, funding, grants, policy
Economic	High unemployment rate	H	Retraining opportunities
	Declining enrollment	H	Loss in tuition revenue
	Declining financial support	H	Loss in revenue; can lead to rise in tuition cost or program and personnel cuts

(*continued*)

Table 5.2 *(continued)*

PESTEL factors	Source of evidence	**Impact** L (low), M (medium), H (high), U (unknown)	Implications
Social	Changing demographics / decline in number of international students	H	Revenue loss, change in campus diversity, potential loss of international partnership programs
	Stakeholder perception of college cost	H	Increased competition
	Increase in student mental health issues	M, H	Negative impact on student success and degree completion
Technological	Artificial intelligence	U	Changes to college majors
	Emerging technology (robot professor)	U, L	Altered delivery options
Environmental/ ecological	Hurricane damage on building infrastructure	H, U	Extensive damage to campus buildings and widespread flooding leads to closure Length of closure will depend on extent of damage and recovery
Legal	Current or pending legislation that will impact funding formulas; performance-based funding (PBF)	H, U	Impacts public institution revenue Metrics of PBF may alter academic decisions

Similar to a SWOT analysis, use of PESTEL as an environmental scanning tool can be scaled up or down (program, department, unit, college, university) and can include multiple sources of evidence in each area. Environmental scanning involves looking outside the institution's walls to assess how external trends influence college planning processes. How might your institution benefit from conducting SWOT and PESTEL analyses?

Appreciative Inquiry

Appreciative inquiry (AI) is another approach that can be used to scan the organizational environment and create a vision for the future. Cooperrider, Whitney, and Stavros (2008) describe appreciative inquiry as a process for positive change that can be used for "strategic planning, culture transformation, and leadership development" (p. 127). Appreciative inquiry was originally developed by Cooperrider in the late 1980s and was considered "a radical departure from traditional deficit-based change to a positive, strengths-based change process" (Cooperrider, n.d.). The SWOT analysis tool reviewed in this chapter can be used to illustrate the difference in approaches. The SWOT is used to identify strengths and opportunities, as well as weaknesses and threats to the organization, whereas an AI approach is only focused on the positive "core strengths" of the organization.

In higher education, we frequently hear about the many problems we face. Rather than focusing on what is wrong with higher education, the appreciative inquiry approach focuses on our positive core and explores how the core can be used to bolster future aspirations (Cockell & McArthur-Blair, 2012). For example, every question employed in the appreciate inquiry process is framed as a positive and is used to create a more conducive environment for open dialogue and stakeholder engagement.

The appreciative inquiry process is based on the 4-D framework (Cooperrider, Whitney, & Stavros, 2008) and is composed of four steps that involve inquiry around a specific topic. The following describes each of the four steps in the 4-D framework and establishes a strategic vision for an organization as an example topic:

- *Discovery (What gives work/life purpose?):* In the discovery phase, stakeholders describe the best of what is in the organization. Sharing ideals and values leads to collective appreciation and a shared vision of the organization. The discovery phase identifies the "positive core."
- *Dream (What might be?):* In the dream phase, stakeholders envision new possibilities for the future based on the positive core. The positive core established in discovery often gives rise to creative thinking and positive imaging of what the future may hold.
- *Design (How can it be?):* In the design phase, stakeholders construct the future by designing strategic steps and plans that can be utilized to realize the possibilities for the future identified in the dream phase.
- *Destiny (What will it be?):* In the destiny phase, stakeholders continue to build on the momentum established through design and move from plans to action. Innovative ideas and action steps are implemented to move future possibilities for the organization to a reality.

Appreciative inquiry is a positive approach to organizational analysis and learning. Throughout the process, stakeholders search for knowledge, appreciate ongoing positive activities, and discover collective ways to value the past and articulate a shared vision for the future (Cooperrider et al., 2008). The strength of this approach lies in the positivity it generates and the stakeholder bonding that occurs through shared visioning.

The appreciative inquiry 4-D model can be adapted to many different topics in higher education and can be used to analyze and learn more about issues related to institutions, colleges, departments, units, curriculums, governance structures, assessment, and so forth. Learning how to apply the model to a variety of topical areas is an important skill set to develop. Cockell and McArthur-Blair (2012) note, "leadership, at its best, builds from an appreciative place and fosters the capacity of others in higher education" (p. 93). The central tenet of a focus on building capacity among campus members underscores the role of networked leadership. As an emerging leader, you have many resources available to help you get started in facilitating an appreciative inquiry approach.

Data-Informed Decision-Making

Institutional leaders using data to inform decision-making is nothing new and has increased as more effective performance indicators are desired for comparative purposes, to identify achievement levels, to guide strategy and decision-making, and to inform resource allocation and funding (J. Taylor, 2014). Data collection in higher education has shifted from a compliance mode to a culture of inquiry in which institutional leaders are utilizing robust data to answer complex questions and guide decision-making (Hyde, 2018). As technological advancements have accelerated the creation of data-rich environments, leaders can spend less time collecting data and more time learning from it.

As the United States experiences a decline in the number of high school graduates between 2014 and 2023 (Bransberger & Michelau, 2016), enrollment managers in higher education are facing greater enrollment challenges and are looking for more effective ways to recruit and retain students. Higher education institutions are turning to big-data firms, such as EAB and Capture Higher Ed to assist in research and data collection for a myriad of purposes, including targeted recruitment of students (Korn, 2018). Big-data analytics is defined as the "ability to link disparate data sources, apply quantitative methods of analysis, and convey results interactively" (Salisbury, 2017). The use of analytics on student data, including course-taking patterns, enrollment trends, and learning, contributes to the institutional decision-making process. For example, knowing that students access the learning-management system for a class most frequently between 1:00 a.m. and 3:00 a.m. the night before an exam can inform faculty instructors on strategies to employ prior to the exam to assure more student interaction with the course material.

Increasing complexity in all aspects of higher education has led to the evolution of strategic enrollment management (SEM) systems that are capable of a comprehensive and more sophisticated data-driven approach (Hill, n.d.). Data-driven SEM systems are often marketed with great promise to streamline recruitment, influence the appeal of the institution to prospective students, and increase retention. However, it is important that administrators understand that data collection and analysis are only one part of the process. Even though big-data systems help identify problems in areas like student retention, a human touch is needed to design, implement, and assess interventions (Salisbury, 2017).

Other innovative technologies, such as predictive modeling techniques and data analytics, are also transforming how higher education institutions are collecting and analyzing data to enhance organizational performance and learning. By analyzing demographic and performance data, institutions can drill down and predict "whether a student will enroll at an institution, stay on track in her courses, or require support so that she does not fall behind. Using data in this way is known as predictive analytics" (Ekowa & Palmer, 2017, p. 2). Ekowa and Palmer (2017) note that there are both benefits and ethical concerns embedded in predictive analytics. The specter of Big Brother watching students' every move can lead to concerns over privacy.

Leaders are eager to find more effective ways to utilize data to inform decision-making and, ultimately, to enhance institutional outcomes, but employing big-data systems in practice is often easier said than done. The perceived benefits of such systems may not justify the cost, especially for smaller institutions. More evidence is needed to confirm that usage of these tools will indeed produce the desired results (Salisbury, 2017). These innovations clearly hold promise and are likely to continue to evolve over time. A starting place in using data to drive decision-making is the formation of questions that leaders and institutions hope to answer once they have data in hand. Strategic thinking practices and scenario building can provide a starting point for formulating guiding questions. As data-informed decision-making becomes more precise, so too will the allocation of resources.

On any given day in higher education, students, faculty, and staff are looking for funding to offset such things as paying conference fees, conducting research, bringing in a speaker, holding a campus event, providing food for meetings, buying equipment, replacing technology, purchasing software, and so on. Administrators are also looking for resources to fund facilities, technology infrastructure, research labs, personnel, advancement campaigns, athletics, university events, security enhancements, and so on. The list of resources needed is far reaching, and while many expenditures are included in annual budgets, requests for additional funding are ongoing. Chief financial officers, in conjunction with the president and Board of Trustees, are tasked with implementing business models to efficiently and effectively manage the university.

Johnson (2016) notes the tensions inherent in decision-making, resource allocation, and alignment to priorities. He argues, "As in any business, postsecondary leaders who pay attention only to short-term priorities at the expense of longer-term objectives related to quality, reputation, stakeholder perceptions and satisfaction, will eventually run into big problems. On the other hand, when short-term incentives are misaligned with long-term priorities, institutions are forced to trade one against another, with a significant downside either way" (p. 5). The strategic planning process and data-driven practices discussed in this chapter provide a solid framework for decision-making. There are advantages to using the strategic plan to guide resource allocation (Hinton, 2012). First, institutional stakeholders are more keenly aware of the plan and the decision-making driving the allocation of resources. Second, resources are more effectively used when focused and aligned to institutional priorities. There will always be those individuals who try to leverage their power or position to garner more resources for any given need or initiative; however, leaders can resolve the issue if they "stick to their knitting" and consistently prioritize requests that are directly in alignment to the strategic plan.

When we think about data-driven decisions to allocate resources, it is also important to remember alignment of these decisions with institutional mission and values. Leaders at all levels who are making budget decisions need to understand and analyze "how processes, technologies, and resources are used to deliver value" (Soares, Steele,

& Wayt, 2016, p. i). As the expense for a college education continues to soar, parents, students, and stakeholders increasingly question the value of a college degree and call for a more cost-effective approach with a greater return on investment. To contain costs and optimize performance, the novice leader must be keenly aware of the linkage between revenue and outcomes and align and allocate resources accordingly.

Shared Leadership

Leading in institutions of higher education is a complex endeavor that is messy. As argued throughout this book, the collective efforts of many people are required to advance the mission and plans of the organization. Shared or team leadership enhances decision-making and implementation as members are actively engaged in the creation of a shared vision, shared goals, and a shared accountability for institutional outcomes (Kezar & Holcombe, 2017). Leadership conceptualized in this way builds from Follett's (1924) early insight into managerial power and privilege. According to Follett, "Leadership is not defined by the exercise of power but by the capacity to increase the sense of power among those being led. The most essential work of the leaders is to create more leaders" from within the organization (qtd. in Hamel & Breen 2007, p. 186). Here, Follett addresses the role of shared power, which she terms "coactive" compared to "coercive" (1924, p. 6). By balancing power in the process of planning and decision-making, more campus stakeholders become invested in the process.

Kezar and Holcombe (2017) describe several forms of shared leadership that you are likely to see in practice across higher education institutions: coleadership, team leadership, and distributed leadership. Even though these vary with regard to shared roles and responsibilities, they all share the following common characteristics:

- There is a greater number of individuals in leadership than in traditional models.
- Leaders and followers are seen as interchangeable.

- Leadership is not based on position or authority.
- Multiple perspectives and expertise are capitalized on for problem solving, innovation, and change.
- Collaboration and interactions across the organization are typically emphasized. (p. 3)

Traditional approaches for managing institutions are inadequate for today's campuses, in light of dynamic social, technical, and economic changes continually reshaping the environment (Siemens, Dawson, & Eshleman, 2018). Shared leadership models create organizations built on layers of leadership (see chapter 7 for more information on networked leadership). The skills, knowledge, and expertise needed for decision-making run vertically as well as horizontally across higher education institutions (McPhail, 2016). Collaborative leadership at all levels requires active engagement and shared responsibility for outcomes.

"Shared leadership" and "shared governance" are common terms in higher education, but they are distinct. Shared leadership is more flexible and relies on the relevant expertise of individuals, whereas shared governance is based on "principles of faculty and administration having distinct areas of delegated authority and decision-making" (Kezar & Holcombe, 2017, p. 6). Shared governance is more complex and is often misunderstood by both faculty and administration (Olson, 2009). Olson describes shared governance as a balancing act between faculty participation in planning and decision-making and administrative accountability for such decisions.

The tensions in strategic planning revolve around the need to involve multiple constituencies *and* the need to implement the plan. As noted earlier, a majority of planning and change efforts fail (Kotter, 2014). Implementation efforts can become more successful when strategic consensus is achieved (Kellermanns, Walter, Floyd, Lechner, & Shaw, 2011). Essentially, this type of consensus involves getting campus members on the same page regarding the strategic direction of the institution, which can be supported by enhanced communication throughout the institution (Rapert, Velliquette, & Garretson, 2002). At the center of shared leadership is top-level leaders having the ability to scan the horizon regarding trends and bringing in other campus leaders to help implement actions that have been formulated from shared strategic thinking. The more encompassing the leaders network, the more individuals involved to help with change.

Institutions of higher education are facing several concurrent challenges. Leaders must have a robust skill set in planning how to help campus members address the threats facing the sector. Using strategic thinking and scenario building exercises can help you foresee issues before they become overwhelming or a crisis. The ability to synthesize a wide range of sources of information can be aided by environmental scanning, as it is difficult to plan for something that is unknown. Environmental scanning not only helps identify the threats facing an institution or the weaknesses inherent in current operations but also provides a chance to envision a different and new future. Understanding better the opportunities open to the institution and campus members and the strengths inherent in programs, human resources, and market location can open up pathways of possibility.

The use of PESTEL as an environmental scanning tool provides a wide-angle lens of the environment. Certainly, elements inherent in this process also contribute to a SWOT analysis, but this tool targets specific arenas that impact higher education as a sector. Appreciative inquiry is also an effective way to gather information and frame issues in a positive light. Planning efforts cannot occur in a vacuum, and not understanding the environmental context is akin to leading while wearing a blindfold. Effective leaders take advantage of available tools. Leveraging the skills of leaders throughout the institution provides more human resources and taps potential in generating new ideas and solutions.

Making This Personal

The questions posed throughout this chapter provide several opportunities for reflecting on personal scenarios. Take time to become familiar with your institution's strategic plan and your unit's strategic plan too, if available. How hard is it to locate a copy of these plans? How well does your unit's plan align with the institutional plan? Understanding the steps of the strategic planning process can enable a more effective contribution to the process. Even when there is no planning process under way, practicing the skills of strategic thinking and scenario planning begin to build an inquiry mind-set. Scanning any of the popular daily higher education news outlets, such as *The Chronicle of Higher Ed* or *Inside Higher Ed*, provides a ready source of material and data to inform perspectives regarding the status of higher education.

Try conducting a SWOT analysis for an issue currently plaguing your unit. The simple format provided in this chapter is helpful to walk you through what is evident for strengths, weaknesses, opportunities, and threats. Engage others in this process if possible, as the power of more input helps identify more elements. It is important to determine where you can find data to help you in your thinking. Consider how data can help challenge persistent myths, such as how students make their way through a program curriculum, the level of research productivity of faculty, and the amount of funding spent on auxiliary services. Identifying where you can find institutional data should be a priority for novice and senior leaders alike.

Key Chapter Points

- Effective leadership relies on strategic thinking and planning that ultimately results in aligning resources and actions to advance the vision, mission, and strategic priorities of the institution.
- Scenario building is an essential component of strategic thinking and planning. Scenario building helps leaders anticipate the institutional response needed when the unexpected occurs.

- Environmental scanning is a valuable tool for identifying internal and external driving forces and recognizing the implications these may have for the institution.
- Leaders often face competing objectives and must clearly articulate institutional priorities through strategic planning, evidence-based decision-making, and alignment and allocation of resources.

Web Resources

- David L. Cooperrider Center for Appreciative Inquiry, Champlain College:
  https://www.champlain.edu/centers-of-excellence/david-l-cooperrider-center-for-appreciative-inquiry-
- EDUCAUSE strategic planning framework:
  https://er.educause.edu/articles/2018/6/data-driven-it-strategic-planning-a-framework-for-analysis
- Integrated Postsecondary Education Data System:
  https://nces.ed.gov/ipeds/use-the-data
- PESTEL analysis templates:
  https://www.tcc-net.com/resources/templates/pestle-analysis
- SWOT analysis templates:
  http://templatelab.com/swot-analysis-templates/

Leadership Training

- ACE Center for Policy Research and Strategy:
  https://www.acenet.edu/news-room/Pages/Center-for-Policy-Research-and-Strategy.aspx
- Balanced Scorecard Institute:
  https://www.balancedscorecard.org/
- Harvard focused topic institutes:
  https://www.gse.harvard.edu/leadership-programs-focused-topics

CHAPTER 6

Student Success

Tools That Matter

The focus on the completion agenda, which has the goal of increasing college graduation rates, and public demands for accountability require all leaders to concentrate efforts on leveraging campus resources to support student success. A large amount of research examines tactics to improve student outcomes, but this information typically exists in small programs or projects with minimal focus on effectively scaling up programs that work (Mehaffy, 2018). This chapter reviews evidence-based research that documents strategies contributing to student success that leaders can use, but it also includes coverage of the challenges that have prevented other programs from achieving expected levels of change. At the core of this chapter is helping leaders develop a culture that supports student success and builds on an understanding of social justice and inclusive teaching. The type of deep change required to support all students requires courageous leaders who question assumptions, push for changes in culture, and build shared purpose among campus stakeholders (Kezar, 2014). Tips are provided on what leaders can do to improve teaching practices, curriculums, and support services for students.

Learning Objectives

- Planning for student success
- Building an equity culture of student success
- Academic leadership
- Student engagement

Planning for Student Success

Campus leaders receive a deluge of information on ways to improve student success. Various higher education associations, for-profit agencies, donors, and student advocacy groups all have perspectives on how to best support students. The roots of focusing on students, and in particular student learning, run deep. In 1995, Barr and Tagg wrote a seminal article calling attention to a move from a focus on teaching to one centered on learning. They advocated that a learning paradigm requires a focus on building powerful learning environments, achieving success for diverse students, creating classes with active learning, and acknowledging that individual experiences shape how students learn.

One might ask, if we knew this information at the turn of the last century, why are we still talking about student success in a learning environment? This question is at the heart of recent work by the American Association of State Colleges and Universities (AASCU). George Mehaffy, vice president for the Division of Academic Leadership and Change at AASCU, wrote about the association's approach to student success. According to Mehaffy (2018), "The higher education community does not have a knowledge problem; it has an implementation problem" (p. 9). Proven practices for student success exist, but they are isolated and not implemented with coordination on individual campuses or across the sector. Mehaffy also argues that we need to think about the practice of blaming students for failure to complete. To be sure, students need to be invested and take ownership of their roles in their own success, but institutional policies and practices serve as barriers—especially for students in the most need of support. The gaps in achievement are exacerbated by growing economic inequalities. As Chetty and colleagues (2017) report, low-income students make gains when they complete college, but some institutions reinforce inequality instead of eliminating it. Changing campus practices requires transformative leadership that disrupts current norms (Shields, 2010).

The AASCU created a new initiative—"Re-Imagining the First Year"—that focuses on initial college success and structures of inequality. The participating institutions were "asked to attempt substantial change at scale by innovating in at least four areas: institutional intentionality, curriculum, faculty and staff, and students" (Mehaffy, 2018, p. 13). Though the initiative is early in its implementation, an emerging issue and barrier to change has been the leadership turnover at the participating colleges, which slows down and challenges institutional transformation. Mehaffy (2018) concludes his essay with this troubling insight: "We are tyrannized by legacy practices and outdated policies" (p. 14). Trying to reimagine student success requires second-order change and questioning what we assume about college teaching and learning. Leaders must address needed changes to institutional structures that help remove barriers to learning and that are sustainable when they leave and new leaders transition on campus.

Yet not all hope is lost, as institutions can show results for students. Consider the work of the sociologists Attewell and Lavin (2007), who tracked 60 percent of two thousand women students who started college during the open-admissions experiment at the City University of New York (CUNY) in the 1970s. Importantly, a full 70 percent of these women graduated. After investigating the impacts on these women some thirty years later, the true legacy of this program was evident in the positive impact on the women's children. Not only did these children have higher rates of educational attainment and associated incomes, but they also were more involved in their communities and had more stable family units. This historical example highlights how the investment in student success today has downstream impact and is an important area for leaders to address (Romano & Eddy, 2017).

A driving leadership question in institutions of higher education is how to support student success. Central to student success is having an intentional plan. Integrating learning between students' in-class experiences and cocurricular activities provides students with increased opportunities to apply learning to their lived experiences, ultimately leveraging what is learned. Developing classroom faculty who use inclusive teaching practices begins to address the issue of meeting students where they are and supporting students who historically have been marginalized in higher education settings. The following sections discuss each of these central issues that leaders can address on their campuses.

Academic Plan

Beginning with the end in mind is the core of backward curriculum mapping (Udelhofen, 2005). Thus, contemplating student success, often defined as completion of a certificate or college degree, requires identifying and defining desired student outcomes at the end of an academic program. Degree-program curriculums provide the road map to obtaining these learning outcomes. Planning the curriculum becomes central to supporting student success. Lattuca and Stark (2009) assert that "the academic plan definition implies a deliberate planning process that focuses attention on important educational considerations, which will vary by field of study, instructors, students, institutional goals, and so on" (p. 3). On the basis of previous research, the authors devised an eight-step academic plan to use as faculty, program leaders, and academic affairs officers build academic pathways for students:

1. *Purposes:* knowledge, skills, and attitudes to be learned
2. *Content:* subject matter selected to convey specific knowledge, skills, and attitudes
3. *Sequence:* an arrangement of the subject matter and experiences intended to lead to specific outcomes for learners
4. *Learners:* how the plan will address a specific group of learners

5 *Instructional processes:* the instructional activities by which learning may be achieved

6 *Instructional resources:* the materials and settings to be used in the learning process

7 *Evaluation:* the strategies used to determine whether decisions about the elements of the academic plan are optional

8 *Adjustment:* enhancements to the plan based on experience and evaluation (Lattuca & Stark, 2009, pp. 3–4)

The academic plan outline may apply to an entire disciplinary major, a specific course, or an individual class session. The applicability of the plan on these different levels provides good versatility and cohesiveness in the planning process.

Other factors influence the academic plan. For example, external influences may include the market demand for particular majors, accreditation standards, or standards in the discipline or field of study. Likewise, internal influences that campus leaders should consider may include college mission, institutional resources, the goals of faculty and students, and potentially location and context. These internal influences impact how the plan is developed and implemented. A student seeking a short-term, just-in-time certificate comes to learning with a different orientation relative to a student looking for a four-year university program to prepare for medical school. Location and context can dictate how an institution and its faculty approach curriculum and academic plan mapping.

Bailey, Jaggars, and Jenkins (2015) investigated how to redesign America's community college and report that the current "cafeteria or self-service" (p. 13) model of the colleges leaves students on their own to navigate their way through their academic plan. Many students, especially first-generation college students, lack the skills or know-how to make curricular decisions without support. Indeed, Ellerbe (2018) has found that course-taking patterns predicted vertical transfer from community colleges to four-year institutions, which is one measure of student success. Given that advising services are already stretched thin at community colleges, students may feel that they are on their own. Instead of self-advising, Bailey and colleagues (2015) propose designing guided pathways to student success. At the heart of their argument is a call for systemic reform and a redesign of the ways in which students first connect to the college, the type of programs available, and the type of instruction and support services. In essence, the redesign advocates for second-order organizational change to occur (Bartunek & Moch, 1987) and for the development of an academic plan (Lattuca & Stark, 2009). Institutional leaders need to define final learning outcomes for degrees, certificates, and programs and question processes, procedures, and practices currently in place that may hinder student success.

Since this initial advocacy for more structured academic pathways in community colleges, approximately 20 percent of community colleges have engaged in large-scale program reforms using the fundamental practice areas, including (1) mapping pathways to student end goals, (2) helping students choose and enter a program pathway, (3) keeping students on path, and (4) ensuring that students are learning (Jenkins, Lahr, Fink, & Ganga, 2018). Similar to community colleges, open-access four-year colleges must now consider how to provide an easy-to-navigate path for program entry, as this pathway proves to be a critical first step toward ultimate student success. Students need to understand more clearly the choices they are making by selecting a particular program area. For example, incoming students may know they like the health professions, but deciding on which specific major or area of study within the health professions requires more information.

At this stage, high-quality advising with accurate data helps make the path more navigable. When students can see their progress via personalized dashboards or readily accessible degree plans, they can envision future choices with much more clarity. Data prove critical in supporting student success—data for students to see, data for faculty to understand measures of student learning, and data for institutional leaders to understand if real change is occurring in degree completion. Leaders focused on student success must look holistically at changes to best support student learning.

Integration of Learning

An intended outcome in obtaining a college degree or certificate is the ability to think critically and to draw connections among disparate subjects and perspectives. Barber (2012) defines the term "integration of learning" as "the demonstrated ability to connect, apply, and/or synthesize information coherently from disparate contexts and perspectives, and make use of these new insights in multiple contexts" (p. 593). Linking together various strands of information not only across subject areas but also across contexts of work, school, and community serves as a marker of student success. As in other types of learning, integration of learning occurs developmentally for students. When leaders understand this learning process, they can advocate better for programming, policies, and resources to support student learning.

Barber (2012) has found that students engage in integrated learning in three ways: establishing a connection, applying across contexts, and synthesizing to build a new whole. *Connection* occurs when students see links between and among concepts and experiences. Connections may occur across courses in a student's major or when students see how a class topic helps them solve a problem at work. *Application* happens when an idea or skill is used in a different context. For example, a business major sees how a class lesson ties to her work as the treasurer for a student group. *Synthesis* requires more complex processes as two or more ideas come together to build new uses of formally disparate ideas or skills. Here, opportunities exist for students to have a moment of recognition. However, the integration of learning is not a linear, lockstep process but rather is a holistic developmental process.

Barber (2014) draws from the concept of self-authorship (Baxter Magolda, 1999) as he discusses how students develop their integration of learning. The evolution of development moves from drawing more from external frameworks and influences (e.g., parents, teachers) to becoming more internally driven. How students integrate and connect what they are learning depends on their individual development. "As a student's developmental level (as measured by self-authorship) increases, the frequency of integration also increases, and students use connection, application, and synthesis more equally" (Barber, 2014, p. 11). Yet many college programs are compartmentalized rather than intentionally drawing on interdisciplinarity (Augsburg & Henry, 2009) and do not connect in-class learning with the learning that students do in cocurricular activities or in other out-of-class experiences. As a result of this type of disconnection, students often lack the opportunity and faculty support to scaffold and integrate course content to better reflect on their overall learning. Consider students who study abroad and the transformation that they say results from these experiences (Rowan-Kenyon & Niehaus, 2011). When students return to campus, there is a shortage of occasions to link their transformation in thinking to their classroom or cocurricular experiences (Eddy et al., 2013).

Building orthogonality into learning outcomes provides campuses a way to determine what all students should know regardless of major and identifies where in the curriculum students see concepts reinforced in different contexts (Leslie, 2014). Leaders have the ability to see the larger picture of possibilities for connections given their macro view of campus operations (Heifetz, 1994). This type of intentionally builds opportunities for students to integrate their learning. For example, the American College Personnel Association (ACPA) addressed the role of student affairs practitioners in supporting student learning when it proposed its 2013 *Student Learning Imperative.* This document focused on ways college professionals could create conditions to support both student learning and student personal development. At the center of this work was recognition of the complexity of the ways in which students learn both in classroom settings and in nonacademic settings. How students are able to bridge these two worlds and integrate their learning influences whether graduates leave college being able to connect ideas that they have learned in different contexts (Whitt et al., 2008).

Planning for student success provides a cohesive process to support all students and builds an institutional culture of expectations that students will gain learning skills during their time in college. Imperative in this scenario is strong, courageous leadership centered on this mission and collaboration across the institution and in some cases across the state's system of higher education (Maliszewski, Crabill, & Nespoli, 2012). When Kinzie and Kuh (2004) investigated practices on twenty campuses to learn how students were being engaged, they found some commonalities present. One of the areas of focus was a "widely shared sense of responsibility for educational quality and student success" (p. 2). In this case, four conditions helped build an expectational culture for students: leadership, partnerships between academic and student affairs personnel, student agency, and what the team defined as the "power of one" (p. 2). Throughout this book, attributes of leadership, partnering, and influence are discussed to help prepare leaders to build the type of culture required to support student success.

Theory into Practice

Throughout this book, the emphasis is on putting ideas into action, specifically addressing Mehaffy's (2018) point regarding the need to implement good practices. In preparing initiatives to support student success, it is important for leaders to first understand the current context. As outlined in chapter 5, conducting an environmental scan of the status of outcomes on campus and on what others have implemented can provide a critical first step.

To illustrate the points outlined in this chapter, the examples highlighted here focus on community colleges, as these institutions enroll almost half of all undergraduates (NCES, 2017). Community colleges are often in the public crosshairs due to their students' lack of program completion or transfer. The Aspen Prize for Community College Excellence serves as a counter to the typical deficit rhetoric around these institutions. In every other year since 2011, the Aspen Prize honors community colleges "that deliver exceptional student outcomes in the following four areas: (1) retention and completion, (2) learning, (3) student employment and earnings, (4) equity for the underserved (measures and selection process may be found at http://highered.aspeninstitute.org/aspen-prize/). Wyner (2014) investigated what the Aspen Prize winners were doing for student success, in order to help others replicate successful practices. Wyner focused on elements contributing to completion and transfer, the role of access on developmental education outcomes, engaging faculty in defining learning outcomes, and tying learning and credentials to jobs and the community. A commonality among the award-winning institutions were leaders focused on student success and excellence. Institutional decision-making revolved around the central question, How will this action/decision help students succeed? The corollary question becomes, What is preventing students from succeeding?

The road map laid out by successful campuses and college leaders includes specific steps to follow to help increase completion rates. Pointedly, the current use of guided pathways (Bailey et al., 2015) in community colleges around the country is designed to help provide clear steps and strategies for students as they explore degree programs and seek transfer programs. Complementing this work is programming on four-year campuses to support transfer students. Not all transfer students come from community colleges (vertical transfer), as many also transfer from other four-year institutions (lateral transfer). The high level of student "swirl" (Borden, 2004, p. 10) among college programs often makes it difficult for students to navigate degree-program requirements. Students may start out at one college, transfer to another, take summer courses at yet another, stop out of college for a time, and reenroll later. This constant swirl may result in a bundle of credits that do not map onto a degree program. Understanding the need to develop academic plans that allow for flexibility of *where* program learning occurs and *how* the patchwork of courses fits together is critical. Structured transfer pathways (R. Baker, 2016) and clear articulation policies (Roksa, 2009) provide tools to help achieve these goals.

Not only is coordination among institutions required to achieve better student outcomes, but so too is collaboration within the institution. Understanding how student affairs professionals can support the integration of learning and how academics can help support student engagement becomes critical (ACPA, 2013; Kuh, 2009; Whitt et al., 2008). Complicating some of this collaboration are the needs of different populations of students, such as international students (Glass, Gesing, Hales, & Cong, 2017), men of color (Hrabowski et al., 2014), and first-generation college students (Pascarella, Pierson, Wolniak, & Terenzini, 2004). Leaders must ask what barriers exist in current policies and structures that prevent student success. Once the barriers are identified, leaders must systematically work to remove them. This type of questioning by leaders helps disrupt what is taken for granted and highlight areas of injustice and inequity (Shields, 2010). Building a culture with an inquiry mind-set helps involve all campus members in the process of building an environment of social justice and equity that ultimately benefits all students.

Campus leaders can help build pathways and plans to help students succeed. These plans will differ based on institutional type, mission, community needs, student aspirations, and the culture of the college. However, top-level leadership turnover (Gagliardi et al., 2017) contributes to rocky starts to initiatives for organizational change to support student success (Mehaffy, 2018). It is necessary to have a two-prong approach to address leadership issues: one that focuses on top-level leadership buy-in to influence culture and organizational processes and one that leverages midlevel leaders who are apt to stay in their positions for longer durations to see change through. Campuses with long-serving presidents have more opportunity to implement strategies, but the current reality is for a shorter length of service by college presidents (Gagliardi et al., 2017).

Case #9: Learning versus Completing: Faculty Connecting the Dots

Tensions were mounting at Northwest College. The comprehensive college was preparing for its accreditation visit, and a faculty committee was in the midst of writing the college's self-study report. The state recently launched a performance-based funding initiative that tied campus budgets to an increased number of graduates. As a result, campus leaders put in place fast-track degree programs that allowed for bundling credits earned by students throughout their college-going years. With this program, students could bundle together college credits they took in dual-enrollment programs, credits earned in summer courses at a nearby community college, and credits at Northwest to complete programs. Provost Jerome Snyder often commented to faculty and students, "All credits are good credits!" This campaign for compiling credits resulted in a 5 percent increase in the college's graduation rate and translated directly to increased funds for the campus. Despite this outcome, the faculty were uncovering the underbelly of the story of bundling credits together as they worked on the college's self-study report.

Molly Hernandez, chair of the Biology Department, was chairing the faculty senate and assigned to the self-study team. Molly recounted to the self-study team some of the unintended consequences of the new policy of bundling credits. She said, "One of my bio grads this year took only half of the major requirements with us because he was able to bring in credits earned in high school and from his transfer college. Even though this helped him graduate, he missed out on the sequence we have in place to build up skill levels." Molly's comments triggered a tirade from other faculty members on the committee. John Riddle, a professor of history, added that his department had to rethink prerequisites as they were unsure what courses to assume students had taken for a prior foundation. John added, "The problem is deeper than the bundling of credits. Our own department can't agree on what is important for graduates to know." Others voiced additional issues:

- "I'm a junior faculty who wants to add some new ideas into our curriculum that I saw work in my doctoral program, but the need to push students through the program means no additions to the curriculum even when it would help our students!"
- "The students are looking for shortcuts to get their degree, so they can get a job. They aren't really interested in learning anything."
- "I tried to implement one of the new active-learning strategies we heard about in our last professional development session, but the students did not have a shared background knowledge. I'm going back to lecturing the basics!"
- "We are tired of central administration and the state telling us to push students through to graduate, as they don't know anything about our curriculum. I wish they would leave us alone!

The meeting spiraled down from here. Molly was trying to make sense of what she was hearing and began thinking, "How can I turn this self-study group around to get to some answers about how to improve student learning?"

Guiding Questions

The push for accountability and student success is important, but faculty members and the institution often lack agreement about how to measure and define student outcomes. As the self-study committee at Northwest College looks ahead to determine strategies to improve student success—with regard to both completion and student learning—it is faced with many challenges.

1 What advice would you give the self-study team to determine the efficacy of bundling credits together to increase graduation rates?

2 How might departments use academic planning to design program curriculums?

3 What strategies could individual faculty members employ to support student success? What strategies could campus leaders employ?

4 How might Northwest campus members integrate learning for students?

Case Discussion

Shifting from tracking the number of students entering college or in programs to tracking completion rates and student learning changes how colleges plan and support student outcomes. Considering the case information, how might the eight-step academic plan outlined earlier (Lattuca & Stark, 2009) help guide the dialogue of the self-study team? Consider how faculty, departmental leaders, and divisions must first define student learning outcomes. Backward mapping can then outline the building blocks of courses to get to these outcomes. Knowing what partnerships exist between academic affairs and student affairs can map out the opportunities that exist for students to integrate their learning. Nurturing a supportive culture can provide students the opportunity to engage with mentors, to develop a significant connection with campus faculty or support staff, and to forge a clear path to completion. Leadership is critical in identifying the institutional barriers that exist; here leaders need to instill in staff members the ability to ask why existing procedures exist and if improvements are possible to smooth out the path for students. Figure 6.3 outlines how to craft a plan that ultimately supports student success, including actions to take using each leadership frame (Bolman & Deal, 2013).

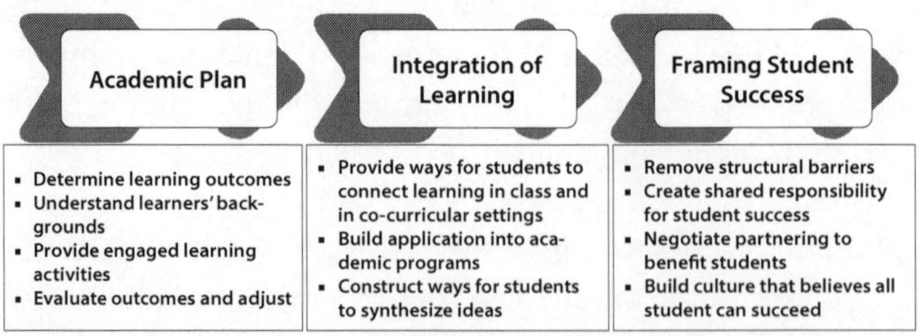

Figure 6.3. Building a leadership plan for student success

Building an Equity Culture of Teaching and Learning

Chapter 1 discussed the importance of culture in organizations. Building on the key elements of artifacts, espoused values, and basic underlying assumptions (Schein, 1992) that represent levels of culture provides an outline to creating a culture of equity to support student success. In seeking to build an equity culture that promotes social justice, it is important to understand the building blocks required to move from mere counting of numbers for diversity to building transformative mind-sets.

Equity and social justice initiatives employ strategies that provide students, staff, and faculty what they need to be successful, as opposed to diversity and inclusion strategies that are based on equality and treating everyone the same (Stewart, 2017). "Social justice is about understanding and interrogating how different individuals or groups are faring in comparison with others in a specific context (such as a university) or more broadly in society" (Wilson-Strydom, 2015, p. 145). Sen (1985, 1999) and Nussbaum (2000, 2011) put forth a capabilities approach to social justice that starts with the welfare of individuals and then focuses on their quality of life—what can they do or what can they be? Here, the consideration is not on having all students achieve the same outcome but rather on different students having the same ability to achieve the same outcome. When leaders question the processes and systems in place that may prevent injustices from occurring, equity is possible. Establishing an equity-mindedness is the first step in creating an equity culture for student success.

Equity-Mindedness

Research underscores the growing socioeconomic stratification of higher education (Astin & Oseguera, 2004; Chetty, Friedman, Saez, Turner, & Yagan, 2017), which exacerbates issues of class and race. Yet a focus on class alone or as a proxy for race falls short as race-based inequities require specific approaches (Malcom-Piqueux & Bensimon, 2017). Bensimon (2004) began to develop a diversity scorecard in 2001 to provide institutional leaders a form of self-assessment regarding the influence of race on student success that is based on evidence. The scorecard showcases how race plays a role in student success. "The Equity Scorecard is an intervention designed to accomplish the following changes among higher education practitioners: (1) develop awareness of race-based inequalities in educational outcomes; (2) learn to interpret race-based disparities in academic outcomes through the lens of equity; and (3) view inequalities in outcomes as a problem of institutional accountability that calls for collective action" (Bensimon, 2006, p. 3). The framework for the scorecard includes access indicators, retention rates, institutional receptiveness, and measures of excellence. First, by disaggregating data, institutional leaders can see how various subpopulations of underrepresented groups fare. Second, setting goals for each of the pillars of the framework sets the stage for meaningful change. Third, data reporting provides campus leadership teams feedback to make continuous improvement—ultimately leading to second-order change (Bartunek & Moch, 1987).

A focus on an equity mind-set specifically counters deficit cognitive frameworks of thinking (Valencia, 1997) that place blame on students for any difficulty in making achievements in school. Here, transformative leaders interrogate current practices that result in perpetuating social injustices on campus and focus instead on building capabilities (Nussbaum, 2011; Shields, 2010). According to Bensimon (2006), "Equity minded individuals are more cognizant that exclusionary practices, institutionalized racism, and power asymmetries have a negative impact on opportunities and outcomes for African American and Latina/o students" (p. 5). Using evidence-based practice to question differences in access, retention, and achievement recasts perspectives of student success. Specific steps to achieve an equity mind-set include the following:

1 Being color conscious (not color blind) in an affirmative sense. To be color conscious means noticing and questioning patterns of educational outcomes that reveal unexplainable differences for

minority students, viewing inequalities in the context of a history of exclusion, discrimination, and educational apartheid.

2 Being aware that beliefs, expectations, and practices can be racialized unintentionally. Examples of racialization include attributing unequal outcomes to students' cultural predispositions and basing academic practices on assumptions about the capacity or ambitions of minority students.

3 Being willing to assume responsibility for the elimination of inequality. Rather than viewing inequalities as predictable and natural, an equity-minded practitioner would allow for the possibility that they might be created or exacerbated by taken-for-granted practices and policies, inadequate knowledge, a lack of cultural know-how, or the absence of institutional support.

4 Being able to demonstrate authentic caring (Valenzuela, 1999) via authentic leadership. To care authentically means to reach out to students proactively and give them the tools they need to succeed—for example, teaching them how to study or showing them how to format a paper. Authentic care encompasses substantial help-giving actions and should not be confused with being understanding or sympathetic. While understanding and sympathy may provide the motivation for help-giving actions, they are not sufficient to make a difference in minority students' lives. (Bensimon, Rueda, Dowd, & Harris, 2007, pp. 33–34)

Using an equity mind-set begins shaping how campus members understand student experiences on campus, in particular, students of color. At the center of this mind-set are elements of second-order change, namely, that courageous leaders must help others in questioning assumptions, use data and evidence to provide feedback regarding outcomes, and move away from a deficit framework.

Consider the following example. On a recent college campus visit, a student recounted that the students in his math class had all done poorly on an exam. As the student related, the faculty member admonished the class and stated that he told them the course work would take several hours a week to master—implying that the class had apparently not spent the time studying. This deficit mind-set held by the faculty member never allowed him to question how his teaching approach failed to support student learning or his lack of authentic caring, both of which ultimately perpetuated inequities. Leaders must help build campus cultures that challenge this type of behavior and dedicate resources to faculty development focused on implicit bias and validation theories.

Strategies for Equity, Strategies for Success

Work over the past decade by Bensimon, Dowd, and Witham (2016) seeks to advance building equity cultures in colleges and universities. Using the lessons learned by institutions since the start of work on the equity scorecard builds strategies for others to use (see table 6.1). Even though the practices outlined in table 6.1 underscore the need for institution-wide application, leaders of smaller units such as departments or schools can also employ these strategies.

A starting place to achieving an equity mind-set is the recognition of stereotype threat (C. Steele, 2011) and implicit bias (Staats, 2016). "Stereotype threat is being at risk of confirming, as self-characteristic, a negative stereotype about one's group" (Steele & Aronson, 1995, p. 797). With stereotype threat, individuals internalize negative external assumptions about their abilities. Implicit bias represents "the attitudes or stereotypes that affect our understanding, actions, and decisions in an unconscious manner" (Staats, 2016, p. 29). In this case, individuals make split-second decisions based on their subconscious beliefs. Leaders must work to become aware of and check their own implicit biases and help support training opportunities for campus members to learn more about how biases and stereotype threat build barriers for student success.

Consider how a woman may buy into the stereotype of girls not being good at math and, as a result, perform poorly on an exam. C. Steele (2011) documents that when women in a math class are prepped

Table 6.1. Principles to Build Equity by Design

Principle	Elements	Campus practices
1	Language, goals, and measures should be clear.	Avoiding exclusionary language (e.g., "at risk") Displaying data in infographics that provide a clear story Disaggregating data to heighten awareness
2	Equity-mindedness should be the guiding paradigm for language and action.	Noticing patterns of inequity Recognizing stereotype threat Questioning institutional practices
3	Equitable practice and policies are designed to accommodate differences in the contexts of students' learning—not to treat all students the same.	Supporting students according to their needs Questioning what conditions allow hegemony to continue Asking who is not at the table and whose views are not present
4	Enacting equity requires a continual process of learning, disaggregating data, and questioning assumptions about relevance and effectiveness.	Engaging in continuous improvement practices Providing campus members with skills for critical reflection Conveying the story told by the data
5	Equity must be enacted as a pervasive institution- and system-wide principle.	Employing systems thinking Gaining buy-in to equity-minded change practices Maintaining focus versus a "goal of the year" strategy

Adapted from Bensimon, Dowd, & Witham (2016)

with comments questioning the assumption of women performing poorly in math, they do better on exams. When validation techniques (Rendon, 1994) are employed, students exhibit greater success. In this case of reinforcement, students receive positive and proactive affirmation about their ability to succeed. Recall that Kinzie and Kuh (2004) documented the power of one person to make a difference in a student's success. A student hearing validation from someone about her ability to succeed evinces more resiliency in the face of obstacles (including institutionalized inequities; Scott, 2012). And the power of one can also relate to equally powerful negative reinforcements. The voicing of a single person's implicit bias about a student's abilities can reinforce stereotypes as well. Faculty leadership helps establish norms that questions assumptions about students and reinforces instead a social justice perspective in teaching and learning.

Despite the recognition that everyone has implicit biases that operate on an unconscious level, individuals can work to make these biases more explicit. Harvard's Project Implicit (see https://implicit.harvard.edu/implicit/takeatest.html) provides a series of tests to determine the type of biases individuals hold. "The real-life implications of implicit biases can create invisible barriers to opportunity and achievement for some students" (Staats, 2016, p. 33). Recognizing that biases exist is the first step. The next step is taking time to respond to barriers to achieving an equity mind-set and taking time to deliberate decisions.

To institutionalize equity as a priority, equity-minded leaders should call practitioners to inquiry and action repeatedly.

—Bensimon et al., 2016

Case #10: Learning Hard Truths in the Data: Now What Do We Do?

This case is one that is all too familiar as institutions begin work to change campus cultures. Consider how to apply the information presented in this chapter to craft an equity culture for the fictitious college presented in the case study.

Wheatfield College, a small private institution located in the middle of the country, just welcomed a new president to campus. Caroline Newman joined the college having served most recently as the provost of a private liberal arts college on the East Coast. She was excited to be joining Wheatfield as she saw great potential for the campus to make a difference in the lives of students. During her campus interview, Caroline kept hearing about the institution's commitment to diversity and inclusion. Indeed, it was just this mission that drew her to the campus. Yet, after just a few months on campus, President Newman was finding that the espoused values of diversity did not align with the institution's equity practices.

One of the first tasks Newman initiated when arriving on campus was to meet all the division and department leaders. She offhandedly noted the obvious fact that most of these leaders were white. When Newman pressed these campus leaders for information on diversity and inclusion efforts on campus and demographic data about their staff and students, she learned that data analytics were not commonly used. The president called a special meeting with the head of institutional research, Robert Harvey. Harvey had been on campus for fifteen years and during his tenure had collected a lot of data for the typical institutional reports for accreditation and Board of Trustees meetings. At the start of the meeting, Harvey offered, "No one has ever asked me for departmental level data on students." The president was shocked! A quick review of the data Harvey brought to the meeting highlighted different levels of diversity across the institution, with some areas enrolling fewer women and students of color compared to others.

After the meeting with Harvey, President Newman reflected about next steps. How was she going to help the campus embrace an equity agenda based on social justice that supports success for *all* students? Why were some units on campus more successful enrolling diverse students compared to others—and how might some of the historically male- and female-dominated disciplines become more integrated? Perhaps most distressing to Newman was the deficit language she heard used by some of the leaders and faculty members regarding students' abilities, with comments such as "maybe *they* don't belong in a college like ours." Clearly, Wheatfield had a way to go in walking the talk of diversity, equity, and inclusion. Highlighting select students of color on the college's website was superficial when compared to the realities that students of color experienced in classrooms and in residence halls.

Guiding Questions

Environmental scans of data often highlight trends or showcase problematic areas. In the case of Wheatfield College, a closer look at the data by President Newman found lower levels of diversity and success for students of color than she desired, as well as attitudes of implicit bias regarding the ability of some of the students. Given the important contributions that leaders can make to organizational change and to improving student success, how might you counsel President Newman?

1. What type of additional data would you suggest the president review?
2. How can the president begin to build an equity culture on campus?
3. Who might be allies the president can recruit to help in the efforts to build diversity, equity, and inclusion (DEI) on campus?
4. How can the president surface underlying assumptions about equity regarding policies and processes that perpetuate exclusionary norms?

5 What type of professional development should be implemented to build an equity culture?

Case Discussion

As a new leader on campus, President Newman's first look at institutional data highlights areas in which the college is falling short with regard to equity. Because she has heard firsthand campus members using a deficit mind-set with respect to student ability, a need exists to build an equity mind-set throughout the institution. Using institutional data to build an equity scorecard could provide the president with a forum to begin discussion on campus with faculty and staff regarding issues of equity. In this case, a focus on the role of implicit bias in maintaining stereotypes could be highlighted. Using various forms of professional development sessions could provide support for campus members. It is important that everyone has a shared language and understands what it means to have implicit biases and how stereotype threat might manifest itself in and out of classrooms.

Building an equity culture requires leadership at multiple levels. Knowing that change is hard, it is important for the president and her leadership staff to present equity goals as an urgent institutional issue (Kotter, 2014). Showing graphical evidence of inequities provides one way to highlight the issues of inequity on campus. Yet, knowing that individuals operate from different frameworks, it is also key to present information in a variety of formats that connect with all four of Bolman and Deal's (2013) frames. Using a continuous improvement process provides a way to question the underlying assumptions held by campus members and helps assure that the goal of equity is not viewed merely as a one-time goal. The following section outlines some of the potential leveraging points to achieve a culture that supports all students.

Leading for Student Success

Supporting student success requires courageous leadership action by multiple individuals and units on campus. As noted earlier, individual practices prove critical in engaging students on a pathway to success. Because the greatest amount of time that commuting students spend on campus is in classes, faculty work and students' classroom experiences provide an ideal location for change to improve student success. What happens in the classroom occurs due to the support faculty have for teaching, the translation of content knowledge into engaged teaching strategies, and the scaffolding of student services for students. Yet most faculty members receive little to no training on how to teach (Austin, 2002) and are typically unaware of the large research base on teaching and learning. Despite Boyer's (1990) arguments about the scholarship of teaching and learning as an area of inquiry, many institutions do not equally value this form of research compared to the scholarship of discovery (Fairweather, 2005).

Further, students do not miraculously appear in classes—they must apply for admission and register for classes. Thus, the unseen influence of support offices is important to consider. For example, Wake Technical Community College in Raleigh, North Carolina, instituted a strategic partnership initiative (SAIL—succeed, achieve, improve, learn) to support improvement efforts on campus. This bottom-up focus provides staff, faculty, and midlevel leaders an opportunity to identify a topic and develop a proposal to address a current problem on campus. The institution then selects the winning proposal, regardless of academic or student service origination (Elrod & Mielish, 2018). This approach highlights the intersection of both academic and student services to address processes and barriers facing students on their path to completion.

Tinto (1975, 1997, 2006) has long studied reasons that students depart from college. The focus of Tinto's research is on how students are integrated into campus life. Think of this as the number of "hooks" that connect students to the college. Importantly, knowing why students opt to leave college does not automatically equate to understanding what will make students successful (Tinto & Pusser, 2006), but understanding better what institutional leaders can do to build environments for success begins to remove barriers on the path to completion. Tinto and Pusser (2006) identify five conditions for student success: "institutional commitment, institutional expectations, support, feedback, and involvement or engagement" (p. 6). As in other types of change initiatives, buy-in from top-level leadership is important to obtain outcomes (Kotter, 2014; Wyner, 2014). Yet buy-in alone is not enough. Institutional leaders must build mechanisms that allow for questioning of processes and policies, allow risk-taking to occur, and in general support disruption to the status quo whenever it reinforces inequities. When college leaders focus on student success and continuously ask the question "How will this support student success?" assumptions are questioned about policies and procedures, resources are dedicated to programs with a track record of results, and institutional culture begins to change. Key to improvements in student outcomes are institutional leadership, faculty development, and student engagement.

Institutional Leadership

When institutional leaders commit to student success, they in turn commit to holding high expectations for students—*all* students. As reviewed earlier, building a culture of equity means that campus leaders, faculty, and staff believe that *all* students can be successful. Validation of the ability of students to succeed (Rendon, 1994) can occur in multiple locations on campus and in a variety of ways. Instead of complaining that students are not committed to learning or are not prepared for college, leaders can convey the belief that students hold potential to reach the high bar set for them in college. At the same time, institutions must commit support for students. "Research points to three types of support that promote success: academic, social, and financial" (Tinto & Pusser, 2006, p. 7). Providing advising to get students to the right support offices and programs is important (Drake, 2011). Creating a safe environment in which students can connect with others helps build a support network for all students. Addressing financial need allows students to focus on their learning, yet financial resources differ for students (Chen & DesJardins, 2010).

Consider the investment made in the Accelerated Study in Associate Programs (ASAP) at the City University of New York (CUNY). The program requires full-time study and provides expanded counseling services, a compact curriculum, free tuition and books, and free local transportation. This institutional commitment to student success resulted in an increase of completion rates for students from 22 to 40 percent in three years (Linderman & Kolenovic, 2013). The template for this program is now expanding to other states with similar results (Sommo & Ratledge, 2016). Given the effectiveness of these high-cost programs, leaders must determine how to allocate resources to cover the costs of programming (Romano & Eddy, 2017).

The ASAP program illustrates that individuals, programs, and departments at different levels of the college all must contribute to student support. The overriding expectational culture is influenced by beliefs in equity and that all students can be successful. Top-level leaders set the tone for expectations, not only for students but also for faculty and staff. Valuing teaching and learning sends a clear message to those who work in classrooms and support offices that the work they do matters. Research productivity is the coin of the realm for promotion, tenure, and institutional prestige in four-year colleges and universities (Fairweather, 2005; O'Meara & Bloomgarden, 2011), which results in faculty being productive in either teaching or research (Fairweather, 2002). When student success drives institutional objectives, campus leaders must reward faculty members and offices that help contribute to positive student outcomes via good teaching and support practices. Changes to tenure and promotion policies may be required to highlight a focus on good teaching and learning outcomes and emphasize the value of and commitment to student success.

It is important for students to receive good advice to plan out their program of study most effectively. Poor advising or self-advising often results in students taking courses that do not count toward their degree or missed opportunities (Bailey et al., 2015). Increasingly, colleges are implementing some form of first-year seminar that helps teach students academic skills to succeed. First-year experiences (FYE) provide a path for students to learn study habits, connect with advisors, plan course-taking options, and engage with other students (Upcraft, Gardner, & Barefoot, 2004). One strategy emphasized in FYE programs is to encourage students to engage with their classroom faculty (Chickering & Gamson, 1987). Preparing faculty to provide much-needed advice, to engage in active learning strategies, to provide effective feedback, and to validate learning contributes to positive student outcomes.

Faculty Development

Faculty development provides opportunities for faculty members to hone their teaching practices. Evidence suggests that faculty teaching skills influence student persistence (Braxton, Bray, & Berger, 2000); thus, institutional investment in faculty members holds promise for improving student outcomes. Over time, the focus of faculty development programs has changed (Sorcinelli, Austin, Eddy, & Beach, 2006). The declines in institutional resources often result in cuts to faculty development programming, which leaves faculty members solely responsible for seeking out opportunities to learn more about how to improve their teaching. Yet leaders must invest in faculty to support the end goal of improved student learning. As adult learners, faculty must understand how new teaching strategies connect to their practice and have a chance to practice the newly acquired skills (Eddy, Hao, Markiewicz, & Iverson, 2018).

Today, work in faculty development coalesces around preparation for using evidence to change teaching practices (Beach, Sorcinelli, Austin, & Rivard, 2016). This current era of evidence requires faculty members to understand what teaching strategies have the most impact on student learning and how to assess student learning. Providing feedback to students helps them improve their learning experience and highlights for faculty members areas that need more coverage or explanation. Using assessment evidence on both the course level and the program level provides a feedback loop of continuous improvement to academic programs (Lattuca & Stark, 2009).

Leaders can promote faculty learning communities (FLC; Cox, 2004), which provide a means to bring faculty members together as a common group (e.g., new faculty) or to address a common topic (e.g., active learning). FLCs leverage the components of adult learning theory (Knowles, 1980) as they tap into faculty members' experiences, provide information that is immediately applicable to the classroom, and engage motivated learners around a topic of shared interest. Understanding more about effective teaching strategies, such as active learning, collaborative learning, problem-based learning, and the like, can provide faculty members with the confidence to try out new practices in their classrooms. Supporting faculty teaching is central to student success. How students engage with faculty members and others on campus influences their desire to persist.

Student Engagement

Theories of student persistence all point to the need for students to be academically and socially integrated on campus (Astin, 1993; Kuh, 2003; Tinto, 1997). "The more students are academically and socially involved, the more likely they are to persist and graduate" (Tinto & Pusser, 2006, p. 7). When students are involved, they are more likely to stay in college and learn more while they are there. Leaders can promote partnerships between academic and student affairs units to help improve student engagement (Whitt et al., 2008). Engagement can take a number of different forms. It might be work with a faculty member on a research project, membership in a social club, athletics, or community engagement. Yet, for commuter students, who make up a large proportion of undergraduate students (e.g., 45 percent of all college students attend a community college; NCES, 2017), engagement outside the classroom is rarer. Therefore, it is most important to consider how students are engaging with faculty members and what is occurring in the classroom environment.

Participating in high-impact practices (HIPs) provides students with increased connections during their college years. Kuh (2008) identifies ten types of experiences and contexts that help support retention and learning for students:

- First-year seminars and experiences
- Common intellectual experiences
- Learning communities
- Writing-intensive courses
- Collaborative assignments and projects
- Undergraduate research
- Diversity / global learning
- E-portfolios
- Service learning, community-based learning
- Internships
- Capstone courses and projects

Moving beyond seeing these items as discrete practices requires thinking about the student learning environment and actions institutions can take. Too often "key elements of the college experience are disconnected and not mutually reinforcing" (Wawrzynski & Baldwin, 2014, p. 51). Mapping out where learning occurs across campus and through opportunities connected to the college (e.g., internships) and online is an important first step in strategizing how to improve student engagement (Borrego, 2006). Leaders can use environmental scanning to determine where opportunities to partner exist on campus. "A strategic mapping process should identify places where learning alliances can be promoted to ensure that students' learning is adequately connected and mutually reinforcing" (Wawrzynski & Baldwin, 2014, p. 54). Building a shared language around student engagement between academic leaders and student affairs practitioners can help strengthen learning and connections for students inside and outside the classroom.

The National Survey of Student Engagement (NSSE) and the Community College Survey of Student Engagement (CCSSE) both survey students to assess their perspectives of levels of engagement across a range of domains. The broad areas in the NSSE survey include academic challenge, learning with peers, experiences with faculty, and campus environment, and the CCSSE survey includes academic challenge, active and collaborative learning, student effort, student-faculty interaction, and support for learners. Table 6.2 provides a summary of the 2018 survey responses of first-year students for both surveys.

Although the surveys of students attending four-year colleges and universities (NSSE) and two-year colleges (CCSSE) differ in the

Table 6.2. Summary of 2018 NSSE and CCSSE Surveys

Category	NSSE*	Category	CCSSE**
Academic challenge	Higher-order learning: 37.8 (63/100) Reflective/integrated learning: 35.0 (58.3/100) Learning strategies: 38.0 (63.3/100) Quantitative reasoning: 27.5 (45.8/100)	**Academic challenge**	Worked harder: 2.64/4.0 (66/100) Exams challenge: 4.9/7.0 (70/100) Analyze ideas: 2.92/4.0 (73/100) Form new ideas: 2.89/4.0 (72/100) Evaluate info: 2.66/4.0 (67/100) Apply concepts: 2.76/4.0 (69/100) Perform new skill: 2.88/4.0 (72/100)
Learning with peers	Collaborative learning: 32.3 (53.8/100) Discussions with diverse others: 39.0 (65/100)	**Active and collaborative learning**	In-class group work: 2.60/4.0 (65/100) Worked with others outside of class: 2.0/4.0 (50/100) Discussed ideas with others outside of class: 2.54/4.0 (64/100)

Category	NSSE*	Category	CCSSE**
Experiences with faculty	**Student-faculty interaction: 21.6 (36/100)** Effective teaching practices: 38.4 (64/100)	Student-faculty interactions	Discussed grades/assignment: 2.65/4.00 (66/100) **Discussed ideas with faculty outside of class: 1.83/4.0 (46/100)** Prompt feedback: 2.79/4.0 (70/100)
Campus environment	**Quality of interactions: 41.9 (69.8/100)** Supportive environment: 36.0 (60/100)	Support for learners	**Support to succeed: 3.06/4.0 (77/100)** Encourage contact with different backgrounds: 2.66/4.0 (67/100) Support to thrive: 2.26/4.0 (57/100) Help cope with nonacademic responsibilities: 2.06/4.0 (52/100)
		Student effort	Integrated ideas for paper: 2.87/4.0 (72/100) Prepared drafts for assignments: 2.52/4.0 (63/100) Number of times accessed skills lab during academic year: 0.93

* NSSE reports mean scores ("never" to "very often" scale) of first-year students on a 60-point scale (converted to a 100-point scale in parentheses) (NSSE, n.d.).

** CCSSE uses varied scales ("never" to "very often" scale) for categories (converted to a 100-point scale in parentheses) (CCCSE, n.d.).

precise questions asked, the overarching areas of review are similar. In table 6.2, both the high means and low means for both surveys are in boldface. What is encouraging is how four-year college students rated highly the quality of interactions they have with others on campus (68.9/100) and two-year college students felt the institution provided support to succeed (77/100). Four-year college students identified less engagement with student-faculty interactions (36/100), whereas two-year college students reported fewer interactions with faculty members outside of class (46/100). Given the commuter nature of community colleges, the latter finding is not unexpected. Community college students also reported that working with other students on assignments outside of class occurred less frequently (50/100).

Leaders can look at institutional-level data on student engagement such as this to identify areas in which their institutions, faculty, and staff can work to improve student engagement. Understanding that engaged students are more likely to persist and succeed is a first step. Next, it is important to develop an institutional plan to build an expectational culture in which faculty members are prepared to employ effective teaching strategies to support student learning.

Central to supporting student success are coordinated campus efforts. Interrogating teaching practices that may reinforce stereotype threat (C. Steele, 2011) and understanding how implicit biases held by faculty may limit and create barriers for students (Staats, 2016) are critical. A first step is understanding the student data—admission rates, retention statistics, and graduation rates must be analyzed to better understand the realities on campus. As outlined earlier, the University of Southern California (Bensimon, 2006) built an equity scorecard that serves as a way to see institutional data in disaggregated formats. Complementing this data tool is the university's Benchmarking Equity and Student Success Tool (BESST), which is a web-based system that allows participants a way to see their data in infographic format (see https://cue.usc.edu/tools/data/). Seeing complex data sets in a variety of visual formats provides a way in which leaders can convey the story of current efforts on equity and highlight goals.

Recognition that higher education currently contains systems of inequity is a first step for transformative leaders to change practices (Shields, 2010). Although it is true that the discourse on social justice and equity has expanded over time, equity has not yet been achieved (Bensimon, 2018). Leaders must institutionalize expectations of inquiry and social justice for these practices to become sustainable even when leadership transitions occur. Establishing an equity culture on campus builds practices that allow all students to succeed. Faculty members can use inclusive teaching practices, department chairs and deans can provide professional development opportunities, academic leaders can analyze student data to identify trends, and student affairs leaders can employ practices that validate students. At a minimum, each individual on campus can work to improve the student experience, and collectively exclusionary institutional practices can change to promote an equity culture for student success.

Making This Personal

This chapter has outlined a range of strategies to promote student success. The nation's focus on increasing higher education completion rates requires institutional and individual introspection to determine what type of changes are required to support the success of all students. As you contemplate the information presented, think about what you are doing to advance efforts to support students. How do you recognize your own implicit biases? Does the institution know who is succeeding and who is failing or dropping out? What improvements can be made to build an equity mind-set on campus? Understanding the basic data points of student admission, retention, and completion begins to paint a portrait for the institution, and disaggregating the data helps to identify leaks in the pipeline and areas of disparity among subgroups.

Building a culture of equity requires questioning of underlying assumptions of which students can be successful (avoiding a deficit mind-set with regard to potential) and constantly asking the questions "Who are we missing?" and "What policies and practices create barriers to student success?" What would an equity scorecard show for your campus? Developing an equity-focused orientation to leading requires constant interrogation of assumptions about potential and questioning the role of existing processes and structures that may unintentionally impede students. Knowing that the power of one in determining student success is critical (Kinzie & Kuh, 2004), consider your actions and words carefully. Telling students that you can see a future for them can make all the difference. Likewise, reinforcing an equity mind-set in colleagues can begin building an equity culture on campus.

Key Chapter Points

- Building an academic plan for degree programs requires identification of student outcomes that can map backward into the curriculum.
- The integration of learning built on connection, application, and synthesis requires (a) time for students to reflect and (b) mentors to help guide students' integration.
- Building an equity culture requires intentional focus on equity-minded practices, critical investigation of campus practices and data, and systems-level thinking.
- High-impact practices can support student engagement.
- Examination of institutional data helps identify achievement gaps and identifies areas for improvement.

Web Resources

- Association of American Colleges & Universities, success examples: https://www.aacu.org/resources/student-success
- Center for Urban Education, University of Southern California: https://cue.usc.edu/
- EDUCAUSE, student success: https://library.educause.edu/topics/information-technology-management-and-leadership/student-success
- Gates' Foundation, postsecondary student success: https://postsecondary.gatesfoundation.org/
- Student Success Center Network: https://www.jff.org/what-we-do/impact-stories/student-success-center-network/

Leadership Training

- AAC&U Diversity, Equity, and Student Success: https://www.aacu.org/conferences/dess/2019
- Aspen Institute, College Excellence Program: https://highered.aspeninstitute.org/
- Harvard implicit bias tests: https://implicit.harvard.edu/implicit/takeatest.html
- POD Network: https://podnetwork.org/

CHAPTER 7

Partnering with Others

Networked Leadership

The complexity of institutions today requires collaborating with others, especially in leadership positions. Yet historically promotions were given based on singular excellence or hero-like feats. Shifting to working collaboratively is challenging in college environments that are still firmly attached to hierarchical organizational charts. Networking builds on both individual connections and organizational partnerships (Eddy et al., 2015). Leaders located throughout the college are required to contribute to change and improve colleges and to achieve success both for students and for the college. To best achieve institutional goals, partnering with others either inside the college or with external partners becomes increasingly necessary. This chapter reviews the importance of the type of ties included in one's network, the role of building social capital, and the creation of an environment in which people can participate and engage with others.

Strategies for building strategic partnerships are reviewed first (Eddy & Amey, 2014) and build on chapter 5's focus on strategic planning. Leaders must establish and initiate action toward an end goal of collaboration that meets strategic objectives and achieves change.

As evident throughout this book, leadership plays a central role in supporting and achieving institutional objectives and in developing a culture in which change is possible. Yet it is not just top-level leaders who are important in networked leadership. Communicating to create strategic partnering requires an underlying belief in and reliance on strong leaders throughout the college. We make the argument that leaders and leadership buy-in are required to make change happen and that using networks and partnering aids in the process. Working together in teams capitalizes on the benefits and synergies of spanning traditional boundaries—between institutions of higher education and industry and community agencies, between institutions of higher education and PK–12, and between academic and student affairs units on campus.

Learning Objectives

- Partnerships
- Networked leadership
- Boundary spanners
- Working in teams

Partnerships

Understanding the components of partnerships helps leaders know which levers to move to achieve change. Eddy and Amey (2014) identify three phases of partnering. Phase 1 involves understanding the antecedents to partnering with others. What motivates individuals and organizations to work together? Motivations include mandates—institutions being "told" to work together as part of policy mandates and individuals being instructed to work together as part of transactional leadership strategies (Avolio et al., 1999). Other motivating forces include value alignment and shared ideologies (Fowler, 2013). Here, consortiums may form based on these shared values. Take for example the partnership that Bryn Mawr has with Haverford College and Swarthmore College—all private colleges focused on liberal arts. Students are able to take courses at any of the partnering schools, with some majors only offered in the Tri-College cooperation with Haverford and Swarthmore. The partnership with Haverford (known as the Bi-College cooperation) extends beyond academics to include a shared student newspaper and radio station, with students able to travel by a frequent bus between the two campuses.

Another motivating source emerges through the desire to achieve a particular strategic objective that requires working with another individual, unit, or entity. Leadership networks exist in states in which all the public university presidents or academic leaders meet, as well as on campus with working committees that cover topics such as curriculum, governance, or diversity. These in-place groups provide a ready source for networking. Consider too several of the examples offered in chapter 6 that target student success. A motivating force to partner here is the need to support students on the path to graduation, which requires multiple individuals and units partnering together. Western Governors University (WGU) provides an example of partnering that crosses state boundaries. The genesis of the university was at a 1997 meeting of the Western Governors Association as the group wrestled with how to provide educational opportunities to residents of their states (Western Governors University, n.d.). The founders of the college, which was accredited in 2003, sought to leverage online platforms to provide degree programs that are flexible for students, competency based, and outcomes oriented. By partnering together, the state leaders were able to address a key strategic objective—namely, providing higher education to more state residents.

In phase 2 of partnering, relationships and communication bolster the social process involved in working together as partnership development progresses and becomes institutionalized. Here, relationships prove central to partnering efforts. Individuals bring varying levels of social capital (Coleman, 1988) to bear in the joint efforts. Social capital contributes to the strength of the relationships and is often based on the reputation of each of the individuals involved. What individuals know, whom they know, and what they can do all contribute to the levels of social capital they bring to the table. At the collective level, institutions and units all have organizational capital, which may include reputation, resources, and expertise (Morgan, 2006). Once formed, partnerships may emerge as a separate spin-off entity that also results in partnership capital that is distinct from the initial contributions of the individuals or organizational partners (Eddy & Amey, 2014). Partnerships may emerge at a range of levels—individuals first working together, departments or programs collaborating, or colleges and universities working together or with business and community partners.

When the partnership becomes more robust, communication is essential to build a shared meaning of the new partnering venture. How partnerships are framed and understood by others influences how the partnership is received on campus and how it becomes embedded into institutional practices. For example, a department chair may work with chairs at other programs across the state to host a conference that ultimately leads to the forming of a consortium that develops a shared program in which each department contributes course work. If this partnership is framed as "the chair's program" versus "the university's program," different meanings emerge that influence the permanence of the partnership. When programming aligns with institutional strategic goals rather than occurring through happenstance, the partnership operates differently.

In phase 3, the final phase of partnering, partnership capital may emerge. Partnership capital is built through shared understanding, shared beliefs, and networking that align processes among individual collaborators (Eddy & Amey, 2014). Not all partnerships result in partnership capital; indeed, some traditional partnerships may fulfill an initial goal and dissolve or become defunct when key personnel leave. Understanding the differences between traditional partnerships and strategic partnerships helps leaders in planning how to engage with partners and how to jump-start lasting and effective partnerships.

Traditional Partnerships

A central feature of traditional partnerships is the happenstance nature of their formation. Often, these forms of partnerships emerge due to individual efforts that eventually involve others (Amey, 2010) or are started to meet a specific outcome (C. Johnson, 2007). Mandates—either institutionally driven or grant/legislatively mandated—spur on individuals and institutions to seek out partners to meet specific requirements. Consider how the National Science Foundation and other grant funders increasingly require institutions to partner with others to receive funding.

Typically, the resulting partnership based on these grant-funded efforts is not embedded within the college's or university's organizational structures but rather is person-centric or loosely coupled to campus operations (Weick, 1976). This type of loose configuration works well for exploring innovative or new programs and ideas, but without ties to the institutional structure, the change generated lacks staying power (Kotter, 2014). Shared meaning only exists for those who are directly involved in the partnership, with communication networks often operating in parallel for those within the partnership and to those operating outside the partnership for the entire institution. Critically, the person-centric nature of the partnership presents a risk for the lasting power of the project. Take for example a study-abroad program built by a faculty member in modern languages and that individual's personal network in country. When the faculty member retires, the partnership with the institution abroad may end. Likewise, when grant funds end, a program involving multiple colleges and community partners may not be able to continue. Leaders must understand the goals of the partnership and the infrastructure needed for longevity.

Strategic Partnerships

Strategic partnerships differ from traditional partnership because of the intentional sense of purpose that drives their formation. These types of partnerships emerge to help meet institutional goals and objectives and are motivated by seeking out partners that hold shared values or purposes. The alignment of goals helps create more staying power for the partnerships, even when a partnership is initiated by individual efforts. For example, consider a scenario in which a public school superintendent is charged with planning the opening of a new high school. This leader sees the need to bridge PK–12 and higher education pathways and advocates for a center in the new building that allows high school students the opportunity to take college-level courses. Furthermore, the need for more midlevel skill positions in industry means that not all students need a four-year degree. Thus, the superintendent advocates for another center that focuses on vocational and technical training with college and industry credentials available. Partnering in this case between a PK–12 institution and a higher education institution begins to bridge the educational pipeline. Thus, even though initiated by an individual, this type of partnering with an institution of higher education is strategic as the partners were selected due to the alignment of their goals.

Strategic partnerships engage in continuous improvement, conducting environmental scans to note changes in context and using feedback to make changes as needed. The basis of these types of partnership requires members to question the assumptions they hold about the way things are done and to become open to new ways of addressing problems jointly. Increased capacity results when partners work closely on common goals, resulting in a larger network available to support the strategic partnership. Communication within the partnership is open and robust, as well as connected to the respective institutional and organizational communication networks. Often, strategic partnerships have logos and branding that distinguish them as unique relative to their participating partners.

Partnering is becoming increasingly important given the decline in funding in the higher education sector and due to the complexity of today's institutions of higher education. Table 7.1 highlights the differences between traditional approaches to partnering and strategic approaches to partnering.

Understanding the type of partnership involved helps leaders know what actions to advocate and when to put the actions into practice. If a partnership is needed to address a specific mandate or requirement, top-level leaders may opt to allocate resources and efforts in a

Table 7.1. Differences in Partnering Approaches

Traditional partnering	Strategic partnership
Top-down initiative or individually driven Happenstance or circumstantial Results in first-order change Builds on the status quo Smaller social network emerges Discrete use of individual social capital Separate communication networks	Deliberate leadership actions Linked to institutional goals or strategic plans Results in second-order change Builds expanded capacity Expanded and dynamic social networks emerge Shared vocabulary and complex communication networks

particular way, as opposed to if a partnership is needed to address a strategic goal of the institution. Leaders operating in the middle may also find that they are key actors in partnering opportunities given their individual networks and the strategic needs of their units and programs within the institution. It is important to think about the role that all leaders have in the formation and maintenance of partnerships and resulting networks.

Theory into Practice

At the beginning stages of a partnership, it is important to understand the motivations for coming together as a group. Sometimes the desire to work together stems from past experiences with a person or group that were successful or from a partner's contribution to the process being something you or your institution needs to complement the work being done. It is therefore important in the initial stage to ask questions both at the individual level and at the organizational level. Eddy and Amey (2014) provide a listing of questions or prompts to consider:

- What do we hope to get out of this partnership?
- What do we need in a partner to help us achieve our goals?
  - ▹ Are we hoping to reach short-term goals?
  - ▹ Are we hoping to obtain strategic objectives?
- Can we achieve these goals with one partner, or are multiple partners beneficial?
- What does an environmental scan show regarding potential partners?
- What are the motivations of these potential partners? (p. 19)

Motivations to partner can be bundled into four categories: (1) economic reasons, (2) mandates, (3) value alignment, (4) strategic leadership (Eddy & Amey, 2014). Understanding the motivations to partner can guide actions and decisions about resources. Improving institutional efficiency is often a reason to partner and build traditional consortia, whereas newer or nontraditional assembly of consortia focus instead on improving effectiveness via innovation and creating something new (Forcier, 2011). As partners work together, relationships deepen and trust builds. This foundation can provide for longer-lasting partnerships. Members of long-lasting partnerships have figured out a way to navigate conflict and disagreements, and they embrace a learning orientation in their work. Key to this type of success are adaptive leaders (Heifetz, 1994). Again, leaders here are not always the top-positional leaders of the partnering institutions but rather might be leaders operating from the middle, tasked with overseeing the partnership or involved with a critical participating group process.

Case #11: Leveraging Alliances

This case illustrates a partnership that held potential to be strategic in orientation instead ended up being quite traditional. Consider how different decisions might have resulted in different outcomes. Finally, contemplate how others view a traditional partnership that achieves its initial goals and then dissolves.

A consortium of five colleges of technology was formed in the mid-1990s when the colleges were targeted for potential closure and faced severe resource constraints. The leaders of the colleges banded together to lobby the state's central office for more resources and advocated for the need within their communities. What started as informal meetings of the college presidents morphed into a voluntary consortium when the group was successful in forestalling campus closure. The focus of the group turned to building and sharing online courses among the five colleges, and an initial influx of funds helped each campus jump-start these efforts. Yet this windfall also proved a hurdle as it was not clear how the funds should be divvied up among the campuses. One vice president of administration quipped, "It was like throwing a hunk of meat to a group of lions." Ultimately, a memorandum of understanding (MOU) was completed that laid out enrollment targets for each campus, courses of specialization, and annual reporting requirements for the central office.

The five member colleges varied in size and fiscal health. Two of the larger campuses had more robust budgets given the funding formulas in the state, whereas the three smaller campuses operated on a shoe string. The president of one of the larger colleges reflected, "When the five college presidents ran their group, they could not get consensus. Leaders could not work together for the benefit of all since each of the presidents held the interest of their own campuses before the consortium." Ultimately an executive director was hired to manage the partnership.

The presidents of the smaller colleges needed the consortium to succeed and were more invested. A president of one of the smaller colleges was new to campus and did not have the history of the informal meetings as a reference, and thus she brought an outsider perspective to the group. Her assessment of the presidential group was that despite the message to play nice with one another, tensions existed. She reflected, "The consortium was not always a happy marriage as the partners were holding their cards close to their chest."

On another of the smaller campuses, the message differed. Here, the campus feared that the end goal of the consortium was to merge all the campuses together to form one large technical college. In general, a fear of loss of identity plagued the smaller campuses, not only with the presidents themselves but throughout the campus. Coupled with the unknown future was the lack of shared information about the consortium, which differed by campus due to the ways in which the college presidents framed the process to their respective campus members. Often, it was the presidents themselves sowing the seeds of discontent. Faculty members felt a lack of voice in the process, and midlevel leaders felt a lack of direction. According to one academic vice president, the "message was not always clear, and what was needed was leadership." Strong individual campus leadership was present instead of a consortium leader representing the collective interests of the partnership. One campus president noted, "From a distance, the consortium looks good, but in reality the process has been messy."

A decade after forming, the consortium dissolved. Once the initial funds were spent, the central office held little sway in requiring the colleges to work together as new and different problems became more pressing. The colleges remained open, but a shared online degree among the group never materialized. Changes in campus leadership further contributed to a lack of shared buy-in to collaborating.

Guiding Questions

The voluntary forming of partnerships as opposed to mandated formation results in a different set of initial motivating factors. Chasing funding often serves as an initial reason to work with others, but even so, the possibility exists to develop shared objectives for the group. Considering this case, what might the initial group of college leaders have done differently to leverage their alliance?

1 How could the initial group of leaders identify a set of shared objectives based on their individual campus strategic goals?

2 What could the appointed executive director have done to build this consortium into a strategic partnership?
3 What role did communication play in the way the consortium was received on each campus?
4 How did the social capital of each of the individual presidents sway the consortium process?

Case Discussion

Though the consortium was initially conceived as a lobby effort among the five campus presidents, the outcome of the mandated nature of the consortium shifted the orientation for the group. There was power in the group coming together to advocate for the needs of the technical colleges, but each of the presidents held firmly to negotiating for their individual campuses over consortium interests. On the one hand, the formation of the consortium provided an opportunity for sharing of information among campus functional groups across the five campuses. This improved communication route proved useful for people working within the college and among the faculty. On the other hand, the lack of shared outcomes for the group and the fear of a five-college merger put up barriers to innovation.

Each of the college presidents operated from their own leadership framework. Some were more structural and process oriented, whereas others were more political or symbolic. As in any change process, barriers to change emerge when there is a lack of recognition of differences in leadership frames and the underlying assumptions held by group members. At best, first-order change will occur that does little but advance more of the status quo. In order for deep, second-order change to occur, the campus presidents would need to question the assumptions for working together beyond merely keeping their campus doors open. The capacity to change increases within consortiums when strategic goals are identified. As the scenario in this case unfolded, it was clear that not one of the individual campus presidents took on the leadership role within the group to help identify and achieve larger group goals. Too much concern existed for individual autonomy given the fear of a merger. Leaders looking to partner must ask, What are critical first steps when a partnership begins? How can leaders surface underlying assumptions to achieve second-order change? What type of leadership proves most effective in partnering?

Networked Leadership

The need for leaders in higher education to work with others is critical. The current context demands that collaborative approaches and leadership throughout the institution occur to facilitate problem solving, innovation, and productivity (Kezar & Holcombe, 2017). Connective leadership (Lipman-Blumen, 1996) builds on behavioral theories that are direct, instrumental, and relational. Lipman-Blumen advocates for connective leadership that involves mentoring, helping, joining forces, empowering, networking, persuading, taking charge, outperforming, and excelling. These strategies help build networks within an institution and across organizations with other partners. Networked leadership moves past mere collaborations and short-term partnerships to foster greater connectivity (Eddy et al., 2015) and act as a driver for educational change (Díaz-Gibson, Zaragoza, Daly, Mayayo, & Romani, 2017). This type of leadership differs from team leadership because networked leadership is more open given the fluid nature of who is involved—both inside and outside the institution. Teams are often more temporal in nature, coming together to solve particular problems (e.g., tiger teams) or convening based on functional issues (e.g., student mental health teams).

Networked leadership relies "on sensemaking and boundary-spanning throughout the college, not just at the top levels" (Eddy & Garza Mitchell, 2017, p. 132). Here, sensemaking by leaders helps them understand the type of changes occurring at the college and proves a leveraging point for buy-in (Kezar, 2014). Boundary-spanning provides a means for building connections between campus units and functional areas, as well as with external partners. Think here of how college committees provide a fertile ground for building up boundary-spanning roles in the institution or how the expansion of one-stop centers on campus for students requires staff to know the work of admissions, financial aid, and academic advising. When individuals get to know the work that others do, relationships deepen, which allows for increased connection across units that can lead to change. Likewise, campus members often serve on community boards, volunteer in community agencies and schools, and have friends who work in area businesses. These activities all cross boundaries. Thinking of leadership as occurring via a network emphasizes the unbounded practice of leading beyond positional authority (Perillo, 2008). A critical aspect of networked leadership is recognizing the need to change reward policies that have traditionally been built on individual efforts. Disruption of work, policies, and process that have been historically valued must occur.

Networked leadership requires leaders to learn from their interactions with others (recall from chapter 1 the cognitive approach to leadership) and reflect on the process of collaborating. This form of leadership differs from historical top-down leading and requires moving past traditional hierarchies. A matrix format in the organization (McPhail, 2016) creates more institutional flexibility that allows for both vertical and horizontal chains of authority. In matrix organizations, power is pervasive throughout the organization, rather than being located solely at the top of the organizational chart. Historical forms of power were limited to the people in control. Current expanded concepts of power are more fluid and accessible to people throughout the organizational chart (Heimans & Timms, 2014). Instead of a conception of power as scarce, newer conceptions of power allow individuals within the college to exert leadership. In this case, leaders operating from the middle are linchpins to networked leadership. Recognizing the potential of the people in the middle is important as these individuals tend to stay in their positions longer than top leaders do (Baldwin, DeZure, Shaw, & Moretto, 2008; Gagliardo et al., 2017) and are most often the face of the college to students and faculty. Broad networks allow access to increased diversity too—diversity in thinking, diversity in experience, and diversity in worldviews. This type of depth of intellectual resource is important given the current demands to innovate in higher education. Networked leadership requires thoughtful changes to campus infrastructures, changes in the way leaders are developed, changes in assumptions regarding who can be a leader, and changes in boundaries. More of a group approach is required.

Power is not evidenced by position, but by the ability to work with others.

—John Dever, president emeritus of Thomas Nelson Community College (personal communication, April 24, 2015)

Boundary Spanners

Anyone working in higher education is aware of the number of silos and boundaries that exist. Some of these boundaries are physical on large campuses with branch campus locations, and some are imaginarily fixed, such as those between professional schools and arts and sciences or between functional units. Initially, boundary theory focused on individuals moving back and forth between roles. Boundary theory emerged as a means to understand the ease of movement between home and work responsibilities (Nippert-Eng, 1996), whereas border theory (S. Clark, 2000) viewed the psychological and physical borders between the two life areas. Some people view these borders as a distinct separation of work and home, as opposed to seeing the two areas as more integrated. The concepts provided in both these theories are helpful in understanding organizational boundaries too as boundaries also exist when working within a network or in partnering with others. The permeability of the boundaries depends on the roles and social capital of the individuals involved, both within the institution and across organizations (Daniels, 2011). Organizational processes, varied missions, challenges in effective cross-border communication, and historical conceptions of academic culture and values also contribute to the strength of the boundaries and challenges in networked leadership (Floyd & Fung, 2017).

The ties that connect individuals range from strong to weak. Granovetter (1983) focused on the weak ties among individuals. It is at the nodes of these weak relationships that connections to expanded networks occur. Consider the image of a social network in figure 7.1. In the figure, weak ties are evident in the lines connecting the various clusters within the network. The individuals in the center of the clusters (noted in the figure by a circle around the individuals) are people with multiple ties to various individuals and weak ties to multiple networks. These connections emphasize the role that people with weak ties serve as boundary spanners. These types of weak ties exist within the college and with others outside the college. Leveraging the potential of these boundary spanners is critical in networked leadership. "Individuals that create weak ties often have cognitive flexibility that allows them to become boundary spanners that link networks together" (Eddy & Amey, 2014, p. 54). A key assumption with these boundary spanners is the existence of high levels of trust within their relationships with others. The existence of a strong relationship builds a foundation that provides easier access to others and to other networks on the basis of the trust developed. Figure 7.1 shows how a social network might look.

When networks are expanded, new practices and forms of interacting emerge (Warmington et al., 2004). The boundary spanners are able to operate in both "worlds and translate the cultural models of one group for another" (Hora & Millar, 2011, p. 92). Those individuals with high levels of social capital and strong social networks are adept at navigating within the network. The loose coupling (Weick, 1976) of functional areas within a college and auxiliary operations provides a context for weaker boundaries. In this case, leaders have the chance to frame the network for others and aid in sensemaking of new ways of operating within the network (Pilbeam & Jamieson, 2010).

Depending on the leadership frame in use by leaders, boundary spanners may be viewed as linchpins in the network or as enigmas that do not fit into day-to-day roles and operations. Consider how

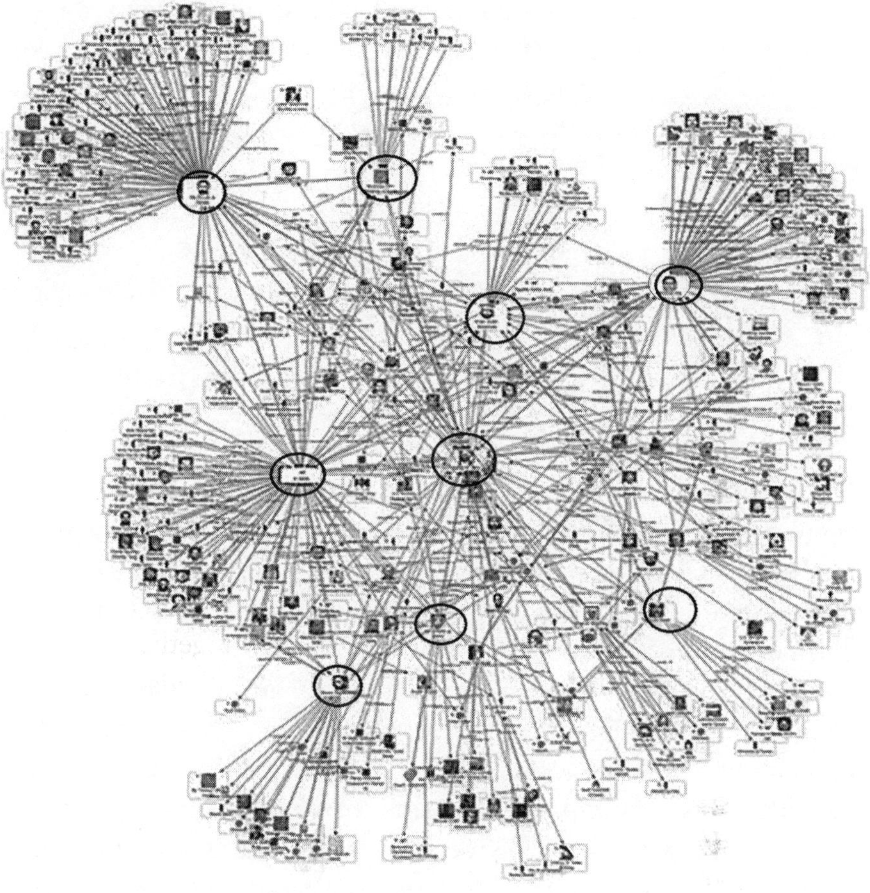

Figure 7.1. Example of a social network

those who operate from a structural frame place emphasis on position and hierarchy, whereas those who use a human resources frame desire to value the contributions of people in the organization. Thus, from a structural orientation, boundary spanners are viewed by their position as opposed to their connections, whereas a human resources orientation would see value in the boundary spanners being able to connect people together. Leaders operating from a political frame may see boundary spanners as central players in negotiating with others or may perceive that boundary spanners have too much individual power and are suspect. Finally, leaders using a symbolic frame may see boundary spanners reinforcing collaborations or may see them as not fitting into the hierarchy (Bolman & Deal, 2013). How leaders frame the role of boundary spanners and the type of collaborative culture in place influences the ultimate effectiveness of these individuals.

Team Leadership

Working in collaboration with others requires teamwork. Ad hoc teams are often formed and have a common goal or objective, have defined tasks, and include individuals with particular skill sets. These types of productive teams generate results that are greater than the sum of what individuals could do on their own (Söderhjelm, Björklund, Sandahl, & Bolander-Laksov, 2018). The move away from top-level leaders telling others what to do and toward multiple individuals working together in a team and network represents a shift in perspective. Here, governance is shared, with all parties having a stake in the outcomes and sharing accountability (Lucey, 2002).

In networks, teams simultaneously share and distribute leadership among team members (Yammarino, Salas, Serban, Shirreffs, & Shuffler, 2012). The role of leader within the team shifts based on the needed experiences and requirements for particular tasks (Kezar & Holcombe, 2017). In a review of presidential teams, Bensimon and Neumann (1993) outline three functions: (1) getting the work done—a utilitarian function; (2) framing problems—an expressive function; and (3) thinking collaboratively to find solutions—a cognitive function. Being able to share ideas and participate in team thinking is central to effective team work, and diverse perspectives are required in productive teams.

To accomplish the team functions, Bensimon and Neumann (1993) define eight thinking roles for presidential teams that apply to teams and networked leadership. The five core roles are the following:

1. *Definer:* frames issues and defines reality
2. *Analyst:* explores and assesses the issues at hand

3 *Interpreter:* translates how others may view decisions outside the group
4 *Critic:* takes on the role of critic and devil's advocate
5 *Synthesizer:* looks broadly at the issues and brings together a summary (p. 59)

Supporting roles include monitoring disparity, tasks, and emotions. Savvy leaders will work to ensure that all these roles are covered within a team to maximize the potential of the group. Networked leadership relies on individuals who are on campus teams to all be contributing members. Using data analytics to monitor progress is becoming de rigueur in higher education, and team productivity is no exception.

A caveat of note regarding teamwork and team leadership is the unequal experiences of leaders on the basis of gender (Eddy, Hartman, & Liu, 2020). Women have largely been absent from top-level leadership roles in higher education. In 2017, only 30.1 percent of college presidents were women, and furthermore, only 16.8 percent were leaders of color (Gagliardi et al., 2017, p. 4). A result of the dearth of women presidents is a reliance on male-dominated forms of leadership and culture. Men generally lead via "task-orientation, aggression, authority, determination, confidence, courage, independence, strength, and vision" (Wheat & Hill, 2016, p. 2), whereas women generally practice and hold traits of "cooperativeness, collaboration of managers and subordinates, lower control for the leader, and problem solving based on intuition and empathy as well as rationality" (Eagly & Johnson, 1990, p. 233). Anticipated leadership turnover and increased calls for collaboration and partnering bode well for a future with more inclusive forms of leading, in particular, the type of networked leadership we argue for in this chapter. In the meantime, recognition of differences based on a range of individual characteristics requires vigilance. Moving forward, it is important to think about who the boundary spanners are in the institution. Focusing on how to develop and expand your professional network is important as it contributes to overall social capital. Think about what is needed to support networked leadership at your college. Contemplating your leadership frame orientation preferences can provide insight into how you interact with others (Bolman & Deal, 2013).

The focus on building networked leadership within colleges and universities requires rethinking individual and functional roles and revisioning what is possible for leaders, faculty, staff, and operations. The staying power of institutions of higher education over time highlights the role of strong academic cultures that have stood the test of time. Often new initiatives falter due to an inability to conceive of roles or processes differently, yet innovation is now demanded in higher education. The movement to new ways of operating establishes a gray area that belies use of traditional roadmaps.

Case #12: Building Bridges

Lixing Liu was recently tenured as an associate professor in psychology at a large urban university located on the West Coast. Her research occurred at the intersection of technology and learning as she investigated the ways in which technology aided learning and how learners' cognitive processes altered due to their interaction with technology. Liu arranged for a sabbatical year with a company located in the state's tech corridor. Her work in the field resulted in many connections within the tech sector and in her disciplinary area. At the last professional conference, Liu organized a symposium involving leaders in the field, representatives from top tech firms, and policy makers.

As Liu's sabbatical leave was nearing the end, she reflected back on her year. She thought to herself, "I can see so many ways that the curriculum should change in the department to allow students to come out better prepared to work in the field of learning science." Her sabbatical work involved using data analytics to determine how people learn best. As a result of this experience, Liu thought, "I can now see how my university can use student learning analytics to improve completion rates!" Her connections within the company opened up an opportunity for a partnership that included roles for faculty members, internships for students, and other funding opportunities. At lunch on her last day at the company, her supervisor commented, "Lixing, I can't wait to get a partnership with your university started. This chance provides an opportunity for the university to get in on the ground floor of an innovative process that could revolutionize how we think about a higher education." Liu was looking forward to reengaging back on campus and bringing new ideas back to her colleagues.

The first thing Liu did when back on campus was set up a meeting with her department chair to debrief him on what she learned on her sabbatical and to lay out plans to initiate collaborating with the tech firm where she spent her sabbatical. In preparation, Liu assembled a list of ideas that included what she saw as a timeline for implementation. On her list were several curricular items, including a required internship, new courses on learning science, and a capstone project that involved working with a tech firm. Liu also envisioned an exchange program in which staff from the tech firm would serve as adjunct faculty in the degree program, and faculty from the program would do research projects at the firm. Liu was also planning on nominating her industry supervisor for a board position in her academic association. Her role as past conference chair of the association held sway in the election process. Liu was on a roll with what she saw as so many great ideas!

Despite Liu's initial enthusiasm, her meeting with her department chair didn't go as well she anticipated. Even though her department chair voiced enthusiasm for the work that Liu was able to do while on sabbatical, he kept responding to each of Liu's suggestions with comments like, "Well, that is a good idea, but . . . ," "Have you thought about . . . ," "There are university policies preventing . . . ," or "How does this fit into your research agenda?" Liu left the meeting more than a little frustrated. She reflected, "How are things ever going to change? I know this type of innovation is what this university needs. I thought with tenure that I'd now have more influence."

Individuals throughout the institution might spark the beginnings of partnering and be part of multiple networks. An advantage for someone in the middle exploring opportunities to work with others is freedom due to the lack of administrative constraints. It is one thing for the president of the university to explore partnering and quite another for a faculty member or director to investigate opportunities. Liu's weak ties have provided a chance for the university to get in on the ground floor of implementing new learning technologies, which may result in redoing requirements in majors, could support additional grant funding, or on the flip side could cost the university money and reputation. Several fragile points of connections occur in the developmental stages of the partnership that can easily derail the process. What is the path to take?

Guiding Questions

Leaders operating from the middle can offer different types of boundary spanning given the number of weak ties they possess with connections in different institutions, with businesses, and in the larger profession. Yet those in the middle often lack access to the resources needed to commit to a burgeoning partnership. Consider how the control that faculty have over curriculum decisions might offer some opportunities for implementing the ideas Liu has. What advice would you provide to Liu as she seeks to change the attitude of "this is the way things are always done at the university"?

1 How can Liu leverage the weak ties she possess within the larger university/business/professional association networks?
2 Given the bureaucracy of the university system, what type of networked leadership might circumvent the barriers presented?
3 How can Liu present her ideas as an opportunity to build a strategic partnership?
4 What type of team role do you think Liu should use with her colleagues.

Case Discussion

Individuals can serve as innovators within higher education, but the infrastructures and rules of universities often make it hard to implement new ideas given a lack of flexibility. Those who are located in the middle, such as Liu in this case, often possess a range of connections and ties with others that open up possibilities for the university to partner within different networks. Although some ideas cost money to implement, others do not. Take for example the curricular suggestions Liu had about providing the students with more authentic learning opportunities (recall from chapter 6 how internships represent a proven high-impact practice that supports student learning). Typically, faculty members control their program curriculum. Working with department colleagues as part of a team effort could provide opportunities to adjust the requirements for the major to include an internship and also to reevaluate current course work with an eye toward expanding learning science course options. Consider how Liu might work with colleagues operating from different leadership frames.

Bringing along allies can help develop partnering opportunities both within the university and with external businesses. Consider how Liu might work with colleagues from the college of education to build jointly offered course work that could fit in both degree programs or with faculty in the computer science department to develop programming on learning analytics. Committee work within the institution also provides opportunities to push for change. University curriculum committees or procedural committees hold responsibility for policies and procedures and, as such, can also change these policies or procedures to reduce red tape. Working with external partners can also provide a venue for them to act as the advocates for new ideas.

Rethinking Organizations

As evident throughout this book, the pressures on higher education to change are rising. The universities of today have retained roughly the same infrastructure over time, which supports siloing of work despite attempts to increase interdisciplinary collaborations. As institutions of higher education seek to become more flexible and nimble to provide relevant learning experiences for students and as they reconceptualize faculty work, change is required (Finger & Lee, 2014). The move to employing more contingent faculty (Kezar & Sam, 2010) results in fewer full-time tenure-track or tenured faculty on campus to support academic functions. For those who are in tenure-track lines, the reward structure is set up in universities to value research productivity that contributes to institutional prestige over teaching or governance work to support change efforts (Fairweather, 2002). Institutions more often reward individual achievement and merit rather than collaborative work. Therefore, conceptualizing how to reenvision the work of faculty is one of the first challenges that new department leaders face in leading change efforts.

Unbundling faculty work is one approach to support change. Consider the work done at Rio Salado College in Arizona, which has unbundled the faculty role and recast the role of adjuncts and other staff in its online programs. "The unbundling of the faculty role occurs when tasks that were all normally performed by a single faculty member—such as course design, course development, presentation of content, interaction, assessment, evaluation, and advisement—are unbundled so that they can be performed by others or through distributed technologies" (V. Smith, 2008, p. 13). The unbundling of tasks by full-time faculty members, adjunct faculty, instructional designers, and other professional staff requires collaboration by all those involved (Smith & Rhoades, 2006). This type of networked leadership provides individuals in a variety of roles the ability to contribute to projects.

As institutions of higher education try to continue to operate as they have done in the past, but with less state support and in an environment of more competition for students, some colleges are going out of business. For example, Busta (2018) reports the closure of fourteen liberal arts colleges since 2016 and more than fifty for-profit colleges closing in that same time period. A 2016 report by Ernst and Young found 735 small institutions at risk, and another 70 large institutions operating inefficiently (p. 4). Partnering with other institutions provides a strategy to reconfigure failing college prospects. One form of partnering is merging with another college (McBain, 2009; Tugend, 2018). Consider the 2019 merger of New England College with New Hampshire Institute of Art (Brooks, 2019) or Wheelock College and Boston University in 2018 (Brown & Chard, 2018). In both cases, the struggles of smaller colleges motivated institutional leaders to seek out partners with complementary institutional values.

Other types of mergers involve larger, system-wide consolidations. Take for example the way Georgia merged fourteen of its colleges into seven new institutions (L. Gardner, 2017). The need to come to agreement on shared operations is difficult given the combination of institutional cultures and practices, not to mention the need to determine how to name the newly combined institution. Another large-scale restructuring and merger is being staged in Wisconsin. The University of Wisconsin system, started in 1971, is merging its thirteen two-year colleges with the seven four-year universities in the state. The intention of the system merger is to more tightly couple the pipeline from the community colleges into the four-year universities, as universities will now award associate's degrees (Meyerhofer, 2018). The creation of regional clusters provides opportunities for partnerships to develop within and across communities. The sixteen technical colleges in the state and their forty-nine campuses will continue to operate independently. These two state mergers highlight different ends of the spectrum. In Georgia, high school graduation rates are on the increase, and the state thus needs to provide more capacity for access to higher education (L. Gardner, 2017); whereas in Wisconsin, the state is experiencing a decline in high school graduation rates and a need to provide more efficiency in its offering of higher education options (Meyerhofer, 2018). The lessons here showcase a glimpse into the future for other higher education leaders and outline the need to be thinking of partnering opportunities sooner rather than later.

The future is built on the ability to work with others. Networked leadership recognizes the need to involve all talent within the college as opposed to relying on singular leadership at the top. This type of shift in leading requires changes in behaviors, a recognition that working with teams of leaders requires different skill sets, and an end to operating from an authoritative perspective. Building networks, leveraging weak ties, and altering infrastructures to matrix formats provides institutional nimbleness. The complexity of today's higher education environment demands flexibility and innovation.

Making This Personal

Understanding more about the partnering process and the potential for networked leadership opens up possibilities in practice. For those who are new to leadership, being savvy about the inner workings of teams and networks can provide for a quicker learning curve. Reflection on individual approaches and past experiences working with others can outline the type of team role one typically fills but can also show the availability of other team contribution opportunities. In constructing teams and working within networks, it is important to have diverse roles. On the one hand, individuals often do not like working in situations containing conflict, which may emerge when different viewpoints are included. On the other hand, a voice acting as the devil's advocate is important to provide for a reality check. Knowing the blind spots one has as well as the blind spots of the larger team is important to avoid pitfalls.

Current organizational structures and historical practices run counter to networked leadership. Expectations for individuals to hold particular roles often eliminates a wider range of voices and ideas being presented. What can be done to change practices? Think of the numerous activities occurring on campus that remain unquestioned. As the need to collaborate with others, both inside the college and with external partners, becomes more prevalent, it is important to consider what practices should remain, how much higher education should subjugate itself to external business demands that commodify education, and how individuals without positions of authority can contribute to needed innovations. Contemplate what you need to prepare for working in this type of environment and whom you need in your network for support.

Key Chapter Points

- Traditional and strategic partnerships have different starting motivations.
- Traditional partnerships based on individual efforts or mandates are often short-lived.
- Strategic partnerships are based on goals that align with the institutional mission and vision.
- The complexities in higher education require more focus on collaborative efforts and networked leadership.
- Networked leadership relies on boundary spanners and teamwork.
- Boundary spanners possess weak ties with others within the institution and with outside stakeholders that provide leverage to partnering and developing networks.
- Team leadership provides opportunities for a range of roles for individuals and builds on the premise that working together gets you further than going it alone.

Web Resources

- American Council on Education, international partnerships: https://www.acenet.edu/news-room/Pages/Collaboration-and-Partnerships.aspx
- Jack Cooke Kent partnership initiative: https://www.jkcf.org/research/partnerships-that-promote-success-lessons-and-findings-from-the-evaluation-of-the-jack-kent-cooke-foundations-community-college-transfer-initiative/

- National Conference of State Legislators toolkit: http://www.ncsl.org/Portals/1/Documents/educ/ReorgAlignMergers_v03.pdf
- The New Network Leader: https://ssir.org/network_entrepreneurs

Leadership Training

- Center for Creative Leadership: https://www.ccl.org/blog/top-6-rules-leadership-networking/
- Collaborative Leadership: https://www.extension.harvard.edu/professional-development/programs/collaborative-leadership-building-organization-future
- Team leadership model: https://www.sagepub.com/sites/default/files/upm-binaries/47444_chp_12.pdf
- The Leadership Laboratory: https://www.leadershipdevelopmentlab.com/
- "The 10 Effective Qualities of a Team Leader": https://smallbusiness.chron.com/10-effective-qualities-team-leader-23281.html

CHAPTER 8

Preparing to Address Higher Education Trends

The following quote has often been attributed to Charles Darwin, "It is not the strongest of the species that survives, nor the most intelligent, but the one most responsive to change." Higher education leaders, educators, and stakeholders are serving in a constant state of flux as institutions face numerous challenges that are likely to continue well into the future. Prolonged financial volatility, constrained state and federal funding, and growing needs for student financial aid coupled with ongoing competition for students from for-profit organizations and online and open-source options are just some of the many factors contributing to a tumultuous higher education environment (Selingo, 2017). Change leaders hoping to develop leadership efficacy amid this turbulence must keep their eyes on emergent trends in higher education that hold promise to shape policy and forecast the future (Fowler, 2013). Understanding more about current trends in higher education helps leaders prepare for and anticipate needed adjustments within their institutions.

Rising tuition costs and student debt have contributed to increasing public skepticism regarding the value of higher education (Juszkiewicz, 2017; Weise & Christensen, 2014) and public inquiry into the adequacy of preparation for the workforce. Yet higher education has proven to be critical for social mobility and higher lifetime income levels (U.S. Department of Education, 2016). In a recent report by the College Board, statistical analyses demonstrate the significance of higher educational attainment and subsequent benefits in employment and earnings (Ma, Pender, & Welch, 2016). Parents and students want to know if there will be a significant return on their investment and, ultimately, if their education leads to a good job.

The Georgetown Center on Education and the Workforce's report *Three Educational Pathways to Good Jobs: High School, Middle Skills, and Bachelor's Degree* (Carnevale, Strohl, Ridley, & Gulish, 2018) defines what is considered a good job and the percentage of jobs available through each of the three pathways. Good jobs are defined as those that pay at least $35,000 for workers aged twenty-five to forty-four and at least $45,000 for workers aged forty-five to sixty-four. These jobs pay median earnings of $56,000 for workers with less than a bachelor's degree and $65,000 for bachelor's degree and higher. Table 8.1 comprises key points from the report, which according to the authors, "highlights the growing value of post-secondary education in the modern economy" (Carnevale et al., 2018, p. 15).

Signals of change are happening all around us, all the time. Initially, the signals may be weak and sporadic. Some fade away, while others become more prominent. The middle skills pathway is an example of a rapidly growing area signaling change in educational attainment that may have significant impact on higher education. Carnevale and colleagues (2018) report that individuals moving along this pathway now have educational opportunities that have expanded beyond traditional community college and internship approaches and include options such as certificates, badges, prior learning credit, micro credentials, career-technical preparation, and for-profit college education (p. 13). The increase in the array of alternative credentialing combined with technological advancements that allow for rapid delivery is gaining momentum and driving change throughout the education sector. What remains to be seen is whether the alternative credentials will increase in perceived value and become a tipping

Table 8.1. Educational Pathways and Job Opportunities

Pathway	Workers	Pros and cons
High school Accounts for 20% of good jobs (13 million)	Workers with a high school diploma or less	Pathway has persisted despite massive disruption of manufacturing market. Employment opportunities continued to decline precipitously. Most good jobs are primarily for men and described as blue collar.
Middle skills Accounts for 24% of good jobs (16 million)	Workers with more than a high school diploma but less than a bachelor's degree (good jobs are growing faster for workers with associate degrees)	Pathway is growing and transforming from blue-collar to skilled services. Rise in skilled services industry has created an abundance of opportunity.
Bachelor's pathway Accounts for 56% of good jobs (37 million)	Workers with bachelor's and advanced degrees	This is considered the premier pathway to economic opportunity. It comprises a majority of professional and technical jobs. The largest growth within skilled services is on the bachelor's pathway (good jobs doubled between 1991 and 2016).

Adapted from Carnevale, Strohl, Ridley, & Gulish (2018)

point for those who are currently following the premier higher education pathway.

This chapter explores just a few of the significant changes that are creating challenges and opportunities for higher education. Three key areas are explored: changing student demographics, the role of technology in education, and alternative forms of credentialing educational outcomes. Campus leaders must embrace and navigate the change process as they seek ways to better position their institutions for the future. Scanning the environment to understand current conditions and future direction is necessary to effectively align and allocate resources. The future can seem daunting unless courageous leaders are well informed, keep a strong pulse on their institution, and have the capacity to reimagine and forge ahead in innovative ways.

Learning Objectives

- Trends
  - Changing student demographics
  - Technological advancements
  - Alternative credentialing
- Leadership skills for the future

Changing Demographics Reshaping Higher Education

After a substantial period of growth, the number of high school graduates in the United States has leveled off and is projected to decline through 2023 (Heckman & LaFontaine, 2010). Even though an overall decline is anticipated nationally, the number of high school graduates will vary greatly by regions, nationwide. Areas in the South and West are expected to grow, whereas the Midwest and Northeast are predicted to remain stagnant or decline (Bransberger & Michelau, 2016). Because the number of high school graduates predicts future enrollment for higher education, it should come as no surprise that enrollment is down in higher education institutions. Data reported from the National Student Clearinghouse Research Center (2018) confirm that for the seventh year in a row, student enrollment in college in the United States has declined. As a result, more attention is shifting to recruiting adult students (Blumenstyk, 2018a) and international students, though the latter student population is currently on the decline (Redden, 2018).

Colleges and universities saw large increases in international student populations over the past twenty years. Yet now international student enrollment is also an area of concern for many universities. The most recent data reported by the Institute of International Education's (2017) annual Open Doors survey indicates that the growth rate in the number of new international students declined 3.3 percent in 2016–17. Even though the total number of international students in the United States was at an all-time high of 1,078,822, this high is attributed to existing students who have probably extended their stay due to work or scholarship (Redden, 2018). Redden (2018) reports that the decline in new international students is not distributed equally across institutions, and based on the results of an Open Doors "snapshot survey" of five hundred institutions in fall 2017, the average decline in enrollment was 7 percent (Baer, 2017).

Student enrollment "is the heart of the economic engine that drives universities that do not have large endowments or research grants" (Pelletier, 2007, p. 4). Thus, the decline in student enrollment has hit some institutions harder than others; it has particularly affected small private colleges, predominantly in the Midwest and Northeast regions. In some cases, this has resulted in mergers and closings (Kim, 2018). (See chapter 7 for more on campus mergers and closures.) Moody's Investors Service, one of the nation's leading providers of credit ratings and financial risk analysis, predicted an increase in mergers and closures in 2015, and to date private college closures have increased from an average of four per year since 2012 to eleven per year from 2015 to 2017 (Seltzer, 2018). Further, Moody's 2018 outlook for the higher education sector was downgraded from stable to negative due to expectations for stagnant revenue streams, increased expenses, and uncertainty of federal funding and policy (Moody's Investors Service, 2017).

Community colleges have experienced the steepest decline in enrollments, with an overall enrollment drop of ninety-seven thousand students between 2011 and 2017 (Marcus, 2017). One of the most significant factors for this decline is the steady recovery of our national economy (Chen, 2018). Community colleges have often experienced an ebb and flow in enrollment. Typically, when the economy is good, potential students are in the workforce (Romano & Palmer, 2015). When unemployment rises, workers often return to community colleges to add to their skill sets and enhance career options. Experience with managing these cyclical changes builds resilience within institutions. However, when these trends are coupled with a continual decline in federal funding for higher education, an increased dependence on high school dual-enrolled students, and an incoming student population purported to be less prepared and unlikely to persist to completion (A. Smith, 2018), it could be a sign of a more disruptive trend (Sydow & Alfred, 2012). Leaders must understand that disruptions to historical approaches to higher education require new leadership tactics and strategies.

In addition, the racial and ethnic profile of the United States is rapidly changing. Immigration has been the driver of this change, with approximately fifty-nine million immigrants who have immigrated to the United States over the past fifty years. The majority of immigrants are from Latin America and Asia, and this trend is predicted to continue for the next fifty years (Cohn & Caumont, 2016). Higher education institutions across the nation are admitting an unprecedented number of racially and ethnically diverse students who also have an even greater need for resources and financial aid (Selingo, Chheng, & Clark, 2017). This shift in population demographics signals a period of transformation for higher education as faculty, staff, alumni, and other stakeholders adapt to more diverse perspectives and communities.

How to build capacity within, and prepare for, a diverse student body is something with which many institutions have already been wrestling, especially community colleges, as collectively they already serve the most diverse student populations in the nation. In a fall 2017 comparison of all undergraduate students enrolled in the United States, 56 percent of all Native American, 52 percent of all Hispanic, 42 percent of all black, and 39 percent of all Asian Pacific Islander undergraduates were enrolled in community colleges (American Association of Community Colleges, 2019). Campus leaders can learn through the lived experiences, challenges, and successes that community colleges have had in responding to a large demographic shift.

Research has also helped to identify best practices targeted for promoting student body diversity and inclusion. The U.S. Department of Education (2016) identified the following elements to support diversity and inclusion on campus:

- Institutional commitment
- Diversity across all levels of the institution
- Outreach and recruitment of prospective students
- Support services for students
- Inclusive campus climate

In higher education, chief diversity officers or related staff positions are tasked with moving the needle on diversity, equity, and inclusion (DEI) in their institutions. While the number of permanent DEI-related positions is growing across campuses, these are typically not senior-level positions. Senior leaders are often better positioned to use their influence and networked leadership approaches to enact change. Damon Williams, founder of the Center for Strategic Diversity Leadership and Social Innovation, noted that after analyzing three hundred chief diversity officer positions across the nation, only one hundred of them could be considered senior level (Valbrun, 2018).

Implementing best practices for DEI necessitates building the institutional infrastructure needed to serve growing numbers of diverse students through resources, action, and commitment from all levels of the organization. The equity scorecard (Bensimon, 2006) and the Benchmarking Equity and Student Success Tool (BESST) developed at the University of Southern California are tools that can be used for institutional change and support for student success (see chapter 6). In an era in which resources are declining on many campuses, support for DEI efforts may require reprioritization and shifting of resource allocations.

Leaders at all levels can benefit from a wide range of professional development in DEI to build personal skill sets and leadership capacity to instill diversity education and awareness across all levels of the institution, develop supportive structures for students, and create inclusive learning environments that invite full participation for all members of the campus community. Online self-assessments, cultural competency trainings, webinars, conferences, and courses are just a few of the many avenues available for enhancing DEI competencies. Examples are included in the resource section at the end of this chapter.

Research confirms that the typical college student today is nontraditional and is defined as having one or more of the following characteristics:

- Is financially independent from one's parents
- Has a child or other dependent
- Is a single caregiver
- Lacks traditional high school diploma
- Delays postsecondary enrollment
- Attends school part-time
- Is employed full-time (Nadworny & Depenbrock, 2018)

Nearly a decade ago, Stephen Pelletier (2010) stated, "Looking at the demographics of today's student body, nontraditional is the new traditional" (p. 1). Hence, understanding the characteristics and needs of what was formerly conceived of as nontraditional students is essential to navigating this demographic shift and the implications it holds for teaching, learning, and degree attainment. Challenges embedded within any one of the characteristics just listed tell us that these students are prone to more stress, financial hardship, and demands on their time that may impede degree progress and persistence to completion. The additional burdens carried by nontraditional students imply that some, if not many, need greater support to help them succeed. In a study examining adult undergraduates, Gianacola, Grawitch, and Borchert (2009) found the added challenges of juggling work, home, and school for these students have a significant impact on their well-being, stress levels, and degree attainment. As population demographics continue to change, it is important to review institutional support systems and ensure that there are some specifically designed for adult students.

Large national data sets help generalize the typical student profile; however, it is also important to note that given the unique variables across all institutions, this profile may not hold true for all. For example, a small, private liberal arts college is likely to attract a much different student than an urban community college or rural four-year university. Fortunately, institutional data can accurately identify the market sectors where students are coming from, their demographics, and the programs/degrees they seek. Understanding the student profile unique to each institution is essential for marketing, recruitment, and fostering student success. Resource allocation should be carefully aligned to attract prospective students and to provide an infrastructure for success designed to meet students' needs once they have enrolled.

Technological Advancement: Challenges and Opportunities

Technology integration will continue to alter the higher education ecosystem as faculty become more adept in using multimedia and digital tools to design and augment the curriculum. Fully online and blended learning approaches are predicted to be the norm in coming years; these approaches result in unbundling of traditional face-to-face courses (V. Smith, 2008). Advancements in learning analytics, data dashboards, and personalized adaptive learning platforms are on the rise and are already shaping innovative ways to measure and enhance student achievement (Ferguson, 2012). In addition, open-education resources, microcredentialing, and competency-based education models are creating alternative forms of recording educational accomplishments and providing greater flexibility, optimization of curriculum, and acceleration of degree completion (Mintz, 2014).

Technological advancement, automation, and artificial intelligence are the stimuli behind a digital transformation under way in business and higher education (Credly, 2018). Rapid changes in and broad access to technology continue to disrupt how students learn as emergent trends such as smart classrooms, active learning spaces, gamification, virtual reality, and simulations become more prevalent (Lister, 2015). New technologies that fall under the umbrella of artificial intelligence are also transforming college campuses today in a variety of ways. Artificial intelligence (AI) is a term used to describe "a branch of computer science dealing with the simulation intelligent behavior in computers" ("Artificial Intelligence," n.d.) and is used in reference to the ways in which machines perform functions that mirror intelligent human behavior. Data analytic systems have advanced the capacity for universities to make decisions more quickly and accurately in multiple areas, such as admissions, enrollment, course scheduling, and advising (Picciano, 2012).

Artificial intelligence is also having an impact on teaching and learning, as professors deploy new tools to enhance instruction, personalize learning for students, and assist in grading and evaluation. Virtual teaching assistants can teach students foreign language, and conversation agents can promote online discussion among students (McMurtrie, 2018; McKenzie, 2018). Chatbots, another name used to describe artificial intelligence conversation tools, are potential game changers in education, according to Singh (2018); Singh notes that these bots were "built to improve student interaction and collaboration" and are used in novel ways such as intelligent tutoring systems, online course assistants, and student feedback systems. Institutions are also turning to chatbots to assist with recruiting, enrolling, and retaining students (McKenzie, 2018).

Early alert advising systems offer a good example of how automation is being combined with personal advising to support student success. Systems are customized to the institution and designed to include such things as appointment scheduling, generating grade and attendance notifications, and nudging students to make an advising appointment or register for classes. These systems are maximized when combined with follow-up by advisors who can intervene early when problems arise (Reddick, Trifilo, Asby, Majewski, & Geissler, 2014).

The future world of work for students is also rapidly changing, as advancements in technology in areas such as artificial intelligence, automations, and robotics have accelerated in all economic sectors, altering the concepts of work (Merisotis, 2018). As these technologies continue to gain traction, there becomes a "no collar" workforce in which humans and technology enter into a symbiotic, mutually beneficial relationship. Deloitte's *Tech Trends 2018* report describes how human performance may be augmented by automating certain parts of a task more conducive to artificial intelligence, while interfacing with humans who provide elements of a task that involve cognitive tools such as empathy, social skills, and emotional intelligence (Abbatiello, Boehm, & Schwartz, 2017).

The implications for a paradigm shift in higher education are significant as we move to more learner-centric systems augmented by networked technology (Schieber, 2018). Leaders in higher education must prepare their institutions to maximize the potential embedded in emergent technologies and lead the way in providing learning pathways that are more personable and adaptable for lifelong learning. Networked leadership is particularly aligned with the needs of this shifting, technical environment because of how technology helps eliminate the need for place-bound instruction. The current environment is ripe for innovation, and alternative credentials are emerging as a serious contender in providing what may become a lifelong learning system with linkages to education and the workplace.

Alternative Credentialing

Higher education has a long-standing and nearly exclusive history as the provider for academic credentials that are recognized by employers as an indicator of a quality education and future success (Thelin, 2011). Credentials such as transcripts, certificates, and diplomas have been the gold standard and described as the "coin of the realm," or the currency students utilize to access occupational opportunities (Pittinsky, 2015; Selingo, 2017). The monopoly that higher education institutions have held on credentials is currently being challenged by a number of alternative credentialing providers (Selingo, 2017). Alternative credentials provide educational pathways and include such things as certificates based on job-relevant skills and competencies, credit-bearing certificates that are stackable and may count toward degrees (MicroMasters degree), and nonaccredited course work or credentials that may be granted college credit ("On-Ramps," 2018).

Microcredentials and Digital Badges

Microcredentials are defined as "digital artifacts that can be used to recognize, display, and transmit information about an individual student's skills, abilities, and knowledge" (Fishman, Teasley, & Cederquist, 2018, p. 1). The term often refers to a variety of shortened learning components—modules, digital badges, a course or series of courses, nano degrees, and MicroMasters (Gallagher, 2018). Digital badges are defined by the MacArthur Foundation (n.d.) as "an assessment and credentialing mechanism that is housed and manned online. Badges are designed to make visible and validate learning in both formal and informal settings, and hold potential to help transform where and how learning is valued." Digital platform systems, created by providers such as Credly, Mozilla Open Badges, and others, are where badges can be created, issued, shared with other social media platforms, and utilized by the consumer for a personal or professional benefit.

The wide range of providers and credentials available has diversified educational pathways and can be confusing to students, employers, and other educational stakeholders trying to make sense of how they can be utilized effectively. The Lumina Foundation (2015b) argues that "in most cases, there's little clarity about what these credentials mean—their value, their quality, and how they connect" (p. 3). A recent study of human resources experts also confirmed that employers' awareness and experience with candidates holding nondegree microcredentials are low and that alternative credentials are "serving as supplements rather than substitutes for traditional degrees" (Gallagher, 2018, p. 3). What remains unknown is how long it will be before this type of credential is ultimately recognized as a means to evaluate knowledge and skill levels for individuals seeking employment.

In an effort to create a common language and structure to communicate and compare the value of varying credentials, the Lumina Foundation (2015a) has created a comprehensive beta Credentials Framework that incorporates all forms of postsecondary credentials, including microcredentials, badges, and degrees. Such frameworks are needed to translate diverse learning experiences, validate quality, and determine market viability and demand.

As microcredentialing initiatives continue to gain traction, higher education thought leaders and stakeholders are experimenting and engaging in research to understand current opportunities and threats and to maintain a pulse on how the field is developing. There are numerous examples of microcredentials and badging already in use in higher education. For example, some students simultaneously complete course work and industry certifications, complete certificates that may be stacked together for graduate degrees, or earn badges to demonstrate acquisition of nonacademic skills. The following are key research studies and further examples of such efforts:

- The American Council on Education (ACE) conducted a three-year pilot study (*Alternative Credit Project to Increase Attainment Levels for Nontraditional Learners with Some College, No Degree*, 2015–2018) involving fifty-eight traditional and nontraditional education providers in their efforts to create a more flexible pathway to college degree attainment for nontraditional learners through acceptance of credits from alternative education providers (P. Steele, 2018).
- In November 2017, the University Professional and Continuing Education Association (UPCEA) convened an invitation-only group of higher education leaders to understand the current status of alternative credentials and issues related to future expansion, use, and acceptance (UPCEA, 2018).
- A National Science Foundation (NSF)–funded workshop in May 2017 at the University of Michigan's School of Information was held to explore the pros and cons of microcredentials as evidence of college readiness and usage in the admissions process (Fishman, Teasley, & Cederquist, 2018).

As further research and study of trends in microcredentialing occur over time, best practices and models will no doubt emerge. It will take courageous leaders willing to accept risk to first test the waters of this type of credentialing. Leaders should stay attuned to these trends to determine the ways in which their institutions should embrace the practices—or not.

Competency-Based Education (CBE)

Competency-based education (CBE) is an area of growing interest in K–12 and higher education. The K–12 sector has seen a dramatic increase in state policy activity related to competency-based learning. In 2012, twenty-seven states had reached either advanced (building capacity), developing (transition), or emerging (task force) levels in policy development to move K–12 instruction toward competency-based learning design. By 2016, forty-five states had some level of competency-based policy activity occurring in the public education sector (Patrick & Sturgis, 2017).

Competency-based learning is linked to credentialing and is defined by Patrick and Sturgis (2017) as having the following five components:

- Students advance upon demonstrated mastery.
- Students receive timely differentiated support based on their individual learning needs.
- Competencies include explicit, measurable, transferable learning objectives that empower students.
- Assessment is meaningful and a positive learning experience for students.
- Learning outcomes emphasize competencies that include application and creation of knowledge along with the development of important skills and dispositions.

Currently competency-based education is focused heavily in K–12 education systems; however, the implications for higher education will become significant as these students cross the university threshold with different learning expectations. In higher education, Western Governors University (n.d.) took the lead as the first institution to offer fully online competency-based bachelor's and master's degrees. Southern New Hampshire University's College for America (n.d.) degree programs offer another example of competency and project-based pathways leading to associate's and bachelor's degrees at just a fraction of the cost of traditional degree programs. In an effort to create a more seamless pathway from K–12 to employment and to develop a student pipeline, Southern New Hampshire University (SNHU) is expanding its outreach to fourteen- to twenty-four-year-olds in a unique way. Students will have the opportunity to earn free or low-cost badges through game-based learning and use these credentials to count toward a competency-based degree program (McKenzie, 2018). Indeed, Blumenstyk (2018b) comments on SNHU's expansion, "Higher education's leadership has yet to reckon with the potential of these emerging mega-universities, or even to determine how to define them." Strategies employed by SNHU include "comfort with being better known for advising than for academic matters, a willingness to invest in its capacity to grow and innovate, and a reliance on corporate-style practices in activities as diverse as marketing, faculty oversight, and employee training" (Blumenstyk, 2018b). New forms of academic governance, nimble organizational structures, a focus on the student experience, corporate partnerships, and large-scale recruitment are hallmarks of the institution. The scale of SNHU and its reimagination of its organizational structure provide the university with flexibility when trying new approaches to learning and assessment of competencies.

Weise and Christensen (2014) believe that online CBE is revolutionary and has the potential to disrupt higher education. They state, "it marks the convergence of multiple vectors: the right learning model, the right technologies, the right customers, and the right business model" (p. iv). CBE is not a new initiative, but digitizing and packaging learning in new ways generates new opportunities to translate cost-effective learning modules into flexible pathways. Whether the future market demand for online CBE significantly disrupts higher education depends on many factors, including student preference and recognition as valuable by employers in business and industry.

To contemplate trends in higher education and the future of learning, consider the following questions:

- Will alternative credentials carry the same weight with regard to quality and rigor? How will these credentials be measured and valued by individuals and employers?
- In what ways are higher education institutions poised to adapt to a new generation of students who may prefer competency-based and alternative credentialing models of instruction? In what ways are higher education institutions constrained?
- Competition often drives organizational change. What kind of structural or pedagogical changes are on the horizon for higher education institutions? Do you find evidence of these changes currently at your institution?
- Will higher education remain the premier pathway for educational attainment and career advancement, or will alternative routes emerge as a better value proposition and a more viable option?

Leadership Skills for the Future

Higher education leaders are challenged by the sector's current complexity and rapid pace of change. Mrig and Sanaghan (2017) suggest that we have reached a tipping point in which the changing student demographic and financial need is coupled with declining financial support for higher education. This confluence of factors has created a contradictory situation for which there are no immediate solutions. Building the leadership capacity to adapt to the changes under way in higher education may be the greatest challenge of all. Visionary leaders who can "adopt an opportunity rather than scarcity mindset and foster creativity and innovation to blaze a new path forward" (Mrig & Sanaghan, 2017, p. 3) are needed to reimagine higher education in the midst of a changing landscape. Just as pilots must be trained to navigate unexpected or prolonged turbulence, higher education leaders need a similar skill set to help them effectively manage uncharted territory across U.S. colleges and universities. Adaptive leadership and anticipatory leaders can provide one means to address these demands (Heifetz, 1994). Two components are central to this form of leading: having the courage to make tough choices and engaging in a network of leaders to accomplish the tasks required for this type of innovative, deep change.

Anticipatory leaders are defined by their exceptional ability to continually scan the external environment in search of future direction and opportunities. These individuals are often able to mobilize others through their positive energy and capacity to create synergies and shared vision for their organizations. Using tools such as SWOT analysis and environmental scanning (see chapter 5) helps identify potential options and current constraints. Anticipatory leaders generally possess a rare combination of three traits: futurist, strategist, and integrator (Savage & Sales, 2008). These traits packaged together provide individuals with a robust advantage to make predictions about future direction, identify threats and opportunities, and integrate resources and execute strategic action plans. Instead of being surprised or derailed by change, anticipatory leaders are prepared to respond and well positioned to drive growth through new and aligned initiatives. So what are these skills, and what does this look like in practice?

Futurists

Futurists are described as "individuals who are skilled in listening to and interpreting signals, which are harbingers of what's to come" (Webb, 2017, p. 1). In essence, futurists develop an anticipatory mindset by studying past and emergent trends; identifying repetition, patterns, and developments in other sectors; building scenarios; and formulating predictions for their organizations. They readily engage with their networks to access a wider span of information.

For example, enrollment is always a top priority in higher education institutions. Considerations regarding related areas such as staffing, housing, programming, tuition, and allocation of scholarship funds require short- and long-term insight, as well as evidence-based decision-making.

Strategists

Strategists are described by Savage and Sales (2008) as individuals who have a keen understanding of dynamics in play and who use their insight to communicate and collaborate with stakeholders. In doing so, strategists and stakeholder partners develop effective strategies to either adapt to changing circumstances or take advantage of emergent opportunities. Those who use a political frame are particularly adept at this type of negotiation (Bolman & Deal, 2013).

For example, as staffing shortages begin to emerge in various areas, such as education and health professions, higher education leaders can be responsive through programming that includes alternative pathways to certification, off-campus offerings, prior learning credit, online course work, or other approaches that support individuals seeking professional credentials to match industry areas of need.

Integrators

Integrators are defined as synergistic in their ability to draw connections and bring together diverse collaborators around common bonds or collective purpose. Savage and Sales (2008) describe integrators as those who fully embrace new ideas and "engage their organizations in dialogue and mutual discovery of possibilities" (p. 29). This type of collaborative leadership approach draws on a wide network. Integrators are weavers, who engage and motivate the passion and interests of others in strategic ways.

For example, the executive director of a new, interdisciplinary center for health and wellness demonstrates extraordinary skills in bringing diverse stakeholders together around emergent ideas that may have a connection to their guiding mission and interests. The director communicates information across many different channels and creates opportunities to bring individuals and groups together to explore, discover, and take collective action on shared initiatives.

Together, these leadership characteristics, when applied systemically, have the potential to create sustaining organizations by optimizing the collective expertise and intelligence of people within the organization (Savage & Sales, 2008). The adaptive and anticipatory leader is forward thinking and able to envision and mobilize action and embed new practices to create dynamic cultures that are responsive to change in effective ways, ensuring a stable and sustainable organizational future. The courageous leaders advocated for in this book are poised to flourish in this type of changing environment.

Building a Culture of Innovation

As argued throughout this book, recognizing the importance of culture in leading change is critical. Building an institutional culture that supports the values of campus members, supports equity, and results in student success requires intentional actions. Innovation is the watchword in higher education—and long has been. In 1972, Trow first foretold about the transformation of higher education resulting from the period of mass expansion of higher education that occurred after World War II. The American system of higher education, built on a tradition of different institutional types and departmental organization, provided a good structure to expand education into the 1960s. But Trow argued, "I think that we . . . will find it necessary to transform our institutions, and not merely expand them. We will find it more difficult, precisely because of the past success of the American system of higher education, and of the grip that these familiar forms have on our imagination and expectations" (p. 66). Indeed, that era witnessed a breakdown in consensus regarding the academic values of higher education. Coming on the heels of a period of 1960s student activism, there was a desire to move toward more action-oriented outcomes of education and engagement. At the time, Trow (1972) argued for institutional structural responses that allowed easy entry, exit, and reentry for stop-out periods, options for part-time adult learners to engage in higher education, and the development of programs that recognize prior learning. Today, higher education is currently witnessing the same breakdown in value consensus. As evident from a quick perusal of current literature on higher education, these recommendations feel like déjà vu.

Historically, access was the focus within higher education. Now, the sector is being tasked to provide accountability for student outcomes at affordable prices, including students formerly not served well in colleges—namely, low-income students and students of color (Christensen et al., 2011). Christensen and colleagues provide the following definition: "Disruptive innovation is the process by which a sector that has previously served only a limited few because its products and services were complicated, expensive, and inaccessible, is transformed into one whose products and services are simple, affordable, and convenient and serves many no matter their wealth or expertise. The new innovation does so by redefining quality in a simple and often disparaged application at first and then gradually improves such that it takes more and more market share over time as it becomes able to tackle more complicated problems" (p. 2). Online education is an example of a disruption in higher education. Higher education systems need to adjust to account for different ways of engaging with students and faculty (see chapter 7 and the example of Southern New Hampshire University in this chapter). As noted earlier, assumptions about teaching and learning were tested and new forms of operation built at SNHU. Sustaining and encouraging innovation requires a change in culture (Zhu & Engels, 2014; Zhu, 2015). Innovation occurs when risks are taken, but with risk comes failures. James Lorenson, former president of Gogebic Community College, advocates for the "fast fail": "Not everything will work. Learn from mistakes and move on. We need to develop different ways of looking at the issues and problems we try to solve. We can't take a year or two years to develop programs. We say we're responsive, but we're not" (personal communication, August 26, 2013).

Key to failing, even fast failing, is learning from failure. An environment conducive to failure is one in which leaders understand that risk-taking does not always result in positive results. According to Tierney (2014), "an innovative organization will function in a different way from a stable one" (p. 9). In particular, he argues that barriers to innovation include "weak incentives to change, regulation, micromanagement, and standardization" (p. 12). A culture of innovation instead provides an environment in which campus members become more creative and one in which leaders question the need for existing structures. Table 8.2 outlines the seven conditions that Tierney posits are necessary to build a culture of innovation.

Table 8.2. Steps to Building a Culture of Innovation

Step	Leaders	Structure
Risk-taking	Match campus members' skills with needs of college Align motivation strategies to the individual	Aligns rewards with risks Allows for a "fast fail" Accesses talent throughout the institution
Personal autonomy	Accept multiple paths to outcomes Support a risk-taking culture Do not micromanage	Is built on a matrix structure Has flexible job roles
Goal-setting	Establish stable goals Articulate goals so they are known throughout the college	Has clear rewards for achieving goals Aligns goals throughout the institution
Decision-making	Clearly identify what needs to get done, with those close to the decision deciding how to get it done Recognize that progress will be in fits and starts	Identifies scope of autonomy in job descriptions Provides venues and processes for hearing individual voices

(*continued*)

Table 8.2 (*continued*)

Step	Leaders	Structure
Teamwork	Build shared vision Value diverse perspectives Construct teams with an understanding of team roles	Instills processes to avoid groupthink Gives rewards and incentives based on team performance Networks to connect individuals
Fiscal and temporal resources	Link budgets to addressing strategic goals Provide time to innovators	Allocates seed funding for innovative ideas Recognizes differentiated job roles
Organizational excitement	Use symbolism to build excitement Verbally acknowledge and support innovators	Celebrates innovative wins Ties innovation to strategic goals

Building a culture of innovation requires both individual work and changes to structures in higher education (Stempfle, 2011). Borrowing from business practices provides strategies to support innovation, but strong academic cultures of critique often serve to squash innovative ideas (Shen & Tian, 2012; Tierney, 2014). Thus, supporting a culture of innovation demands changes in personal and organizational practices. It is important for leaders to assess if their institution is poised to support innovation. As a leader, it is also critical to understand what one must do to help in supporting innovative change.

Making This Personal

This book has presented tools to help leaders throughout the institution to improve their practice. Developing an anticipatory mind-set based on the tenets of networked leadership can help individuals in personal and professional pursuits, and contemplating how to apply the various theories and strategies is an ongoing process. The prompts that follow serve to aid in the reflective process of what it means to lead in today's colleges and universities.

- How would you describe the typical college student today at your institution: traditional or nontraditional? What information are you using to make that conclusion? Explore your institutional data set for your department, college, or university. Also, review your corresponding website, resources, and marketing messaging and student photographs. Is there alignment between the profile and your target student audience?
- Understanding the projections for shifts in high school graduation rates and changing demographics in your region is of critical importance for leaders in higher education at all levels. The Western Interstate Commission for Higher Education (WICHE) has been conducting research in this area for decades, and current information and projections are found at the Knocking at the College Door data dashboard (https://knocking.wiche.edu/nation-region-profile/). Access the link and explore national projections. Home in on your region and compare to the national trend. As a leader, what implications for your institution are embedded in these projections?
- How is technology employed at your institution to support student learning? How are faculty developed to use the technology to its fullest potential? What type of data analytics are in place to understand learning outcomes for students?
- How does or could your institution use alternative forms of accounting for learning, such as competency-based education? What forms of measures exist at your institution to evaluate prior learning? What is in place to accommodate adult learners?
- What type of leadership development is available to develop as an anticipatory leader? A networked leader? How can you fine-tune your skills to best support exploring, discovering, and embodying information to become the best, most courageous leader you can be?

Several current trends are evident in higher education. Leaders must be mindful of the changes in the environment around them to be most effective. Understanding what is emerging as important allows leaders an opportunity to prepare themselves and their campuses for what is coming. Critical to success in addressing the challenges facing higher education is to capitalize on the concurrent opportunities that are also present. When leaders help foster a culture of innovation on campus, all staff members become engaged in providing solutions and contributions to meeting strategic goals.

What is obvious throughout this book is the need to work with others to accomplish tasks and to meet institutional objectives. Developing leaders throughout the organization who all contribute their talent, who are team players, and who are willing to take risks requires rethinking the structures of today's colleges and universities. Successful colleges and universities require leaders who are adaptive (Heifetz, 1994) and institutions that allow space for innovation (Kezar, 2014; Kotter, 2014). The number of recent college closures and mergers (Busta, 2018) serves as a warning to others to innovate or run the risk of becoming obsolete. The information presented in the chapters of this book is intended to provide leaders with skills to address the challenges facing higher education. We are in an era in which courageous leaders are needed—ones who ask the hard questions, who work on restructuring how colleges and universities function, and who rely on a network as opposed to thinking they can go it alone.

Key Chapter Points

- Shifting student demographics are resulting in a more diverse student body in higher education.
- Technological advancements continue to change the nature of learning and the future of work as automation, artificial intelligence, and robotics become more embedded throughout systems and society.
- Alternative credentialing and competency-based education are expanding and hold promise for the creation and establishment of lifelong learning systems.

- Higher education leaders need to be forward thinking and capable of energizing their organizations in strategic ways that will ensure stability and sustainability in the future.

Web Resources

- College Board, "Trends in Higher Education": https://trends.collegeboard.org/
- "Committing to Equity and Inclusive Excellence": https://www.aacu.org/committing-to-equity
- OnLeadership video series exploring trends and relevant topics for higher ed leaders: https://www.chronicle.com/specialreport/On-Leadership/29?cid=UCHESIDENAV2
- "Step Up & Lead for Equity: What Higher Education Can Do to Reverse Our Deepening Divides": https://www.aacu.org/publications/step-up-and-lead

Leadership Training

- Hawaii Research Center for Future Studies: http://futures.hawaii.edu
- National Coalition Building Institute, Leadership for Diversity Institute: http://ncbi.org/leadership-for-diversity-institute/
- The Futurist Institute: https://www.futuristinstitute.org/
- University of Houston College of Technology Foresight Program: http://houstonfutures.org
- World Future Society: https://www.worldfuture.org/

Acknowledgments

This book evolved over time as we both advanced and converged along varied leadership paths throughout our careers. As we shared experiences, conversation always circled back to the topic of leadership in higher education and the unique challenges embedded within this context. Some years ago, we co-led a study-abroad trip to Ireland for graduate students studying educational leadership. As we traveled on a chartered bus across the Irish countryside, we encouraged students to take advantage of this travel time to form impromptu salons to engage in conversations about their learning but also to use this bus time to share their research ideas, dissertation topics, and career hopes and dreams. On one such ride, the two of us formed our own conversational group and talked about what we affectionately termed "crazy making" in higher education. As seasoned administrators, we turned our conversation to some of the outlandish displays of leadership we had witnessed and recognized, which were often the result of ill-prepared leaders working within a complex environment for which they lacked essential skills and knowledge.

We ruminated on how we could write a book, filled with examples of leadership gone awry and containing helpful tools to help others avoid some of the pitfalls common for new leaders. Leadership positions in higher education are often filled by individuals who have emerged from faculty ranks and who have had little, if any, administrative experience. We determined that what seemed obvious to us as leadership scholars with administrative experience was not so clear to someone trained as a disciplinary expert in the arts and sciences. We sought to contribute a practical source to help remedy this situation. This book is intended to provide an overarching set of skills for new leaders that apply to a wide range of topics and that are explored in authentic case study vignettes. Our thinking was guided by our own experiences and by those of others who have answered the leadership call and who continue to navigate the many challenges and opportunities that encompass the journey. The book provides a glimpse of the realities of leadership in higher education today and provides an introduction to the skills and training needed for success.

Our writing drew from a large group of scholars who have studied leadership in a variety of settings. The scholarship of Debra Bragg, Estella Bensimon, and Alicia Dowd helped in our thinking about equity. Studies by the community college scholars Marilyn Amey and John Levin reminded us to consider the full spectrum of leadership contexts. The writing of John Kotter and Adrianna Kezar pushed our conceptions on change in higher education. Adrianna helped us think about how our work bridges the disparate subsets of leadership research and pushed us to consider how to translate complex theory for use in practice. For her guidance, we are immensely grateful.

A special thanks to Dr. Tracey Schneider, graduate of William & Mary. Tracey reviewed our chapters, asked provocative questions, and applied strong editing skills through completion of the text. Her close read of our work helped produce a more polished book, though we bear responsibility for any errors. We are also grateful to the anonymous reviewer of this book whose insight helped provide additional clarity.

Appendix

Summary of Case Studies

Case	Chapter	Topic	Main issues
#1: Out with the Old; In with the New (Part 1)	1	Leadership theories & new leaders	Breaking a history of authoritarian leadership New regimes and transitioning of leadership styles Bolman & Deal's four frames Power and control
#1: Out with the Old; In with the New (Part 2)	1	Leadership theories & new leaders	Identifying and changing culture Finding leadership voice in an engrained culture Alternative strategies within a given cultural context
#2: Father Knows Best: Leading without Input	2	Leadership actions and stakeholder reactions	Constituent participation in decision-making Change theory Building trust
#3: The Sky Is Falling!	2	Gauging a crisis	Setting priorities with limited resources Developing the leadership team Supporting initiatives
#4: It's All about How You Ask	3	Communication: telling the story	Framing the issue Identifying the communication network Mental maps to guide change

Case	Chapter	Topic	Main issues
#5: The President versus the Faculty Blog	3	Communication: social media	Communication frames Strategies for communication in response to attacks on leadership Managing social media
#6: Stealing the Limelight	4	Managing expectations	Identifying sources of conflict Understanding the roots of conflict Ego versus collective
#7: The Question of Professional Competency	4	Conflict management among staff	Identifying the facts Management issues Clarity of policy
#8: Follow the Money	5	Strategic planning	Implementation of institutional strategic plans Linking of overarching plans to unit-level planning Accountability during implementation
#9: Learning versus Completing: Faculty Connecting the Dots	6	Planning for student success	Defining student success Identifying metrics for student success Getting faculty buy-in
#10: Learning Hard Truths in the Data: Now What Do We Do?	6	Equity	Looking for patterns of equity in data Building an equity mind-set Defining elements for an equity culture
#11: Leveraging Alliances	7	Traditional partnerships	Motivations for partnering Imbalances in partnering Opportunities for collective action
#12: Building Bridges	7	Partnership roles	Individuals as a catalyst for partnering Building on weak ties Institutionalizing initiatives

References

Abbatiello, A., Boehm, T., & Schwartz, J. (2017). No-collar workforce. In *Tech trends 2018: The symphonic enterprise* (pp. 24–39). Retrieved from https://www2.deloitte.com/content/dam/insights/us/articles/Tech-Trends-2018/4109_TechTrends-2018_FINAL.pdf.

ABC Action News. (2018, August 10). *A timeline of the deadly weekend in Charlottesville, Virginia*. Retrieved from https://6abc.com/a-timeline-of-events-in-charlottesville-virginia/2305769/.

Akechi, H., Senju, A., Uibo, H., Kikuchi, Y., Hasegawa, T., & Hietanen, J. K. (2013). Attention to eye contact in the West and East: Autonomic responses and evaluative ratings. *PloS One*, *8*(3), e59312. Retrieved from https://doi.org/10.1371/journal.pone.0059312.

American Association of Community Colleges. (2019). *Fast facts 2019*. Retrieved from https://www.aacc.nche.edu/research-trends/fast-facts/aacc-2019-fact-sheet.

American Association of State Colleges and Universities (AASCU). (2018). *Higher education state policy issues for 2018*. Retrieved from https://www.aascu.org/policy/publications/policy-matters/Top10Issues2018.pdf.

American College Personnel Association (ACPA). (2013). *The student learning imperative: Implications for student affairs*. Retrieved from http://co.myacpa.org/wp-content/uploads/2015/01/acpas_student_learning_imperative.pdf.

American Council on Education. (2012). *American college president*. Washington, DC: Author.

American Institute of Stress. (n.d.). *Workplace stress*. Retrieved from https://www.stress.org/workplace-stress.

American Psychological Association. (2016). *2016 work and well-being survey*. Retrieved from https://www.apaexcellence.org/assets/general/2016-work-and-wellbeing-survey-results.pdf.

American Psychological Association. (n.d.). *How stress affects your health*. Retrieved from https://www.apa.org/images/stress-facts_tcm7-166363.pdf.

Amey, M. J. (2010). Administrative perspectives on international partnerships. In P. L. Eddy (Ed.), *International collaborations: Institutional frameworks and faculty roles*. New Directions for Higher Education, no. 150. San Francisco: Jossey-Bass.

Amey, M. J. (2013). Leadership: Community college transitions. In J. S. Levin & S. T. Kater (Eds.), *Understanding community colleges* (pp. 135–152). New York: Routledge.

Amey, M. J., & Twombly, S. (1992). Re-visioning leadership in community colleges. *Review of Higher Education*, 15(2), 125–150.

Archibald, R., & Feldman, D. H. (2010). *Why does college cost so much?* Oxford: Oxford University Press.

Argyris, C., & Schön, D. A. (1974). *Theory in practice: Increasing professional effectiveness*. San Francisco: Jossey-Bass.

Argyris, C., & Schön, D. A. (1996). *Organisational learning II: Theory, method and practice*. Boston: Addison-Wesley.

Artificial intelligence. (n.d.). In *Merriam-Webster's online dictionary* (11th ed.). Retrieved from https://www.merriam-webster.com/dictionary/artificial%20intelligence.

Aspen Institute. (2014). *Hiring exceptional community college presidents: Tools for hiring leaders who advance student access and success*. Washington, DC: Author. Retrieved from https://assets.aspeninstitute.org/content/uploads/files/content/docs/pubs/Hiring%20Tools,%20Full%20Report,%20FINAL.pdf.

Astin, A. W. (1993). *What matters in college? Four critical years revisited*. San Francisco: Jossey-Bass.

Astin, A. W., & Astin, H. S. (2000). *Leadership reconsidered: Engaging higher education in social change*. Battle Creek, MI: W. K. Kellogg Foundation.

Astin, A. W., & Oseguera, L. (2004). The declining "equity" of American higher education. *The Review of Higher Education*, 27(3), 321–341.

Attewell, P., & Lavin, D. E. (2007). *Passing the torch*. New York: Russell Sage Foundation.

Augsburg, T., & Henry, S. (Eds.). (2009). *The politics of interdisciplinary studies: Essays on transformations in American undergraduate programs*. Jefferson, NC: McFarland.

Austin, A. E. (2002). Preparing the next generation of faculty: Graduate school as socialization to the academic career. *The Journal of Higher Education*, 73(1), 94–122.

Avolio, B. J., Bass, B. M., & Jung, D. I. (1999). Re-examining the components of transformational and transactional leadership using the Multifactor Leadership Questionnaire. *Journal of Occupational and Organizational Psychology*, 72(4), 441–462.

Baer, J. (2017). *Fall 2017 international student enrollment hot topics survey*. New York: IE Center for Academic Mobility Research and Impact. Retrieved from https://www.iie.org/Research-and-Insights/Open-Doors/Data/Fall-International-Enrollments-Snapshot-Reports.

Bailey, T. R., Jaggars, S. S., & Jenkins, D. (2015). *Redesigning America's community colleges*. Cambridge, MA: Harvard University Press.

Baker, R. (2016). The effects of structured transfer pathways in community colleges. *Educational Evaluation and Policy Analysis*, *38*(4), 626–646.

Baker, W. (2012). From cultural awareness to intercultural awareness: Culture in ELT. *ELT Journal*, *66*(1), 62–70.

Baldwin, R., DeZure, D., Shaw, A., & Moretto, K. (2008). Mapping the terrain of mid-career faculty at a research university: Implications for faculty and academic leaders. *Change: The Magazine of Higher Learning*, *40*(5), 46–55.

Barber, J. P. (2012). Integration of learning: A grounded theory analysis of college students' learning. *American Educational Research Journal*, *49*(3), 590–617.

Barber, J. P. (2014). Integration of learning model: How college students integrate learning. In P. L. Eddy (Ed.), *Connecting learning across the institution*. New Directions for Higher Education, no. 165 (pp. 7–18). San Francisco: Jossey-Bass. Retrieved from https://doi.org/10.1002/he.20082.

Barr, M. J., & McClellan, G. S. (2011). *Budgets and financial management in higher education*. San Francisco: John Wiley & Sons.

Barr, R. B., & Tagg, J. (1995). From teaching to learning, *Change*, *27*(6), 12–25.

Bartunek, J. M., & Moch, F. J. (1987). The effects of organizational restructuring on frames of reference and cooperation. *Journal of Management*, *14*(4), 579–592.

Bass, B. M. (1985). *Leadership and performance beyond expectations*. New York: Free Press.

Bass, B. M. (1991). From transactional to transformational leadership: Learning to share the vision. *Organizational Dynamics*, *18*(3), 19–31.

Bass, B. M. (1997). Does the transactional-transformational leadership paradigm transcend organizational and national boundaries? *American Psychologist*, 52(2), 130–139.

Bass, B. M., & Avolio, B. J. (1993). Transformational leadership: A response to critiques. In M. M. Chemers & R. Ayman (Eds.), *Leadership theory and research: Perspectives and directions* (pp. 49–80). San Diego: Academic Press.

Bass, B. M., & Avolio, B. J. (1994). Shatter the glass ceiling: Women may make better managers. *Human Resource Management*, *33*(4), 549–560.

Bass, B. M., & Stogdill, R. M. (1990). *Bass & Stogdill's handbook of leadership: Theory, research, and managerial applications*. New York: Simon & Schuster.

Baxtor Magolda, M. B. (1999). *Creating contexts for learning and self-authorship: Constructive-developmental pedagogy*. Nashville, TN: Vanderbilt University Press.

Beach, A. L., Sorcinelli, M. D., Austin, A. E., & Rivard, J. K. (2016). *Faculty development in the age of evidence: Current practices, future imperatives*. Sterling, VA: Stylus.

Bensimon, E. M. (1990a). The new president and understanding the campus as a culture. In W. G. Tierney (Ed.), *Assessing academic climates and cultures*, New directions for institutional research, no. 68 (pp. 75–86). San Francisco: Jossey-Bass.

Bensimon, E. M. (1990b). Viewing the presidency: Perceptual congruence between presidents and leaders on their campuses. *Leadership Quarterly*, *1*(2), 71–90.

Bensimon, E. M. (2004). The diversity scorecard: A learning approach to institutional change. *Change: The Magazine of Higher Learning*, *36*(1), 44–52.

Bensimon, E. M. (2006). Learning equity-mindedness: Equality in educational outcomes. *The Academic Workplace*, *1*(17), 2–21.

Bensimon, E. M. (2018). Reclaiming racial justice in equity. *Change: The Magazine of Higher Learning*, *50*(3), 95–98.

Bensimon, E. M., Dowd, A. C., & Witham, K. (2016). Five principles for enacting equity by design. *Diversity and Democracy, the Equity Imperative*, *19*(1).

Bensimon, E. M., & Neumann, A. (1993). *Redesigning collegiate leadership: Teams and teamwork in higher education*. Baltimore: Johns Hopkins University Press.

Bensimon, E. M., Neumann, A., & Birnbaum, R. (1989). *Making sense of administrative leadership* (ASHE-ERIC Higher Education Report No. 1). Washington, DC: George Washington University.

Bensimon, E. M., Rueda, R., Dowd, A. C., & Harris III, F. (2007). Accountability, equity, and practitioner learning and change. *Metropolitan Universities*, *18*(3), 28–45.

Berquist, W. H., & Pawlak, K. (2008). *Engaging the six cultures of the academy*. San Francisco: Jossey-Bass.

Bess, J. L., & Dee, J. R. (2014). *Bridging the divide between faculty and administration: A guide to understanding conflict in the academy*. New York: Routledge.

Black, J. S., & Gregersen, H. B. (2002). *Leading strategic change: Breaking through the brain barrier*. Upper Saddle River, NJ: Pearson Education.

Black, J. S., & Gregersen, H. B. (2013). *It starts with one: Changing individuals, changing organizations* (3rd ed.). Upper Saddle River, NJ: Pearson Education.

Black, S. A. (2015). Qualities of effective leadership in higher education. *Open Journal of Leadership*, *4*, 54–66.

Blake, R. R., & Mouton, J. S. (1994). *The managerial grid: Leadership styles for achieving production through people*. Houston: Gulf.

Blumenstyk, G. (2018a). The adult student: The population colleges—and the nation—can't afford to ignore. *The Chronicle of Higher Education*, 4–53.

Blumenstyk, G. (2018b, November 11). Meet the new mega-university: Can the fast-growing Southern New Hampshire U. transform higher education? *The Chronicle of Higher Education*. Retrieved from https://www.chronicle.com/article/Meet-the-New-Mega-University/245049.

Bolden, R., Petrov, G., & Gosling, J. (2009). Distributed leadership in higher education rhetoric and reality. *Educational Management Administration & Leadership*, *37*(2), 257–277.

Bolman, L. G., & Deal, T. E. (2013). *Reframing organizations: Artistry, choice and leadership* (5th ed.). San Francisco: Jossey-Bass.

Borden, V. M. (2004). Accommodating student swirl: When traditional students are no longer the tradition. *Change: The Magazine of Higher Learning*, *36*(2), 10–17.

Bornstein, R. (2014). Leadership legitimacy, managed authenticity, and emotional stability. In K. A. Longman & S. R. Madsen (Eds.), *Women & Leadership in Higher Education* (pp. 189–196). Charlotte, NC: Information Age.

Borrego, S. (2006). Mapping the learning environment. In R. P. Keeling (Ed.), *Learning reconsidered 2: A practical guide to implementing a campus-wide focus on the student experience* (pp. 11–16). Washington, DC: ACPA, ACUHOI, ACUI, NACADA, NACA, NASPA, NIRSA.

Bowen, W. G., & Tobin, E. M. (2015). *Locus of authority: The evolution of faculty roles in the governance of higher education* (Vol. 85). Princeton, NJ: Princeton University Press.

Boyer, E. L. (1990). *Scholarship reconsidered: Priorities of the professoriate*. Princeton, NJ: Princeton University Press.

Bradfield, R., Wright, G., Burt, G., Cairns, G., & Van Der Heijden, K. (2005). The origins and evolution of scenario techniques in long range business planning. *Futures*, *37*(8), 795–812.

Bragg, D. D., & Durham, B. (2012). Perspectives on access and equity in the era of (community) college completion. *Community College Review*, *40*(2), 106–125.

Bragg, D. D., Kirby, C., Witt, M. A., Richie, D., Mix, S., Feldbaum, M., & Mason, M. (2014). *Transformative change initiative*. Champaign, IL: Office of Community College Research and Leadership. Retrieved from https://eric.ed.gov/?id=ED558790.

Bransberger P., & Michelau, D. K. (2016, December). *Knocking at the college door: Projections of high school graduates*. Boulder, CO: Western Interstate Commission for Higher Education (WICHE). Retrieved from https://static1.squarespace.com/static/57f269e19de4bb8a69b470ae/t/58d2ebfc3e00be70a4278e16/1490217985173/Knocking2016ExecutiveSummaryFINAL.pdf.

Braxton, J. M., Bray, N. J., & Berger, J. B. (2000). Faculty teaching skills and their influence on the college student departure process. *Journal of College Student Development*, *41*(2), 215–226.

Bright, D. E., & Richards, M. P. (2001). *The academic deanship: Individual careers and institutional roles*. San Francisco: Jossey-Bass.

Brooks, D. (2019, January 2). New England College merger with N.H. Institute of Art is official. *Concord Monitor*. Retrieved from https://www.concordmonitor.com/NEC-New-England-College-Henniker-arts-22504707.

Brown, E. (2013). *The great man theory: Strengths and weakness of charismatic leadership*. Kindle Edition. Retrieved from https://www.amazon.com/Great-Man-Theory-Weaknesses-Charismatic-ebook/dp/B00HHN7P6K.

Brown, R. A., & Chard, D. J. (2018, August 7). Lessons learned from a college merger. *Inside Higher Ed*. Retrieved from https://www.insidehighered.com/views/2018/08/07/two-presidents-provide-lessons-their-merger-opinion.

Bryman, A. (2007). Effective leadership in higher education: A literature review. *Studies in Higher Education*, *32*(6), 693–710. doi:10.1080/03075070701685114.

Bryson, J. M. (2018). *Strategic planning for public and nonprofit organizations: A guide to strengthening and sustaining organizational achievement*. Hoboken, NJ: John Wiley & Sons.

Bukowski, S., & Michael, J. (2012). *Environmental scanning: Looking for strategic intelligence*. Retrieved from https://extension.psu.edu/environmental-scanning-looking-for-strategic-intelligence.

Buller, J. L. (2013). *Positive academic leadership: How to stop putting out fires and start making a difference*. New York: John Wiley & Sons.

Buller, J. L. (2014). *Change leadership in higher education: A practical guide to academic transformation*. New York: John Wiley & Sons.

Burns, J. M. (1978). *Leadership*. New York: Harper & Row.

Busta, H. (2018). *How many colleges and universities have closed since 2016?* Retrieved from https://www.educationdive.com/news/how-many-colleges-and-universities-have-closed-since-2016/539379/.

Butler, D., & Geis, F. L. (1990). Nonverbal affect responses to male and female leaders: Implications for leadership evaluations. *Journal of Personality and Social Psychology*, *58*(1), 48.

Campus Conflict Management Guidelines Committee. (2003). *Institutional and program level guidelines for conflict management in higher education*. Retrieved from http://campus-adr.org.

Carlson, S. (2009, April 17). Campus officials seek building efficiencies, one square foot at a time. *The Chronicle of Higher Education*. Retrieved from https://www.chronicle.com/article/Campus-Officials-Seek-Building/3292.

Carnevale, A. P., Strohl, J., Ridley, N., & Gulish, A. (2018). *Three educational pathways to good jobs: High school, middle skills, and bachelor's degree*. Washington, DC: Center on Education and the Workforce, Georgetown University.

Retrieved form https://1gyhoq479ufd3yna29x7ubjn-wpengine.netdna-ssl.com/wp-content/uploads/3ways-FR.pdf.

Carroll, J. B., & Wolverton, M. (2004, Summer). Who becomes a chair? [Electronic version]. *New Directions for Higher Education, 126*, 3–10.

Center for Community College Student Engagement (CCCSE). (n.d.). *Benchmark survey results: CCSSE respondents*. Retrieved from https://www.ccsse.org/survey/national3.cfm.

Chaffee, E. E. (1983). *Rational decision-making in higher education: An NCHEMS executive summary*. Boulder, CO: National Center for Higher Education Management Systems.

Charity Hudley, A. H., & Mallinson, C. (2010). *Understanding English language variation in U.S. schools*. New York: Teachers College Press Multicultural Education Series.

Cheldelin, S. I., & Lucas, A. F. (2004). *The Jossey-Bass academic administrator's guide to conflict resolution*. San Francisco: Jossey-Bass.

Chen, G. (2018, November 16). Post-recession cliff looms for community colleges. *Why Community College* (Community College Review). Retrieved from https://www.communitycollegereview.com/blog/post-recession-cliff-looms-for-community-colleges.

Chen, R., & DesJardins, S. L. (2010). Investigating the impact of financial aid on student dropout risks: Racial and ethnic differences. *The Journal of Higher Education, 81*(2), 179–208.

Chetty, R., Friedman, J. N., Saez, E., Turner, N., & Yagan, D. (2017). *Mobility report cards: The role of colleges in intergenerational mobility*. Stanford, CA: Equality of Opportunity Project. Retrieved from http://www.equality-of-opportunity.org/papers/coll_mrc_paper.pdf.

Chickering, A. W., & Gamson, Z. F. (1987). Seven principles for good practice in undergraduate education. *AAHE Bulletin, 3*, 3–7.

Christensen, C. M., Horn, M. B., Caldera, L., & Soares, L. (2011). *Disrupting college: How disruptive innovation can deliver quality and affordability to postsecondary education*. Boston: Center for American Progress.

Clark, B. R. (1972). The organizational saga in higher education. *Administrative Science Quarterly, 17*(2), 178–184.

Clark, S. C. (2000). Work/family border theory: A new theory of work/family balance. *Human Relations, 53*(6), 747–770.

Cockell, J., & McArthur-Blair, J. (2012). *Appreciative inquiry in higher education: A transformative force*. San Francisco: Jossey-Bass.

Coffman, J. R. (2005). *Work and peace in academe: Leveraging time, money, and intellectual energy through managing conflict*. Bolton, MA: Anker.

Cohn, D., & Caumont, A. (2016, March 31). *Ten demographic trends that are shaping the U.S. and the world.* Washington, DC: Fact Tank, Pew Research Center. Retrieved from http://www.pewresearch.org/fact-tank/2016/03/31/10-demographic-trends-that-are-shaping-the-u-s-and-the-world/.

Coleman, J. S. (1988). Social capital in the creation of human capital. *The American Journal of Sociology, 94*, S95.

Conger, J. A., & Kanungo, R. N. (1987). Toward a behavioral theory of charismatic leadership in organizational settings. *Academy of Management Review, 12*(4), 637–647.

Cooperrider, D. L. (n.d.). *What is appreciative inquiry?* Retrieved from http://www.davidcooperrider.com/ai-process/.

Cooperrider, D. L., Whitney, D. D., & Stavros, J. M. (2008). *The appreciative inquiry handbook: For leaders of change*. Brunswick, OH: Crown.

Cox, M. D. (2004). Introduction to faculty learning communities. *New Directions for Teaching and Learning, 2004*(97), 5–23.

Credly. (2018, August 22). The future of human capital management: How organizations benefit from issuing digital credentials. *Credly Blog*. Retrieved from https://credly.com/blog/post/hcm-white-paper-organizations.

Crowe, C. (2018, December). "Culture of indifference" and "institutional protection" at Michigan State stymied investigation of Larry Nassar. *The Chronicle of Higher Education*. Retrieved from https://www.chronicle.com/article/Culture-of-Indifference-/245379.

Cyert, R. M., & March, J. G. (1963). *A behavioral theory of the firm*. Englewood Cliffs, NJ: Prentice-Hall.

Dane, E., & Pratt, M. G. (2007). Exploring intuition and its role in managerial decision making. *Academy of Management Review, 32*(1), 33–54.

Daniels, H. (2011). The shaping of communication across boundaries. *International Journal of Educational Research, 50*(1), 40–47.

Day, D. V., & Antonakis, J. (2012). *The nature of leadership* (2nd ed.). Thousand Oaks, CA: Sage.

Deetz, S., & Simpson, J. (2003). Critical organizational dialogue: Open formation and the demand for "otherness." In R. Anderson, L. A. Baxter, & K. N. Cissna (Eds.), *Dialogue: Theorizing difference in community studies* (pp. 141–158). Thousand Oaks, CA: Sage.

DeZure, D., Shaw, A., & Rojewski, J. (2014). Cultivating the next generation of academic leaders: Implications for administrators and faculty. *Change*, Jan./Feb., 6–12.

Díaz-Gibson, J., Zaragoza, M. C., Daly, A. J., Mayayo, J. L., & Romani, J. R. (2017). Networked leadership in educational collaborative networks. *Educational Management Administration & Leadership*, 45(6), 1040–1059.

Diaz-Saenz, H. R. (2011). Transformational leadership. In A. Bryman, D. Collinson, K. Grint, B. Jackson & M. Uhl-Bien (Eds.). *The Sage handbook of leadership* (pp. 37–50). Thousand Oaks, CA: Sage.

Dickey, J. (2016, May 16). Revolution on America's campuses. *Time*. Retrieved from http://time.com/4347099/college-campus-protests/.

Dinh, J. E., Lord, R. G., Gardner, W. L., Meuser, J. D., Liden, R. C., & Hu, J. (2014). Leadership theory and research in the new millennium: Current theoretical trends and changing perspectives. *Leadership Quarterly*, *25*(1), 36–62.

Donahue, W. A., & Kolt, R. (1992). *Managing interpersonal conflict*. Newbury Park, CA: Sage.

Dooris, M. J., Kelley, J. M., & Trainer, J. F. (2004). Strategic planning in higher education. *New Directions for Institutional Research*, *2004*(123), 5–11.

Dougherty, K. J., & Townsend, B. K. (2006). Community college missions: A theoretical and historical perspective. *New Directions for Community Colleges*, *2006*(136), 5–13.

Drake, J. K. (2011). The role of academic advising in student retention and persistence. *About Campus*, *16*(3), 8–12.

Duffy, F. M. (2008). Strategic communication during times of great change. *School Administrator*, *65*(4), 22–25.

EAB. (n.d.). *What we do*. Retrieved from https://www.eab.com/.

Eagly, A. H., Johannesen-Schmidt, M. C., & Van Engen, M. L. (2003). Transformational, transactional, and laissez-faire leadership styles: A meta-analysis comparing women and men. *Psychological Bulletin*, *129*(4), 569–591.

Eagly, A. H., & Johnson, B. T. (1990). Gender and leadership style: A meta-analysis. *Psychological Bulletin*, *108*(2), 233.

Earley, P. C. (2002). Redefining interactions across cultures and organizations: Moving forward with cultural intelligence. *Research in Organizational Behavior*, *24*, 271–299.

Earley, P. C., & Mosakowski, E. (2004, October). Cultural intelligence. *Harvard Business Review*, *82*(10), 139–146.

Eckel, P. D., & Kezar, A. (2003). *Taking the reins: Institutional transformation in higher education*. Westport, CT: American Council on Education and Praeger.

Eddy, P. L. (2003). Sensemaking on campus: How community college presidents frame change. *Community College Journal of Research and Practice*, *27*(6), 453–471.

Eddy, P. L. (2010). *Community college leadership: A multidimensional model for leading change*. Sterling, VA: Stylus.

Eddy, P. L., & Amey, M. (2014). *Creating strategic partnerships: A guide for educational institutions and their partners*. Sterling, VA: Stylus.

Eddy, P. L., Barber, J. P., Holly, N., Brush, K., Bohon, L., & Green, M. F. (2013). Internationalizing a campus: From colonial to modern times. *Change: The Magazine of Higher Learning*, *45*(6), 43–50.

Eddy, P. L., & Garza Mitchell, R. L. (2017). Preparing community college leaders to meet tomorrow's challenges. *Journal for the Study of Postsecondary and Tertiary Education*, 2, 127–145. doi:10.28945/3884.

Eddy, P. L., Garza Mitchell, R., & Amey, M. J. (2016, December 2). Leading from the middle. *The Chronicle of Higher Education*, *68*(15), A48.

Eddy, P. L., Hao, Y., Markiewicz, C., & Iverson, E. (2018). Faculty change agents as adult learners: The power of situated learning. *Community College Journal of Research and Practice*, *43*(8), 539–555. Retrieved from https://doi.org/10.1080/10668926.2018.1507848.

Eddy, P. L., Hartman, C., & Liu, E. (2020). Gender differences in team leadership. In G. Boggs & C. McPhail (Eds.), *Community college team leadership* (pp. 19–40). Sterling, VA: Stylus.

Eddy, P. L., Sydow, D., Alfred, R., & Garza Mitchell, R. (2015). *Developing tomorrow's leaders: Context, challenge, and capacities*. Lanham, MD: Rowman & Littlefield.

Editorial note: Revised definition of "organizational ombuds." (2013, February 1). *The Ombuds Blog*. Retrieved from https://ombuds-blog.blogspot.com/2013/02/editorial-note-revised-definition-of.html.

Ekowa, M., & Palmer, I. (2017, March). *Predictive analytics in higher education: Five guiding practices for ethical use*. Washington, DC: New America. Retrieved from https://na-production.s3.amazonaws.com/documents/Predictive-Analytics-GuidingPractices.pdf.

Ellerbe, L. (2018, December). *Access and equity in an age of completions: Community college course taking patterns that predict vertical transfer*. Unpublished doctoral dissertation, College of William & Mary, Williamsburg, VA.

Elrod, R., & Mielish, J. (2018). Strategic partnerships: Thinking outside the administrative box. *Community College Journal of Research & Practice*, 42, 617–622.

Engleberg, I. N., & Wynn, D. R. (2007). *Working in groups: Communication principles and strategies*. Boston: Allyn & Bacon.

Englehardt, E. E., Pritchard, M. S., Romesburg, K. D., & Schrag, B. (Eds.). (2014). *The ethical challenges of academic administration*. New York: Springer.

Ernst & Young. (2016). *Strength in numbers: Strategies for collaborating in a new era for higher education*. Retrieved from https://cdn.ey.com/parthenon/pdf/perspectives/P-EY_Strength-in-Numbers-Collaboration-Strategies_Paper_Final_082016.pdf.

Eunson, B. (2007). *Conflict management*. Milton: John Wiley & Sons Australia.

Fairhurst, G. T. (2001). Dualisms in leadership research. In F. M. Jablin & L. L. Putnam (Eds.), *The new handbook of organizational communication: Advances in theory, research and methods* (pp. 349–439). Thousand Oaks, CA: Sage.

Fairhurst, G. T. (2011). *The power of framing: Creating the language of leadership*. San Francisco: Jossey-Bass.

Fairhurst, G. T., & Sarr, R. (1996). *The art of framing*. San Francisco: Jossey-Bass.

Fairweather, J. S. (2002). The mythologies of faculty productivity: Implications for institutional policy and decision making. *The Journal of Higher Education*, *73*(1), 26–48.

Fairweather, J. S. (2005). Beyond the rhetoric: Trends in the relative value of teaching and research in faculty salaries. *The Journal of Higher Education*, *76*, 401–422.

Felton, L. (2018, January 17). How colleges foretold the #MeToo movement. *The Atlantic*. Retrieved from https://www.theatlantic.com/education/archive/2018/01/how-colleges-foretold-the-metoo-movement/550613/.

Ferguson, R. (2012). Learning analytics: drivers, developments and challenges. *International Journal of Technology Enhanced Learning*, *4*(5/6), 304–317.

Fiedler, F. E. (1967). *A theory of leadership effectiveness*. New York: McGraw-Hill.

Fiedler, F. E., & Chemers, M. M. (1974). *Leadership and effective management*. Harlow, UK: Longman Higher Education.

Fiedler, F. E., & Chemers, M. M. (1984). *Improving leadership effectiveness: The leader match concept* (2nd ed.). New York: Wiley.

Finger, G., & Lee, M. (2014). Leadership and reshaping schooling in a networked world. *Education Sciences*, *4*(1), 64–86.

Fishman, B., Teasley, S., & Cederquist, S. (2018). *Micro-credentials as evidence of college readiness: Report of an NSF workshop*. Ann Arbor: University of Michigan. http://hdl.handle.net/2027.42/143851.

Floyd, A., & Fung, D. (2017). Focusing the kaleidoscope: Exploring distributed leadership in an English university. *Studies in Higher Education*, *42*(8), 1488–1503.

Follett, M. P. (1924). *Creative experience*. New York: Longmans, Green. Retrieved from https://pqm-online.com/assets/files/lib/books/follett.pdf.

Forcier, M. F. (2011). Innovation through collaboration: New pathways to success. *Trusteeship*, *19*(5), 8–12.

Fortunato, J. A., Gigliotti, R. A., & Ruben, B. D. (2017). Racial incidents at the University of Missouri: The value of leadership communication and stakeholder relationships. *International Journal of Business Communication*, *54*(2), 199–209. doi:10.1177/2329488416687056.

Fowler, F. (2013). *Policy studies for educational leaders: An introduction* (4th ed.). Boston: Pearson.

Friedel, J. N., Thornton, Z. M., D'Amico, M. M., & Katsinas, S. G. (2013). *Performance-based funding: The national landscape*. Tuscaloosa: University of Alabama Educational Policy Center.

Frost, R. A., Strom, S. L., Downey, J., Schultz, D. D., & Holland, T. A. (2010). Enhancing student learning with academic and student affairs collaboration. *The Community College Enterprise, 16*(1), 37.

Furlong, G. (2010). *The conflict resolution toolbox: Models and maps for analyzing, diagnosing and resolving conflict*. Mississauga, ON: John Wiley & Sons Canada.

Gagliardi, J. S., Espinosa, L. L., Turk, J. M., & Taylor, M. (2017). *American college president study 2017*. Washington, DC: American Council on Education.

Gallagher, S. R. (2018, December). *Educational credentials come of age: A survey on the use and value of educational credentials in hiring*. Chicago: Northeastern University, Center for the Future of Higher Education and Talent Strategy. Retrieved from https://www.northeastern.edu/cfhets/wp-content/uploads/2018/12/Educational_Credentials_Come_of_Age_2018.pdf.

Gardner, H. (1983). *Frames of mind*. New York: Basic Books.

Gardner, L. (2017, June 19). Georgia's mergers offer lessons, and cautions, to other states. *The Chronicle of Higher Education*. Retrieved from https://www.chronicle.com/article/Georgia-s-Mergers-Offer/240390.

George, J. M. (2000). Emotions and leadership: The role of emotional intelligence. *Human Relations, 53*(8), 1027–1055.

Gianacola, J. K., Grawitch, M. J. & Borchert, D. (2009). Dealing with the stress of college: A model for adult students. *Adult Education Quarterly*, 59, 246–263.

Ginsberg, B. (2011). *The fall of the faculty*. Oxford: Oxford University Press.

Giri, V. (2009). Nonverbal communication theories. In S. W. Littlejohn & K. A. Foss (Eds.), *Encyclopedia of communication theory* (Vol. 1, pp. 691–694). Thousand Oaks, CA: Sage. doi:10.4135/9781412959384.n262.

Gladwell, M. (2007). *Blink: The power of thinking without thinking*. New York: Back Bay Books.

Glass, C. R., Gesing, P., Hales, A., & Cong, C. (2017). Faculty as bridges to co-curricular engagement and community for first-generation international students. *Studies in Higher Education*, 42, 895–910.

Gmelch, W. (2004, Summer). The department chair's balancing act. [Electronic version]. *New Direction for Higher Education, 2004*(126), 69–84.

Goldman, C. A., & Salem, H. (2015). *Getting the most out of university strategic planning: Essential guidance for success and obstacles to avoid*. Santa Monica, CA: Rand Corporation. Retrieved from https://www.rand.org/pubs/perspectives/PE157.html.

Goleman, D. (1995). *Emotional intelligence*. New York: Bantam Books.

Goleman, D. (2000, March–April). *Leadership that gets results*. Boston: Harvard Business Review.

Goleman, D. (2005). *Social intelligence: The revolutionary new science of human relationships*. New York: Bantam Books.

Granovetter, M. (1983). Strength of weak ties: A network theory revisited. *Sociological Theory*, *1*, 201–233.

Halpin, A. W. & Winer, B. J. (1957). A factorial study of the leader behavior descriptions. In R. M. Stogdill & A. E. Coons (Eds.), *Leader behavior: Its description and measurement*. Columbus: Bureau of Business Research, Ohio State University.

Hambrick, D. C. (1982). Environmental scanning and organizational strategy. *Strategic Management Journal*, *3*(2), 159–174.

Hamel, G., & Breen, B. (2007). *The future of management*. Boston: Harvard Business School Press.

Hanover Research. (2013, July). *Strategic planning in higher education-best practices and benchmarking*. Academy Administration Practice. Washington, DC: Author.

Hansen, C. (2018, July 20). More than 100 Ohio State alumni allege abuse by former university sports doctor. *The Chronicle of Higher Education*. Retrieved from https://www.chronicle.com/article/More-Than-100-Ohio-State/243979.

Harvard Business Review. (2014). *Running meetings (20-minute manager series)*. Boston: Harvard Business Review Press.

Hearn, J. C., & McLendon, M. K. (2012). Governance research from adolescence to maturity. In M. Bastedo (Ed.), *The organization of higher education managing colleges for a new era* (pp. 45–85). Baltimore: John Hopkins University Press.

Heckman, J. J., & LaFontaine, P. A. (2010). The American high school graduation rate: Trends and levels. *The Review of Economics and Statistics*, 92(2), 244–262.

Heifetz, R. (1994). *Leadership without easy answers*. Cambridge, MA: Harvard University University Press.

Heimans, J., & Timms, H. (2014). Understanding "new power." *Harvard Business Review*, *92*(12), 48–56.

Helgesen, S. (2005). *The web of inclusion: Architecture for building great organizations*. Frederick, MD: Beard Books.

Herold, D. M., & Fedor, D. B. (2008). *Change the way you lead change: Leadership strategies that really work*. Stanford, CA: Stanford University Press.

Hickman, G. R. (2010). *Leading change in multiple contexts: Concepts and practices in organizational, community, political, social, and global change settings*. Thousand Oaks, CA: Sage.

Hickman, G. R., & Couto, R. A. (2006). Causality, change, and leadership. In G. R. Goethals (Ed.), *The quest for a general theory of leadership* (pp. 152–187). Cheltenham, UK: Edward Elgar.

Higher Education Research Institute. (2016, February 10). *College students' commitment to activism, political and civic engagement reach all-time highs*. Retrieved from http://newsroom.ucla.edu/releases/college-students-commitment-to-activism-political-and-civic-engagement-reach-all-time-highs.

Hill, S. (n.d.). *The history of enrollment management: Part one*. Louisville, KY: Capture Higher Ed.

Hillman, N. W., Tandberg, D. A., & Fryar, A. H. (2015). Evaluating the impacts of "new" performance funding in higher education. *Educational Evaluation and Policy Analysis*, *37*(4), 501–519.

Hinton, K. E. (2012). *A practical guide to strategic planning in higher education*. Ann Arbor, MI: Society for College and University Planning.

Hofstede, G. (1998). Attitudes, values and organizational culture: Disentangling the concepts. *Organization Studies*, *19*(3), 477–493.

Holton, S. A. (1998). *Mending the cracks in the ivory tower: Strategies for conflict management in higher education*. Bolton, MA: Anker.

Hoover, E., & Supiano, B. (2016, December 6). A population in flux forces colleges to adapt. *Chronicle of Higher Education*. Retrieved from https://www.chronicle.com/article/A-Population-in-Flux-Forces/238583.

Hora, M. T., & Millar, S. B. (2011). *A guide to building education partnerships: Navigating diverse cultural contexts to turn challenge into promise*. Sterling, VA: Stylus.

House, R. J. (1977). A 1976 theory of charismatic leadership. In J. G. Hunt & L. L. Larson (Eds.), *Leadership: The cutting edge*. Carbondale: University of Southern Illinois Press.

Hrabowski, F. A., Bitsóí, L., Gordon, E. T., Harper, S. R., Sáenz, V. B., & Teranishi, R. T. (2014). *Men of color in higher education: New foundations for developing models for success*. Sterling, VA: Stylus.

Huber, G. P. (1991). Organizational learning: The contributing processes and the literatures. *Organization Science*, *2*(1), 88–115.

Hyde, K. (2018, November 9). Changing the culture around collecting and using education data. *Capture Higher Ed*. Retrieved from https://capturehighered.com/predictive-modeling/changing-culture-around-education-data/.

Hymes, D. (1974). *Foundations in sociolinguistics: An ethnographic approach*. Philadelphia: University of Pennsylvania Press.

Institute of International Education. (2017). *Open Doors report on international educational exchange 2017*. New York: Author.

International Institute for Education Planning. (2010). *Strategic planning: Concept and rationale*. New York: Author. Retrieved from http://www.iiep.unesco.org/sites/default/files/wp1_sp.pdf.

International Ombudsman Association. (n.d.). *IOA code of ethics*. Retrieved from https://www.ombudsassociation.org/assets/docs/Code_Ethics_1-07.pdf.

Izadi, E. (2015, November 9). The incidents that led to the University of Missouri president's resignation. *The Washington Post*. Retrieved from https://www.washingtonpost.com/news/grade-point/wp/2015/11/09/the-incidents-that-led-to-the-university-of-missouri-presidents-resignation/?utm_term=.bofaf8cc1571.

Jablin, F. M., & Putnam, L. L. (2001). *The new handbook of organizational communication: Advances in theory, research, and methods*. Thousand Oaks, CA: Sage.

Jenkins, P. D., Lahr, H. E., Fink, J., & Ganga, E. C. (2018). *What we are learning about guided pathways*. New York: Community College Research Center, Teachers College, Columbia University.

Johnson, C. (2007). *The role of social capital in creating sustainable partnerships*. Unpublished doctoral dissertation, Central Michigan University, Mt. Pleasant, MI.

Johnson, N. (2016, June). *Aligning student and institution incentives in higher education finance*. Indianapolis: Lumina Foundation.

Jones, J. M. (2018, October 9). Confidence in higher education down since 2015. *Gallop Blog*. Retrieved from https://news.gallup.com/opinion/gallup/242441/confidence-higher-education-down-2015.aspx.

Kantor, J., & Twohey, M. (2017, October 7). Harvey Weinstein paid off sexual harassment accusers for decades. *The New York Times*. Retrieved from https://www.nytimes.com/2017/10/05/us/harvey-weinstein-harassment-allegations.html.

Kaplin, W. A., & Lee, B. A. (2007). *The law of higher education* (4th ed.). San Francisco: John Wiley & Sons.

Katz, D., & Kahn, R. L. (1952). Some recent findings in human relations research in industry. In G. E. Swanson, T. M. Newcomb, & E. Hartley (Eds.), *Readings in social psychology* (pp. 650–665). New York: Holt.

Keashly, L., & Neuman, J. H. (2010). Faculty experiences with bullying in higher education: Causes, consequences, and management. *Administrative Theory & Praxis*, *32*(1), 48–70.

Keller, G. (1983). *Academic strategy: The management revolution in American higher education*. Baltimore: Johns Hopkins University Press.

Kellerman, B. (1984). *Leadership: Multidisciplinary perspectives*. Englewood Cliffs, NJ: Prentice-Hall.

Kellermanns, F. W., Walter, J., Floyd, S. W., Lechner, C., & Shaw, J. C. (2011). To agree or not to agree? A meta-analytical review of strategic consensus and organizational performance. *Journal of Business Research*, *64*(2), 126–133.

Kerr, R., Garvin, J., Heaton, N., & Boyle, E. (2006). Emotional intelligence and leadership effectiveness. *Leadership & Organization Development Journal*, *27*(4), 265–279.

Kezar, A. J. (2009). *Rethinking leadership in a complex, multicultural, and global environment: New concepts and models for higher education*. Sterling, VA: Stylus.

Kezar, A. J. (2014). *How colleges change: Understanding, leading, and enacting change*. New York: Routledge.

Kezar, A. J., & Carducci, R. (2009). Revolutionizing leadership development: Lessons from research and theory. In A. J. Kezar (Ed.), *Rethinking leadership in a complex, multicultural, and global environment* (pp. 1–38). Sterling, VA: Stylus.

Kezar, A. J., & Gehrke, S. (2014). Why are we hiring so many non-tenure-track faculty? *Liberal Education*, *100*(1), 44–51.

Kezar, A. J., & Holcombe, E. M. (2017). *Shared leadership in higher education*. Washington, DC: American Council on Education.

Kezar, A. J., & Maxey. D. (2012). *The Delphi Project on the changing faculty and student success*. Los Angeles: USC Rossier School of Education, Pullias Center for Higher Education.

Kezar, A. J., & Sam, C. (2010). Understanding the new majority: Contingent faculty in higher education. *ASHE Higher Education Report Series*, *36*(4).

Kilmann, R. H. (n.d.). *A brief history of the Thomas-Kilmann Conflict Mode Instrument*. Retrieved from https://kilmanndiagnostics.com/a-brief-history-of-the-thomas-kilmann-conflict-mode-instrument/.

Kilmann Diagnostics. (n.d.). *An overview of the Thomas-Kilmann Conflict Mode Instrument (TKI)*. Retrieved from https://kilmanndiagnostics.com/overview-thomas-kilmann-conflict-mode-instrument-tki/.

Kim, J. H. (2018). Asset specificity and firm value: Evidence from mergers. *Journal of Corporate Finance*, *48*, 375–412.

Kinzie, J., & Kuh, G. D. (2004). Going DEEP: Learning from campuses that share responsibility for student success. *About Campus*, *9*(5), 2–8.

Klofstad, C. A., Anderson, R. C., & Nowicki, S. (2015). Perceptions of competence, strength, and age influence voters to select leaders with lower-pitched voices. *PloS One*, *10*(8), e0133779. Retrieved from https://journals.plos.org/plosone/article?id=10.1371/journal.pone.0133779.

Knowles, M. S. (1980). *The modern practice of adult education: From pedagogy to andragogy* (Revised and updated). Englewood Cliffs, NJ: Cambridge Adult Education.

Korn, M. (2018, July 14). To recruit students, colleges turn to corporate-marketing playbook. *Wall Street Journal*. Retrieved from https://www.wsj.com/articles/to-recruit-students-colleges-turn-to-corporate-marketing-playbook-1531569600.

Kotter, J. P. (2008). *A sense of urgency*. Boston: Harvard Business Press.

Kotter, J. P. (2014). *Accelerate: Building strategic agility for a faster-moving world.* Boston: Harvard Business Review Press.

Kouzes, J. M., & Posner, B. Z. (2010). *The leadership challenge activity book.* San Francisco: Pfeiffer/Wiley.

Kouzes, J. M., & Posner, B. Z. (2011). Leadership is a relationship. In J. M. Kouzes & B. Z. Posner (Eds.), *Credibility* (pp. 1–21). Hoboken, NJ: John Wiley & Sons. doi:10.1002/9781118983867.

Kuh, G. D. (2003). What we're learning about student engagement from NSSE: Benchmarks for effective educational practices. *Change: The Magazine of Higher Learning, 35*(2), 24–32.

Kuh, G. D. (2008). *High-impact educational practices: A brief overview.* Washington, DC: Association of American Colleges & Universities. Retrieved from http://www.aacu. org/leap/hip.

Kuh, G. D. (2009). What student affairs professionals need to know about student engagement. *Journal of College Student Development, 50*, 683–706.

Kuhnert, K. W., & Lewis, P. (1987). Transactional and transformational leadership: A constructive/developmental analysis. *Academy of Management Review, 12*(4), 648–657.

Labrecque, L. I., Markos, E., & Milne, G. R. (2011). Online personal branding: Processes, challenges, and implications. *Journal of Interactive Marketing, 25*(1), 37–50.

Lambert, M. T. (2014). *Privatization and the public good: Public universities in the balance.* Boston: Harvard Education Press.

Lattuca, L. R., & Stark, J. S. (2009). *Shaping the college curriculum: Academic plans in context* (2nd ed.). San Francisco: Jossey-Bass.

Lederman, D. (2018, March 9). Leading in turbulent times: A survey of presidents. *Inside Higher Ed.* Retrieved from https://www.insidehighered.com/news/survey/survey-college-presidents-finds-worry-about-public-attitudes-confidence-finances.

Leisyte, L., & Dee, J. R. (2012). Understanding academic work in a changing institutional environment. In J. C. Smart & M. B. Paulsen (Eds.), *Higher education: Handbook of theory and research* (pp. 123–206). Dordrecht: Springer.

Leslie, D. (2014). "Orthogonality" in learning and assessment. In P. L. Eddy (Ed.), *Connecting learning across the institution.* New Directions for Higher Education, no. 165 (pp. 41–50). San Francisco: Jossey-Bass. doi:10.1002/he.20082.

Lester, J. (2009). Not your child's playground: Workplace bullying among community college faculty. *Community College Journal of Research and Practice, 33*(5), 444–462.

Lewin, K. (1947). Frontiers in group dynamics: Concept, method and reality in social science; equilibrium and social change. *Human Relations, 1*(1), 5–41.

Lewin, K., Lippitt, R., & White, R. K. (1939). Patterns of aggressive behavior in experimentally created "social climates." *Journal of Social Psychology, 10*, 271–299.

Linderman, D., & Kolenovic, Z. (2013). Moving the completion needle at community colleges: CUNY's Accelerated Study in Associate Programs (ASAP). *Change: The Magazine of Higher Learning, 45*(5), 43–50.

Lipman-Blumen, J. (1996). *The connective edge: Leading in an interdependent world.* New York: John Wiley & Sons.

Lipman-Blumen, J. (2000). *Connective leadership: Managing in a changing world.* Oxford: Oxford University Press.

Lister, M. C. (2015). Gamification: The effect on student motivation and performance at the post-secondary level. *Issues and Trends in Educational Technology, 3*(2), 1–22.

Livermore, D. (2015). *Leading with cultural intelligence: The real secret to success* (2nd ed.). New York: American Management Association.

Livermore, D., & Van Dyne, L. (2015). *Cultural intelligence: The essential intelligence for the 21st century.* SHRM Foundation's Effective Practice Guidelines Series. Alexandria, VA: Society for Human Resource Management.

Long, J., Johnson, C., Faught, S., & Street, J. (2013). The need to practice what we teach: Succession management in higher education. *American Journal of Management, 13*(2), 73–78.

Lord, R. G., De Vader, C. L., & Alliger, G. M. (1986). A meta-analysis of the relation between personality traits and leadership perceptions: An application of validity generalization procedures. *Journal of Applied Psychology, 71*(3), 402–410.

Lowe, K. B., Kroeck, K. G., & Sivasubramaniam, N. (1996). Effectiveness correlates of transformational and transactional leadership: A meta-analytic review of the MLQ literature. *Leadership Quarterly, 7*(3), 385–425.

Lucey, C. A. (2002). Civic engagement, shared governance, and community colleges. *Academe, 88*(4), 27.

Lumina Foundation. (2015a, May). *Connecting credentials: A beta credentials framework; Building a system for communicating about and connecting diverse credentials.* Indianapolis: Author.

Lumina Foundation. (2015b, June). *Connecting credentials: Making the case for reforming the U.S. credentialing system.* Indianapolis: Author.

Lunenberg, F. C., & Ornstein, A. C. (2012). *Educational administration: Concepts and practices* (6th ed.). Belmont, CA: Wadsworth.

Ma, J., Pender, M., & Welch, M. (2016). *Education pays 2016: The benefits of higher education for individuals and society* (Trends in Higher Education). Washington, DC: College Board. Retrieved from https://trends.collegeboard.org/sites/default/files/education-pays-2016-full-report.pdf.

MacArthur Foundation. (n.d.). *Digital badges*. Retrieved from https://www.macfound.org/programs/digital-badges/.

Major, C. H. (2015). *Teaching online: A guide to theory, research, and practice*. Baltimore: Johns Hopkins University Press.

Malcom-Piqueux, L., & Bensimon, E. M. (2017). Taking equity-minded action to close equity gaps. *Peer Review, 19*(2), 5.

Maliszewski, C., Crabill, K., & Nespoli, L. (2012). The role of presidential leadership in improving New Jersey's community college transfer experience. *New Directions for Community Colleges, 160*, 69–78.

Marcus, J. (2017, December). *University enrollment decline continues into sixth straight year*. Retrieved from https://hechingerreport.org/university-enrollment-decline-continues-into-sixth-straight-year/.

McBain, L. (2009). *College and university mergers: Recent trends* (Policy matters: A higher education policy brief). Washington, DC: American Association of State Colleges and Universities.

McCarthy, P., & Mayhew, C. (2004). *Safeguarding the organization against violence and bullying: An international perspective*. New York: Palgrave Macmillan.

McCleskey, J. A. (2014). Situational, transformational, and transactional leadership and leadership development. *Journal of Business Studies Quarterly, 5*(4), 117–130.

McKenzie, L. (2018, October 19). Next for SNHU: Game-based learning and digital badges for middle schoolers. *Inside Higher Ed*. Retrieved from https://www.insidehighered.com/digital-learning/article/2018/10/19/acquisition-snhu-seeks-pathway-between-k-12-college-and-work.

McMurtrie, B. (2018, August 12). How artificial intelligence is changing teaching. *The Chronicle of Higher Education*. Retrieved from https://www.chronicle.com/article/How-Artificial-Intelligence-Is/244231.

McPhail, C. (2016). From tall to matrix: Redefining organizational structures. *Change: The Magazine of Higher Learning, 48*(4), 55–62.

Mehaffy, G. L. (2018). Student success: It's not just for students. *Change: The Magazine of Higher Learning, 50*(2), 8–14.

Merisotis, J. (2018, September 28). The future of learning and work: Making sure that all learning counts. *News & Views* (Lumina Foundation). Retrieved from Luminafoundation.org.

Meyerhofer, K. (2018, June 30). UW system merger approved: Here's when the official transfer takes place. *News Republic*. Retrieved from https://www.wiscnews.com/baraboonewsrepublic/news/state-and-regional/uw-system-merger-approved-here-s-when-the-official-transfer/article_782bfa40-a618-5c9d-a557-9974cab32159.html.

Mintz, S. (2014, November 19). Next generation online learning. *Inside Higher Ed*. Retrieved from https://www.insidehighered.com/blogs/higher-ed-gamma/next-generation-online-learning.

Mintzberg, H. (1994). The fall and rise of strategic planning. *Harvard Business Review*, *72*(1), 107–114.

Monge, P. R., & Contractor, N. S. (2001). Emergence of communication networks. In F. M. Jablin & L. L. Putnam (Eds.), *The new handbook of organizational communication: Advances in theory, research, and methods* (pp. 440–502). Thousand Oaks, CA: Sage.

Moody's Investors Service. (2017, December 5). *Moody's: US higher education sector outlook revised to negative as revenue growth prospects soften* (Announcement). Retrieved from https://www.moodys.com/research/Moodys-US-higher-education-sector-outlook-revised-to-negative-as--PR_376587.

Moore, C. W. (2014). *The mediation process: Practical strategies for resolving conflict*. Hoboken, NJ: John Wiley & Sons.

Moran, M., Seaman, J., & Tinti-Kane, H. (2011). *Teaching, learning, and sharing: How today's higher education faculty use social media*. Boston: Pearson, Babson Survey Research Group. Retrieved from http://files.eric.ed.gov/fulltext/ED535130.pdf.

Morgan, G. (2006). *Images of organization*. Thousand Oaks, CA: Sage.

Mrig, A., & Sanaghan, P. (2017). *The skills future higher education leaders need to succeed*. Denver, CO: Academic Impressions. Retrieved from https://www.academicimpressions.com/PDF/future-skillset.pdf.

Mullin, C. M. (2012). Student success: Institutional and individual perspectives. *Community College Review*, *40*(2), 126–144.

Nadworny, E., & Depenbrock, J. (2018, September 4). *Today's college students aren't who you think they are*. Retrieved from https://www.npr.org/sections/ed/2018/09/04/638561407/todays-college-students-arent-who-you-think-they-are.

National Center for Education Statistics (NCES). (2017). *Digest of education statistics*. Washington, DC: Author.

National Student Clearinghouse Research Center. (2018, Spring). *Term enrollment estimates*. Retrieved from https://nscresearchcenter.org/wp-content/uploads/CurrentTermEnrollment-Spring2018.pdf.

National Survey of Student Engagement (NSSE). (n.d.). *The college student report*. Retrieved from http://nsse.indiana.edu/html/about.cfm.

Nesheim, B. E., Guentzel, M. J., Kellogg, A. H., McDonald, W. M., Wells, C. A., & Whitt, E. J. (2007). Outcomes for students of student affairs-academic affairs partnership programs. *Journal of College Student Development*, *48*(4), 435–454.

Neumann, A. (1995). On the making of hard times and good times. *The Journal of Higher Education*, *66*(1), 3–31.

Nippert-Eng, C. E. (1996). *Home and work: Negotiating boundaries through everyday life*. Chicago: University of Chicago Press.

Northouse, P. G. (2015). *Leadership: Theory and practice* (6th ed.). Thousand Oaks, CA: Sage.

Nussbaum, M. C. (2000). *Women and human development: The capabilities approach*. Cambridge: Cambridge University Press.

Nussbaum, M. C. (2011). *Creating capabilities: The human development approach*. Cambridge, MA: Harvard University Press.

Olson, G. (2009, July 23). Exactly what is "shared governance"? *The Chronicle of Higher Education*. Retrieved from https://www.chronicle.com/article/Exactly-What-Is-Shared/47065.

O'Meara, K., & Bloomgarden, A. (2011). The pursuit of prestige: The experience of institutional striving from a faculty perspective. *Journal of the Professoriate*, *4*(1), 39–73.

On-ramps and off-ramps: Alternative credentials and emerging pathways between education and work. (2018, September 19). *Inside Higher Ed*. Retrieved from https://www.insidehighered.com/content/alternative-credentials-and-emerging-pathways-between-education-and-work.

Overton, A. R., & Lowry, A. C. (2013). Conflict management: Difficult conversations with difficult people. *Clinics in Colon and Rectal Surgery*, *26*(4), 259–264. Retrieved from https://doi.org/10.1055/s-0033-1356728.

Pascarella, E. T., Pierson, C. T., Wolniak, G. C., & Terenzini, P. T. (2004). First-generation college students: Additional evidence on college experiences and outcomes. *The Journal of Higher Education*, *75*, 249–284.

Patrick, S., & Sturgis, C. (2017, June 2). *Webinar: Overview of K–12 competency-based education* [PowerPoint slides]. Retrieved from http://www.ncsl.org/Portals/1/Documents/educ/NCSLOverview_K-12Competency_31394.pdf.

Payne, W. L. (1985). *A study of emotion: Developing emotional intelligence, self-integration, relating to fear, pain and desire*. Unpublished doctoral dissertation, Union Institute, Cincinnati, OH.

Pazzanese, C. (2016, July 12). The high price of workplace stress. *The Harvard Gazette*. Retrieved from https://news.harvard.edu/gazette/story/2016/07/the-high-price-of-workplace-stress/.

Pelletier, S. (2010, Fall). Success for adult students. *Public Purpose* (American Association of State Colleges and Universities). Retrieved from https://www.aascu.org/uploadedFiles/AASCU/Content/Root/MediaAndPublications/PublicPurposeMagazines/Issue/10fall_adultstudents.pdf.

Pelletier, S. (2017). Enrollment management and big data in an era of change. *The Chronicle of Higher Education*. Retrieved from https://www.ellucian.com/assets/en/white-paper/whitepaper-enrollment-management-and-big-data-chronicle.pdf.

Perillo, S. J. (2008). Fashioning leadership in schools: An ANT account of leadership as networked practice. *School Leadership & Management*, *28*(2), 189–203.

Perlmutter, D. (2018, February 5). A crash course in crisis communication. *The Chronicle of Higher Education*. Retrieved from https://www.chronicle.com/article/A-Crash-Course-in-Crisis/242443?cid=trend_au&elqTrackId=970f4b77a8174640b4a6d07f757f7993&elq=07bc1021a99641bf8163c182e6281806&elqaid=17747&elqat=1&elqCampaignId=7827.

Peters, L. H., Hartke, D. D., & Pohlmann, J. T. (1985). Fiedler's contingency theory of leadership: An application of the meta-analysis procedures of Schmidt and Hunter. *Psychological Bulletin*, *97*(2), 274.

Picciano, A. G. (2012). The evolution of big data and learning analytics in American higher education. *Journal of Asynchronous Learning Networks*, *16*(3), 9–20.

Pilbeam, C., & Jamieson, I. (2010). Beyond leadership and management: The boundary-spanning role of the pro-vice chancellor. *Educational Management Administration & Leadership*, *38*(6), 758–776.

Pittinsky, M. (2015, March 2). Credentialing in higher education: Current challenge and innovative trends. *EDUCAUSEreview*. Retrieved from https://er.educause.edu/articles/2015/3/credentialing-in-higher-education-current-challenges-and-innovative-trends.

Pondy, L. R. (1967). Organizational conflict: Concepts and models. *Administrative Science Quarterly*, *12*, 296–320.

Rapert, M. I., Velliquette, A., & Garretson, J. A. (2002). The strategic implementation process: Evoking strategic consensus through communication. *Journal of Business Research*, *55*(4), 301–310.

Rasmus, D. (2012, November 3). Why higher education need scenarios. *University Business Magazine*. Retrieved from https://www.universitybusiness.com/article/why-higher-education-needs-scenarios.

Ratnasingam, P. (2005). Trust in inter-organizational exchanges: A case study in business to business electronic commerce. *Decision Support Systems*, *39*(3), 525–544.

Redden, E. (2018, November 13). New international enrollments decline again. *Inside Higher Ed*. Retrieved from https://www.insidehighered.com/news/2018/11/13/new-international-student-enrollments-continue-decline-us-universities.

Reddick, K. W., Trifilo, J., Asby, S.B., Majewski, D., & Geissler, J. (2014, December). Maximizing the use of an early alert system through advisor outreach.

Academic Advising Today, *37*(4). Retrieved from https://www.nacada.ksu.edu/Resources/Academic-Advising-Today/View-Articles/Maximizing-the-Use-of-an-Early-Alert-System-through-Advisor-Outreach.aspx.

Rendon, L. I. (1994). Validating culturally diverse students: Toward a new model of learning and student development. *Innovative Higher Education*, *19*(1), 33–51.

Richmond, R. C. (2015). The future of the university is change. In G. A. Olson & J. W. Presley (Eds.), *The future of higher education: Perspectives from academic leaders* (pp. 31–42). New York: Routledge.

Roksa, J. (2009). Building bridges for student success: Are higher education articulation policies effective? *Teachers College Record*, *111*, 2444–2478.

Romano, R. M., & Eddy, P. L. (2017). Community colleges and social mobility. *Change: The Magazine of Higher Learning*, *49*(6), 55–62.

Romano, R. M., & Palmer, J. C. (2015). *Financing community colleges: Where we are, where we're going*. Lanham, MD: Rowman & Littlefield.

Rosete, D., & Ciarrochi, J. (2005). Emotional intelligence and its relationship to workplace performance outcomes of leadership effectiveness. *Leadership & Organization Development Journal*, *26*, 388–399.

Rowan-Kenyon, H. T., & Niehaus, E. K. (2011). One year later: The influence of short-term study abroad experiences on students. *Journal of Student Affairs Research and Practice*, *48*, 213–228.

Ruben, B. D., De Lisi, R., & Gigliotti, R. A. (2017). *A guide for leaders in higher education: Core concepts, competencies, and tools*. Sterling, VA: Stylus.

Runde, C. E., & Flanagan, T. A. (2008). Conflict competent leadership. *Leader to Leader*, *2008*(47), 46–51.

Salisbury, M. (2017, April 9). Big hopes, scant evidence: Acquiring expensive data tools does not guarantee real improvement. *The Chronicle of Higher Education*. Retrieved from https://www.chronicle.com/article/Big-Hopes-Scant-Evidence/239710.

Salovey, P., & Mayer, J. D. (1990). Emotional intelligence. *Imagination, Cognition, and Personality*, *9*, 185–211. doi:0.2190/DUGG-P24E-52WK-6CDG.

Sanaghan, P. (2009). *Collaborative strategic planning in higher education*. Washington, DC: National Association of College and University Business Officers.

Savage, A., & Sales, M. (2008). The anticipatory leader: Futurist, strategist and integrator. *Strategy & Leadership*, *36*(6), 28–35.

Schein, E. H. (1985). *Organizational culture and leadership* (1st ed.). San Francisco: Jossey-Bass.

Schein, E. H. (1992). *How can organizations learn faster? The problem of entering the Green Room*. Cambridge, MA: Massachusetts Institute of Technology, Sloan School of Management. Retrieved from https://dspace.mit.edu/bitstream/handle/1721.1/2399/SWP-3409-45882883.pdf.

Schein, E. H. (1994). *Organizational culture and leadership* (2nd ed.). San Francisco: Jossey-Bass.

Schieber, C. (2018, January 16). *We are in the midst of a historic paradigm shift in education*. Retrieved from https://www.competencyworks.org/higher-education-2/we-are-in-the-midst-of-a-historic-paradigm-shift-in-education/.

Schoemaker, P. J. (1995). Scenario planning: A tool for strategic thinking. *Sloan Management Review, 36*(2), 25–50.

Scott, J., & Carrington, P. J. (Eds.). (2011). *The Sage handbook of social network analysis*. Thousand Oaks, CA: Sage.

Scott, S. E. (2012). *Emancipated foster youth's transition from care to Virginia community colleges*. Unpublished doctoral dissertation. ProQuest (UMI 3514843).

Selingo, J. J. (2017). *The future of the degree: How colleges can survive the new credential economy*. Washington, DC: Chronicle of Higher Education.

Selingo, J. J., Chheng, S., & Clark, C. (2017). *Pathways to the university presidency: The future of higher education leadership*. Atlanta: Deloitte University Press. Retrieved from https://www2.deloitte.com/content/dam/insights/us/articles/3861_Pathways-to-the-university-presidency/DUP_Pathways-to-the-university-presidency.pdf.

Seltzer, R. (2018, July 25). Moody's: Private-college closures at 11 per year. *Inside Higher Ed*. Retrieved from https://www.insidehighered.com/quicktakes/2018/07/25/moodys-private-college-closures-11-year.

Sen, A. (1985). Well-being, agency & freedom: The Dewey lectures 1984. *The Journal of Philosophy, 52*(4), 169–221.

Sen, A. (1999). *Development as freedom*. Oxford: Oxford University Press.

Senge, P. M. (1990). *The fifth discipline: The art and practice of the learning organization*. New York: Doubleday Currency.

Shapiro, J. P., & Stefkovich, J. A. (2016). *Ethical leadership and decision making in education: Applying theoretical perspectives to complex dilemmas*. New York: Routledge.

Shapiro, P. (2005). Too many leaders? . . . or do we use the term "leader" too freely? *News & Tools Leadership, 1*(2), 1–2.

Shen, X., & Tian, X. (2012). Academic culture and campus culture of universities. *Higher Education Studies, 2*(2), 61–65.

Shields, C. M. (2010). Transformative leadership: Working for equity in diverse contexts. *Educational Administration Quarterly, 46*(4), 558–589.

Siemens, G., Dawson, S., & Eshleman, K. (2018, October 29). Complexity: A leader's framework for understanding and managing change in higher education. *EDUCAUSEreview*. Retrieved from https://er.educause.edu/articles/2018/10/complexity-a-leaders-framework-for-understanding-and-managing-change-in-higher-education.

Singh, R. (2018, May 2). AI and chatbots in education: What does the future hold? *Chatbox Magazine*. Retrieved from https://chatbotsmagazine.com/ai-and-chatbots-in-education-what-does-the-futurehold-9772f5c13960.

Sloan, J. (2017). *Learning to think strategically* (3rd ed.). New York: Routledge.

Smith, A. A. (2018, June 21). No bottom yet in 2 year college enrollments. *Inside Higher Ed*. Retrieved from: https://www.insidehighered.com/news/2018/06/21/community-college-enrollment-rates-expected-keep-falling.

Smith, V. C. (2008). *The unbundling and rebundling of the faculty role in e-learning community college courses*. Unpublished doctoral dissertation. University of Arizona Repository (http://hdl.handle.net/10150/194795).

Smith, V. C., & Rhoades, G. (2006). Community college faculty and web-based classes. *Thought and Action*, *22*, 97–110.

Smorynski, H. W. (2017). Avoiding the common pitfalls of failed strategic plans. *Academic Leader Today*. Retrieved from https://www.magnapubs.com/newsletter/academic-leader/134/Avoiding-the-Common-Pitfalls-of-Failed-Strategic-Plans-13454-1.html.

Soares, L., Steele, P., & Wayt, L. (2016). *Evolving higher education business models: Leading with data to deliver results*. Washington, DC: American Council of Education.

Söderhjelm, T., Björklund, C., Sandahl, C., & Bolander-Laksov, K. (2018). Academic leadership: Management of groups or leadership of teams? A multiple-case study on designing and implementing a team-based development programme for academic leadership. *Studies in Higher Education*, *43*, 201–216.

Solomon, R. C., & Flores, F. (2001). *Building trust in business, politics, relationships, and life*. New York: Oxford University Press.

Sommo, C., & Ratledge, A. (2016). *Bringing CUNY Accelerated Study in Associate Programs (ASAP) to Ohio: Early findings from a demonstration in three community colleges*. MDRC Policy Brief.

Sorcinelli, M. D., Austin, A. E., Eddy, P. L., & Beach, A. L. (2006). *Creating the future of faculty development: Learning from the past, understanding the present*. Bolton, MA: Anker.

Southern New Hampshire University, College for America. (n.d.). *About*. Retrieved from https://collegeforamerica.org/about-college-for-america/.

Staats, C. (2016). Understanding implicit bias: What educators should know. *American Educator*, *39*(4), 29–33, 43.

Steele, C. M. (2011). *Whistling Vivaldi: And other clues to how stereotypes affect us (issues of our time)*. New York: Norton.

Steele, C. M., & Aronson, J. (1995). Stereotype threat and the intellectual test performance of African Americans. *Journal of Personality and Social Psychology*, *69*, 797–811.

Steele, P. (2018). *American Council on Education (ACE) Alternative Credit Project: Final report*. Washington, DC: Higher Ed Insight. Retrieved from https://www.acenet.edu/news-room/Documents/ACE-Alternative-Credit-ProjectFinal-Report.pdf.

Stempfle, J. (2011). Overcoming organizational fixation: Creating and sustaining an innovation culture. *Journal of Creative Behavior*, *45*(2), 116–129.

Stewart, D. L. (2017, March 30). Language of appeasement. *Inside Higher Ed*. Retrieved from https://www.insidehighered.com/views/2017/03/30/colleges-need-language-shift-not-one-you-think-essay.

Suárez, E. (2016, May 4). Navigating conflict. *Inside Higher Ed*. Retrieved from https://www.insidehighered.com/advice/2016/05/04/how-navigate-conflict-higher-education-leader-essay.

Sutcliffe, K. M. (2001). Organizational environments and organizational information processing. In F. M. Jablin & L. L. Putnam (Eds.), *The new handbook of organizational communication: Advances in theory, research, and methods* (pp. 197–230). Thousand Oaks, CA: Sage.

Svrluga, S. (2015, November 9). U. Missouri president, chancellor resign over handling of racial incidents. *The Washington Post*. Retrieved from https://www.washingtonpost.com/news/grade-point/wp/2015/11/09/missouris-student-government-calls-for-university-presidents-removal/?utm_term=.47db17b4f0b4.

Sydow, D., & Alfred, R. L. (2012). *Re-visioning community colleges: Positioning for innovation*. Lanham, MD: Rowman & Littlefield.

Tardanico, S. (2013, January 15). 10 traits of courageous leaders. *Forbes*. Retrieved from http://www.forbes.com/sites/susantardanico/2013/01/15/10-traits-of-courageous-leaders/#2c0fb00a5104.

Taylor, F. W. (1911). *The principles of scientific management*. New York: Harper & Brothers.

Taylor, J. (2014). Informing or distracting? Guiding or driving? The use of performance indicators in higher education. In M. E. Menon, D. G. Terkla, & P. Gibbs (Eds.), *Using data to improve higher education: Research, policy, and practice*. Rotterdam, Netherlands: Sense.

Thelin, J. R. (2011). *A history of American higher education*. Baltimore: Johns Hopkins University Press.

Thomas, D. C., Liao, Y., Aycan, Z., Cerdin, J.-L., Pekerti, A. A., Ravlin, E. C., et al. (2015, December). Cultural intelligence: A theory-based, short form measure. *Journal of International Business Studies*, *46*(9), 1099–1118.

Thomas-Kilmann, K. W. (1974). *Thomas-Kilmann conflict mode survey*. Tuxedo, NY: Xicom.

Thomas-Kilmann, K. W. (2008). Thomas-Kilmann conflict mode. *TKI Profile and Interpretive Report*, 1–11.

Tierney, W. G. (1988). Organizational culture in higher education: Defining the essentials. *The Journal of Higher Education*, *59*(1), 2–21.

Tierney, W. G. (2008). *The impact of culture on organizational decision-making: Theory and practice in higher education*. Sterling, VA: Stylus.

Tierney, W. G. (2014). *Creating a culture of innovation: The challenge in becoming and staying a world-class university*. Los Angeles: Pullias Center for Higher Education. Retrieved from https://files.eric.ed.gov/fulltext/ED559354.pdf.

Tigue, C. C., Borak, D. J., O'Connor, J. J., Schandl, C., & Feinberg, D. R. (2012). Voice pitch influences voting behavior. *Evolution and Human Behavior*, *33*(3), 210–216.

Tinto, V. (1975). Dropout from higher education: A theoretical synthesis of recent research. *Review of Educational Research*, *45*(1), 89–125.

Tinto, V. (1997). Classrooms as communities: Exploring the educational character of student persistence. *The Journal of Higher Education*, *68*, 599–623.

Tinto, V. (2006). Research and practice of student retention: What next? *The Journal of College Student Retention: Research, Theory & Practice*, *8*(1), 1–19.

Tinto, V., & Pusser, B. (2006). *Moving from theory to action: Building a model of institutional action for student success*. Washington, DC: National Postsecondary Education Cooperative. Retrieved from https://nces.ed.gov/npec/pdf/tinto_pusser_report.pdf.

Tovstiga, G. (2015). *Strategy in practice: A practitioner's guide to strategic thinking* (3rd ed.). New York: John Wiley & Sons.

Trow, M. (1972). The expansion and transformation of higher education. *International Review of Education*, *18*(1), 61–84.

Tschannen-Moran, M., & Hoy, W. K. (2000). A multidisciplinary analysis of the nature, meaning, and measurement of trust. *Review of Educational Research*, *70*(4), 547–593.

Tugend, A. (2018, October 21). Mergers can benefit all involved—but they're never easy. *The Chronicle of Higher Education*. Retrieved from https://www.chronicle.com/article/Mergers-Can-Benefit-All/244850.

Twale, D. J., & De Luca, B. M. (2008). *Faculty incivility: The rise of the academic bully and what to do about it*. San Francisco: Jossey-Bass.

Twombly, S. B. (1995). Gendered images of community college leadership: What messages they send. In B. K. Townsend (Ed.), *Gender and power in the community college*. New Directions for Community Colleges, no. 89 (pp. 67–77). San Francisco: Jossey-Bass.

Udelhofen, S. (2005). *Keys to curriculum mapping: Strategies and tools to make it work*. Thousand Oaks, CA: Corwin.

Ulmer, R. R., Sellnow, T. L., & Seeger, M. W. (2017). *Effective crisis communication: Moving from crisis to opportunity*. Thousand Oaks, CA: Sage.

Umbricht, M. R., Fernandez, F., & Ortagus, J. C. (2017). An examination of the (un)intended consequences of performance funding in higher education. *Educational Policy, 31*, 643–673.

United Nations Educational, Scientific, and Cultural Organization (UNESCO). (2010). *Strategic planning: Concept and rationale*. Paris: International Institute for Educational Planning. Retrieved from https://unesdoc.unesco.org/ark:/48223/pf0000189757.

United States Institute of Peace. (n.d.). *Introduction to conflict analysis*. Retrieved from https://www.usip.org/education-training/courses/introduction-conflict-analysis.

University Professional and Continuing Education Association (UPCEA). (2018). *Convening on the future of credentials: Post-event executive summary*. Retrieved from https://upcea.edu/wp-content/uploads/2018/03/UPCEA-Convening-on-the-Future-of-Credentials-Post-Event-Executive-Summary.pdf.

Upcraft, M. L., Gardner, J. N., & Barefoot, B. O. (2004). *Challenging and supporting the first-year student: A handbook for improving the first year of college*. San Francisco: Jossey-Bass.

U.S. Department of Education. (2016, November). *Advancing diversity and inclusion in higher education*. Washington, DC: Office of Planning, Evaluation and Policy Development and Office of the Under Secretary. Retrieved from https://www2.ed.gov/rschstat/research/pubs/advancing-diversity-inclusion.pdf.

Valbrun, M. (2018, May 7). From diversity chief to college president. *Inside Higher Ed*. Retrieved from https://www.insidehighered.com/news/2018/05/07/chief-diversity-officer-position-new-path-presidency.

Valencia, R. R. (1997). Conceptualizing the notion of deficit thinking. In R. R. Valencia (Ed.), *The evolution of deficit thinking: Educational thought and practice* (pp. 1–12). Abingdon, UK: RoutledgeFalmer.

Valenzuela, A. (1999). *Subtractive schooling: Issues of caring in education of US-Mexican youth*. Albany: State University of New York Press.

Warmington, P., Daniels, H., Edwards, A., Brown, S., Leadbetter, J., Martin, D., & Middleton, D. (2004). *Interagency collaboration: A review of the literature*. Bath, UK: Learning in and for Interagency Working Project.

Warters, W. C. (2001). The emergence of campus mediation systems: History in the making. *Conflict Management in Higher Education Report*, 2(1). Retrieved from http://creducation.net/resources/cmher_vol_2_1_warters_a.pdf.

Watson, N. T., Watson, K. L., & Stanley, C. A. (2016). *Conflict management and dialogue in higher education: A global perspective*. Charlotte, NC: Information Age.

Watson, O. M. (1970). *Proxemic behavior: A cross-cultural study*. The Hague: Mouton.

Wawrzynski, M., & Baldwin, R. (2014). Promoting high-impact student learning: Connecting key components of the collegiate experience. In P. L. Eddy (Ed.), *Connecting learning across the institution*. New Directions for Higher Education, no. 165 (pp. 51–62). San Francisco: Jossey-Bass.

Webb, A. (2017, Summer). The flare and focus of future of successful futurist. *MIT Sloan Management Review*, *58*(4). Retrieved from https://ilp.mit.edu/media/news_articles/smr/2017/58412.pdf.

Weber, M. (2009). *From Max Weber: Essays in sociology*. New York: Routledge.

Weick, K. E. (1976). Educational organizations as loosely coupled systems. *Administrative Science Quarterly*, *21*, 1–19.

Weick, K. E. (1995). *Sensemaking in organizations*. Thousand Oaks, CA: Sage.

Weimer, M. (2013). *Learner-centered teaching: Five key changes to practice* (2nd ed.). San Francisco: Jossey-Bass.

Weise, M. R., & Christensen, C. M. (2014). *Hire education: Mastery, modularization, and the workforce revolution*. Redwood City, CA: Clayton Christensen Institute for Disruptive Innovation.

Western Governors University. (n.d.). *About Western Governors University*. https://www.wgu.edu/about.html.

"What happened in Ferguson?" (2015, August 10). *The New York Times*. Retrieved from https://www.nytimes.com/interactive/2014/08/13/us/ferguson-missouri-town-under-siege-after-police-shooting.html.

Wheat, C. A., & Hill, L. H. (2016). Leadership identities, styles, and practices of women university administrators and presidents. *Research in the Schools*, *23*(2), 1–16.

Wheeler, D. W. (2012). *Servant leadership for higher education: Principles and practices*. New York: John Wiley & Sons.

White, R. (2018). Title VII and the# MeToo movement. *Emory Law Journal Online*, *68*, 1014–1033.

Whitt, E. J., Nesheim, B. E., Guentzel, M. J., Kellogg, A. H., McDonald, W. M., & Wells, C. A. (2008). "Principles of good practice" for academic and student affairs partnership programs. *Journal of College Student Development*, *49*(3), 235–249.

Wilmot, W. W., & Hocker. J. (2011). *Interpersonal conflict* (8th ed.). New York: McGraw-Hill.

Wilson-Strydom, M. (2015). University access and theories of social justice: Contributions of the capabilities approach. *Higher Education*, *69*(1), 143–155.

Wood, J. L., & Nevarez, C. (2014). Ethics, decision-making, and praxis. In C. Nevarez & L. J. Wood (Eds.), *Ethical, leadership and the community college:*

Paradigms, decision-making, and praxis (pp. 3–11). Charlotte, NC: Information Age.

Wyner, J. S. (2014). *What excellent community colleges do: Preparing all students for success*. Cambridge, MA: Harvard Education Press.

Yammarino, F. J., Salas, E., Serban, A., Shirreffs, K., & Shuffler, M. L. (2012). Collectivistic leadership approaches: Putting the "we" in leadership science and practice. *Industrial and Organizational Psychology*, *5*(4), 382–402.

Yammarino, F. J., Spangler, W. D., & Bass, B. M. (1993). Transformational leadership and performance: A longitudinal investigation. *Leadership Quarterly*, *4*(1), 81–102.

Yarn, D. H., & Boyens, J. (2004). *A guidebook for implementing the initiative and policy direction on conflict resolution* (4th ed.). Atlanta: University of Georgia.

Yukl, G. A. (2002). *Leadership in organizations*. Englewood, NJ: Prentice-Hall.

Zaccaro, S. J. (2007). Trait-based perspectives of leadership. *American Psychologist*, *62*(1), 6–16.

Zaccaro, S. J., Kemp, C., & Bader, P. (2004). Leader traits and attributes. In J. Antonakis, A. T. Cianciolo, & R. J. Sternberg (Eds.), *Nature of leadership* (pp. 101–124). Thousand Oaks, CA: Sage.

Zhu, C. (2015). Organisational culture and technology-enhanced innovation in higher education. *Technology, Pedagogy and Education*, *24*(1), 65–79.

Zhu, C., & Engels, N. (2014). Organizational culture and instructional innovations in higher education: Perceptions and reactions of teachers and students. *Educational Management Administration & Leadership*, *42*(1), 136–158.

Index

About the Authors

Pamela L. Eddy is a professor and department chair in Educational Policy, Planning, and Leadership at the College of William & Mary. She is the author or editor of twelve books. Her most recent book was a coedited volume entitled *Critical Approaches to Women and Gender in Higher Education* (2017).

Elizabeth Kirby, Ed.D., is the dean of the College of Education and Human Services at Central Michigan University. She has over thirty years of experience in PK–12 and higher education and has held a variety of administrative roles within the college in recent years.